Testimonials

In "The 5 Critical Success Factors," John Goddard offers a r̃ entrepreneurs seeking to succeed in the SME sector. John's decades-long research in the SME sector and his deep experience as a senior career banker shine through this comprehensive analysis of the strengths successful SME principals need to nurture, to be successful. His focus on the five critical success factors of Professional Advice, The Finances, Front-Line Leadership, Time Management and Sustainable Leadership provide concrete steps for readers to follow, ensuring they have access to a realisable roadmap for building a thriving business. What sets the book apart is Goddard's attention to detail, with the chapters on front-line leadership in particular offering his timeless nine tenets for building a customer base and generating revenues. The book is a valuable resource for anyone looking to start or grow a business. Goddard's insights and practical advice make it a must-read for entrepreneurs at any stage of their journey.

Bruce Muirhead, CEO Mind Hive & former CEO of prominent Australian Think Tank – The Eidos Institute.

This is a book we would recommend to our clients. There's a genuine lack of resources available to business owners to help them succeed in the SME space. We have worked with John for a long time and would observe that he offers a wealth of experience from his past leadership roles with deep insights that are invaluable. John's book is easy to read and conveys priceless business principles to the SME owner, no matter how long they have been trading.

Simon Chun, Tax Partner Pitcher Partners, Brisbane Office.

Getting a start in any venture can be the hardest thing, no matter what you're trying to do. There are so many things to consider in leading a successful business, that it's all too easy to become overwhelmed. We all need a map and a compass for where we want to go and John's book delivers on those dimensions together with the essential drill down detail you will require on your journey ahead. 'The 5 Critical Success Factors' connects the strategy to the plan and shines a light on the practicalities you need to ensure you will be successful in executing your plan.'

Daniel Herbert, CEO of SSKB Property & Former Champion Australian Rugby Union International.

John Goddard's extensive experience in business leadership provides all SME leaders, experienced and start-ups alike, with an encyclopaedic reference tool, a veritable treasure trove of insights and lessons learnt over a lifetime of senior leadership experiences across the world: It is a tool with a limitless shelf-life! A must-read guide not least for those executives wishing to advance their careers and keen to avoid the pitfalls often common in inexperienced leaders.

John G. Bowie, AM, BA, M Admin (UNE), Prominent Educator.

SME Leadership: The 5 Critical Success Factors

The 5 Critical Success Factors is a valuable resource for small business owners and aspiring entrepreneurs alike. The book emphasises the importance of strong financial management, effective customer engagement and strategic time management, while fostering a culture of trust and collaboration. Its real-world examples and actionable advice makes it accessible for readers at any stage of their entrepreneurial journey. Especially useful is its clear, concise layout, making complex business principles easy to understand and implement. Whether you're starting out or wanting to refine your business strategies, this guide offers valuable insights and tools to help your business thrive. Overall, it's an essential read for anyone serious about achieving long-term success.

Chander Dhawan, Tax & Business Advisor to the SME Sector. Principal of MaxWealth CA, Chartered Accountants, Canberra ACT.

This book is an accessible, down-to-earth guide on the fundamentals of achieving SME success and should be a must read for anyone contemplating a start-up or looking to improve their existing business operation. Author John Goddard has drawn on his vast experience and valuable learnings accrued while forging a highly successful career over four decades in banking, both in Australia and abroad, and his experience in corporate life as a company director, strategic adviser and business mentor. John's chatty, easy-to-read writing style reflects a warm personality, easy-going nature and an attention to detail which he combines so well with the strong, attentive people skills appreciated and admired by all who know him.

Richard Owen, Journalist & former Business Editor of NewsCorp Queensland Masthead, The Courier Mail.

This is an extremely comprehensive, detailed and pragmatic guide on SME Leadership. I wish I had this book when I was learning my craft in this space. It's written by an expert in SME's, Finance, Leadership and high-end Business Acumen. John's experience is exceptional, and I have the utmost respect for him. On a personal level, I always admired his ability to authentically build powerful relationships and leverage his leadership style for the benefit of his business. It was based on John's credibility and skill, not just his 'networking' skills. I highly recommend this book. Enjoy.

Greg Crocombe, State General Manager Queensland Consumer & Business, Westpac & St George Banks, and Head of Westpac Consumer Banking, London.

The success of the Small Business Sector is one of the most critical link points in building prosperous local communities and achieving sustainable, nation building economic growth. Yet many SMEs are challenged by a multitude of issues that test the very existence of their business and the odds of their ultimate success. John Goddard's book lays out not only the important fundamentals but also provides a pathway to deal with the critical challenges in a way that brings all the essential tools, skills and vital business generating networks together to maximise the best opportunities for success. The book will undoubtedly become your secret weapon in achieving the success you deserve.

Greg Peel, former CEO, Community Sector Banking.

SME Leadership: The 5 Critical Success Factors

I wish I had read John's book before I started my business. Like so many would-be entrepreneurs, I had an idea and set off as fast as I could to make something of it. I soon discovered the importance of John's 5 Critical Success Factors. Building a successful business is a demanding occupation, and John has pulled together almost everything a would-be business owner could need, all in one place. His knowledge and experience about the world of business shines through. He has also written it in a comprehensive and clear way, making the information easily accessible to even the busiest entrepreneur. So, on behalf of the many business owners out there, thank you John!

Michael Morgan, CEO Asia, Herrmann Brain International (HBDI).

This is the sort of book I could have really used when I started out many years ago. It covers literally everything you need to know from finance to business names to legal stuff and how to generate revenue. Some of it is covered in detail with stories, examples and anecdotes that make for a good read. Some of it gives you useful links and pointers to where you can get more information – and that's especially important for the stuff that changes regularly. John has put together a business guide which will be vital to anyone starting a new venture, but it also contains a great deal of useful information for existing business principals wanting to achieve superior outcomes.

Mick Devine, CEO Calxa Accounting Software.

John Goddard's book is a fascinating look into the world of SMEs from both a banker's and businessman's perspective. It covers the technical aspects such as competently managing the finances, tracking performance, complying with Tax Laws and meeting Corporations Law obligations, but also covers the critical qualitative aspects of SME Leadership. Networking, selling, generating revenues, hiring good people, developing a solid brand and building a good reputation are essential ingredients of any successful business. John covers these and a multitude of other subjects, drawing on personal anecdotes and practical illustrations from his own life experience and learnings. John Goddard's book may well become the business textbook of choice for SMEs.

Greg Meek, Former Director Government Services, Gadens Lawyers.

Congratulations on your book. The more I browse the more I appreciate the extraordinary breadth of the material you have covered. I was looking for something you might have missed, but everything I thought of you had, and much, much, more!

Tim Sheehan, Principal/Shareholder SSKB Property.

Through his extensive experience in Australia's finance and business community, John Goddard has compiled this comprehensive "must read" guide of all the critical aspects of business to enable SME leaders to best position themselves and their enterprises for success. The book's well-researched and illustrated critical financial and business management tools have been presented in a form that will be easily understood by readers irrespective of their experience

SME Leadership: The 5 Critical Success Factors

or background. From recruitment to financial management, marketing and that all important networking and selling, John has through his personal experiences, provided SME leaders with all the ingredients they need for success.

Bob Millar, OAM, former Bendigo Community Bank Director and Moreton Bay Region Local Government Councillor.

SME Leadership

The 5 Critical Success Factors

The Essential Skills, Strategies, Tactics & Actions

…keeping the dream alive.

SME Leadership The 5 Critical Success Factors

Published by SME Keystone Leadership Pty Ltd

smekeystone.com/books

Copyright © John A. Goddard, Ian T. Hulbert and
SME Keystone Leadership Pty Ltd 2025

The rights of John A. Goddard and Ian T. Hulbert to be identified as the authors of the work has been asserted by them in accordance with the *Australian Copyright Act* and *The Berne Convention for the Protection of Literary and Artistic Works*.

All rights reserved. No part of this publication may be reproduced, stored in a retrieval system, or transmitted, in any form, or by any means (electronic, mechanical, photocopying, recording, or otherwise) without the prior written consent of the authors and SME Keystone Leadership Pty Ltd, nor may it be otherwise circulated in any form of binding or cover other than that in which it is published, without a similar condition being imposed on the subsequent purchaser.

ISBN: 978-1-7638466-0-9   Format: Softback

Distributed by SME Keystone Leadership Pty Ltd

Dedication

For Leslie Goddard and Sam Goddard

TABLE OF CONTENTS

Testimonials	**1**
Acknowledgments	**1**
About the Authors	**3**
Introduction	5
The Global SME Statistics	5
John's SME Research	6
The Traits of the Highly Competent Generalist	8
Franchise Sector Influences	9
Sporting Sector Influences	10
Academic Research	10
Pulling It All Together	10
A Salute to the SME Entrepreneur	12
Foreword	**14**
Prologue	**16**

About The 5 Critical Success Factors	**17**
Brief Synopsis	**17**
Rapid Learning Strategies	**21**

CRITICAL SUCCESS FACTOR 1:	
THE FOUNDATIONS	**23**
Why Are You Reading This Book?	24
Finding the Right Professional Advisors	25
How Many Banks Do I Have to Rob?	25
What Are My Legal Obligations?	25
What Else Should I Do?	26
Chapter 1: Professional Advice	27
Importance of Retaining an External Tax Accountant	28
Finding the Right Accountant	30
Other Professional Advisors Who May Help	30
Chapter 2: The Trading Structure	32
Sole Trader	32

Partnership	33
Limited Liability Corporation	34
A Trust	36
The Next Steps?	36
Chapter 3: Capital	**38**
Capital Assets	38
Intangible Assets	39
Social Capital	39
The Initial Seed Funding of the Business	39
Shareholding Options for a Company	41
Shareholding Recording and Reporting Priorities	42
Recording and Reporting Priorities for Partnerships	42
Supplementary Private Capital Raisings	43
Chapter 4: Legal Responsibilities & Obligations	**44**
Corporate Law Directors Compliance	44
Director Penalty Regimes and Other Liability Risks	45
Director Protection Options	46
Director / Partner Relationship Management	47
Succession	48
Prenuptial Agreements	49

CRITICAL SUCCESS FACTOR 2: THE FINANCES — 50

Chapter 5: The Bookkeeping Basics	**52**
About Debits, Credits, and Double-Entry Bookkeeping	52
The Principle of Accrual Accounting	53
The Bookkeeping Software Decisions	56
The Chart of Accounts	58
Dealing With Unaccounted for Formation Expenses	59
Establishing Your E-Commerce Platforms	59
The System Feed and Reconciliation Rules with Your Bank	60
Setting up Your Sales Invoice Template	60
Small Business Payrolls	61
Treatment of Stock in the Financial Accounts	61
Dealing With Cash / Out-of-Pocket Expenses	62
'Food for the Table'	63
The Accounting Software Dashboards	63
Accounting Software Community Forums	64
Sales Transactions	64

Expense / Overhead Transactions	64
What to Outsource	65
Bookkeeping Routines That Give the Business Oxygen	65
Who can access your Online Bookkeeping Software?	66
Manual Journal Entry Protocols	66
How secure is Confidential Information Stored on Cloud?	66
Virus Protection Software	67
Disaster Recovery	67
Password Security Protocols Across the Whole Business	67
Chapter 6: Statutory Obligations	**70**
Australian Employment Law and Obligations	70
Enterprise Bargaining Agreements	70
Workers Compensation Insurance	71
Payroll Tax	71
Tax File Number Declaration	71
Superannuation	72
Long Service Leave (LSL)	72
Other Payroll Entitlements	73
Setting up Employees in Your Accounting Software's Payroll Module	73
Withholding Tax Rates	73
Dealing With the Principal / Director's Earnings	74
PAYG Instalment Tax and PAYG Withholding Tax	76
Fringe Benefits Tax (FBT)	76
Goods and Services Tax (GST)	77
Business Activity Statement (BAS) Lodgement Obligations	78
Excise Duty and Customs Duty Obligations	78
Tax Time Accounting and Reporting	79
Other Statutory Compliance Obligations	79
Chapter 7: The Business Performance Metrics	**81**
The Balance Sheet	81
The Profit and Loss Statement	83
The Cash Flow Statement	85
The Three-Way Cash Flow	89
Trend Ratio Analyses	90
Benchmarking your Financial Ratios	93
Breakeven Analyses	95
Annual Budget Time	96
What to Do When Cash Flows Are Stretched to the Limit	98
Dealing with Disasters	99

Chapter 8: Risk Management — 102
- Step 1: Statutory Obligations — 104
- Step 2: Legal Obligations — 104
- Step 3: Other Risks and Opportunities — 105
- Step 4: Contingency Planning — 106
- Workplace Health and Safety (WHS) — 107

Chapter 9: Tax Time Reporting — 109
- Australian Tax Compliance — 109
- Expert Insights About Growing Your Business — 110
- Dealing With Reviews and Disputes — 110
- Dealing With Financial Distress and Insolvency — 111
- Tax Time Accounting, Reporting, and Lodgement — 112
- Tax on Distribution of Business Profits — 113
- Tax Planning — 114
- PAYG Tax Instalments — 115
- Tax Return Lodgement and Payment Dates — 115
- Tax Advisor / Client Relationship — 116

Chapter 10: Dealing with the Bankers — 117
- Typical Lending Options — 118
- A Corporate Credit Card — 118
- Asset and Equipment Financing — 118
- Debt and Invoice Financing and Full-Service Factoring — 119
- Foreign Exchange and Trade Finance — 119
- Overdrafts — 120
- Commercial land and building finance. — 120
- Property Development Financing — 121
- Other Loan Types — 122
- The disclosure sensitivities and required homework. — 122
- My Four Standard Steps for Seeking Credit — 123
- The Loan Security Options — 125
- Typical Debt Covenants and Conditions Precedent — 127

Chapter 11: Buying or Selling a SME — 128
- Stress Test Your Motive for Going Into Business — 128
- About the Business Opportunity & Its Potential to Succeed — 129
- About that *Opportunity of a Lifetime!* — 129
- The Due Diligence Stage — 131
- The Hard Reflections — 132
- On Reaching the Sales Contract Stage — 133
- Purchasing a Turnkey Franchise Business — 134
- Selling an SME — 135

CRITICAL SUCCESS FACTOR 3: THE FRONT LINE — 136

Chapter 12: Dynamic Business Planning	139
A: The First Cut Business Plan	141
B: The Plan Stress Tests	146
C: Future Proofing Tools	149
D: The Business Narratives	150
E: The Projects, Priorities and Timelines	151
F: The Operating Projections	151
Chapter 13: Brand and Positioning	154
My Core Definition of Brand	155
The Importance of Timely Response to Customer Issues	158
How Else Can I Test My Brand Strength	158
Chapter 14: Trade Secrets	160
How Do I Protect My Trade Secrets?	161
Trademarks	162
What's in a Business Name?	164
Copyright	165
Patents	166
Chapter 15: Customers & Revenues	168
Understanding the Buyers' Viewpoint	169
Ned Herrmann's Whole Brain® HBDI®	171
CRM Software	174
Quality Lead Networking	176
Digital Lead Sourcing	179
Planning for Successful Sales Calls	180
Creating the Selling Narratives	182
Remuneration Options for Your Sales Team	185
Managing the Salesperson's Mindset	186
Definition of an Accomplished Salesperson	186
Chapter 16: Collaborative Networking	189
What is Networking?	190
How to Build a Generic Networking Plan	191
A Blueprint for Networking at Business Meetings	192
What You Should Carry in Your Networking *Kit Bag*	193
Author's Collaborative Networking Journey in Queensland	194

Chapter 17: Community Engagement	198
New *Beyond the Bottom-Line* Perspectives on Capitalism	199
Engaging Your Local Community	200
John's Community Engagement Learnings	203
Chapter 18: Mentors & Learning Circles	211
St. George Bank's Jim Sweeney	211
Bendigo Bank's Rob Hunt	213
Building Collaborative Learning Circles	216

CRITICAL SUCCESS FACTOR 4: MANAGING TIME — 219

Chapter 19: Continuous Learning	222
Continuous Learning – A Starting Point	222
The 7 Stages of Learning and Self-Awareness	227
Continuous Learning and the Team	232
A Continuous Learning Checklist for the SME Team:	233
Chapter 20: Daily Personal Journaling	234
The Nuts and Bolts of my Morning Journal	234
End of Day Journal Sign-Off	235
Chapter 21: Habits & Routines	236
Defining Habits, Routines & Paradigms	236
Before Work Habits and Routines	239
Workday Habits	240
End of Workday Shut Down Routine	245
On Your Way Home	245
Ban the *Bull Shit* Bag	246
Chapter 22: Priorities & Time	247
The SME Priority Planner	248
Chapter 23: Front-Line Time Management	251
The Principal's Time Management System	252
Chapter 24: Financial Time Management	259
The Bookkeeper's Time Management System	259

Chapter 25: Managing the Back Office — 264
- Delegation — 264
- Management by Walking About (MBWA) — 266
- Managing Supply Chain Efficiency — 269
- Adopting Franchise Sector Initiatives — 270
- Computers Behaving Badly! — 271

Chapter 26: Making Decisions — 273
- Critical Decision-Making Considerations — 273
- Dealing With Less Consequential Day-To-Day Decision Making — 275

Chapter 27: The Organisation Structure — 276
- The Stages of Small Business Evolution — 276
- Michael Gerber on Building a Structure That Works — 277
- About Individual and Collective Responsibilities — 278
- Dealing With Bureaucracy — 279
- Employee Screening — 279
- Employee Induction — 281
- Just Make Things Happen! — 282
- The Quest for a Workable Customer-Driven Structure — 283
- The Monitoring and Control Framework: — 286
- The Meeting Rules — 287

Chapter 28: The Power of One — 288
- The Sole Trader — 288

CRITICAL SUCCESS FACTOR 5: LEADERSHIP — 290

Chapter 29: The Leadership Basics — 293
- The Pre-hire Stage. — 293
- Hiring Friends and Family — 294
- Ban the Annual Review! — 294
- Dealing With Negativity — 294
- Show That You Care — 297
- Genuine Gestures Do Count — 298

Chapter 30: Sustainable Collaborative Leadership — 299
- The Cultural Value Drivers — 300
- The Capital Leadership Drivers — 302
- The Team Leadership Drivers — 304

Team and Stakeholder Trust	304
Crafting a Proactive Mindset	310
Don't Cheat *the Guy in the Glass*	311
Some Unique Leadership Lessons from Elite Sport	312
The 5 Qs for Thriving as a Leader	315
Chapter 31: Managing Emotions	316
More About Stress and Trauma	317
Mental health in Australia	317
Mental Health in the Typical Workplace	318
Common Workplace Stress Symptoms	318
Useful Mental Health Resources in Australia	319
How to Promote a Mentally Healthy Workplace	321
Chapter 32: Nine Inspiring Leadership Tales from the Trenches	323

Appendix (i)
The 5 Critical Success Factors Rapid Learning Guide   351

Appendix (ii)
Access to the Book Buyer's Essentials Toolkit   355

Appendix (iii)
SME Keystone Web Platform Initiatives   356

Dedication to Sam Goddard   357

Bibliography   358

Acknowledgments

Leslie Goddard: My best friend and confidant-in-chief took what I've referred to as a light-heartedly de facto PhD in Small Business in supporting me with our major writing project. Leslie's quest for deep research was unremitting. She challenged me constantly, asking a multitude of rational questions to test the strength and validity not only of the hard facts in the book but also some of the debatable viewpoints and assumptions. We laughed a lot. We argued a lot, but ho-hum, of course, she was invariably right! And as we worked through our final draft, we sat side by side, stripping down every page and every paragraph, eliminating duplicate words, trite turns of phrase, superfluous overstatements and unnecessary adjectives. I'm proud of the end-product and acknowledge it would not have been fractionally as good without Leslie's valuable input ... and of course, her patience!

Ian Hubert: I first showed Ian the bare bones of my Time Management System in 2013. He came back with some great questions, supported by an excellent *eyes-of-the-beholder* summary that included templates of how he believed my system could work best for him. Ian was also able to demonstrate how he had already adapted management of his outlook diary to incorporate the core habits, routines, priorities and disciplines embedded in my system. Ian followed the same logic in collaborating with me on the Critical Success Factor 4, Managing Time chapters and has already completed a good slice of the early groundwork for a digital version of the system. I thank Ian for his invaluable friendship, support, patience, and his significant contribution to the finished version of the book overall.

My thanks go to our many supporters, mentors, business colleagues and great mates who individually and collectively brought to the table their unique knowledge and skills. Thank you also to our valuable readers of the various drafts of the book who included successful SME principals, bankers, non-bank financiers, accountants, former elite sportsmen, academics, educators, business journalists, and several Australian and US technology vendors with offerings to the SME sector.

I most especially acknowledge and thank the Hon Rachel Nolan; John Bowie AM; Bob Millar OAM; Rob Hunt AM; Tim Sheehan; Daniel Herbert; Bruce Muirhead; Greg Crocombe; Antonio Avolio; Ross McQuinn; Jo Pollard; Michael Morgan; Greg Meek; Mick Divine; Richard Owen; Michael Robertson; Andrew Cooper; Graeme Harding; Mark Mahaffey; Greg Peel; Scott Elkington; David To; Simon Chun; Chander Dhawan, John Mangos; Sally Dodd, Phil Martin and Luke Goddard.

I gained immense on-point learnings about the SME Sector from my decade as chairman of Cooper Property Group, one of South-East Queensland's most successful larger SMEs and Property Developers.

The *Harvard Business Review (HBR)* delivers timely, valuable data and research articles in their short, easy-to-digest editorial *bites*, a number of which I have referenced throughout the book.

The Boston-based *Kauffman Institute is* a long-time supporter of the SME Sector in the US and a valuable resource for SME's in the Developed and Developing World's.

National and Regional *Chambers of Commerce,* not only represent and advocate for every sector of private enterprise but also provides a forum for SME principals to confer with each other. Indeed, The International Chamber of Commerce is the largest collegiate business organization globally with more than 50 million members in 100 countries.

The Council of Small Business of Australia (The COSBOA) has a proud history of advocacy and is Australia's peak body representing the interests of Small Business and we salute them for they work they do.

The Australian Small Business & Family Enterprise Ombudsman provides a most useful resource in its annually updated research report *Small Business Counts: Small Business in the Australian Economy.*

The Bibliography includes the fifty plus reference books we reviewed over several years. While I gained valuable insights from them all, my top ten standout authors are Jim Collins (*Good to Great*); Stephen R. Covey (*First Things First*); Stephen M.R. Covey (*The Speed of Trust*); Dyer, Jawad & Kakabadse (*Leadership Intelligence*); Michael E. Gerber (his *E Myth* book series); Ross Gittins* (*A Life Among Budgets, Bulldust and Bastardry* and *Gittins Guide to Economics*); Jeff Dyer, Hal Gregersen and Clayton Christensen (*The Innovator's DNA*); Jim Kwik (*Limitless: Upgrade Your Brain; Learn Anything Faster and Unlock Your Exceptional Life*); Ned & Anne-Nedhi Herrmann (*Unlocking the Power of Whole Brain Thinking*®); and Carl J. Schramm (*Burn the Business Plan*).

*Ross Gittins, Economics Editor for over five decades at the Sydney Morning Herald and The Melbourne Age is my favourite scribe about all things Economic. Ross is affectionately known as *The GOAT* (the greatest of all time!) because of his unique capacity to break down and explain complex economic concepts, that do a great job of improving public understanding of the 'nuts 'n bolts' of the economy.

About the Authors

John Goddard: During my working life as a senior career banker, I gained solid financial credentials from my early Chartered Accounting studies, a solid rookie banker's education from the Westpac Banking Group, particularly my time with AGC Leasing; and my valuable learnings working for a World Bank and Asian Development Bank funded Financial Institution in the Asia Pacific Region.

In Australia, I had responsibility for large retail, commercial and SME Banking portfolios as Group Chief General Manager Operations and Head of St. George's Retail Bank, CEO of Bendigo Bank's Italian Banking business, Chief Operating Officer of Bendigo Queensland and Chairman of South-East Queensland Community Telco. Following my retirement from

Bendigo, I was Chairman of The Cooper Property Group, one of South-East Queensland's most successful larger SME's.

I sat on many boards, including Public Corporation Entities, Government-Owned Corporations, Industry Bodies, Not-For-Profits, Educational Institutions, and Advisory Boards at University of Queensland and Griffith University. I was also privileged to be able to join advanced executive learning programs at Columbia University in New York and several other respected international business schools.

Ian Hulbert is CEO of SME Keystone Leadership Pty Ltd. He was my valued collaborator in penning my *Critical Successful Factor 4 Time Management* chapters and in his very significant contributions to the book overall. Over the past two decades, Ian has worked in Senior SME leadership roles, where he has been able to leverage his diverse experience in refining and improving Workplace Systems; managing Workplace Health & Safety and Environment programs, driving Quality (HSEQ) Management Systems; dealing with time, management and resource optimisation challenges; constructing sales leadership and customer mapping data for optimal CRM deployment; introducing the benefits of advanced digitisation; and generally in managing change for positive outcomes.

Introduction

The Global SME Statistics

The OECD (Organisation for Economic Co-operation and Development) defines Small to Medium Enterprises (SME's) as non-listed, independent businesses that employ a varying maximum number of employees (e.g., 200 in Australia, 250 in the UK and the European Union, and 500 in the US). Each SME is then sub-categorised as a self-employed sole trader, a micro, a small or a medium business.

Developed World SME's

In *Australia*, there are Circa 2.6 million actively trading SMEs. They represent 99% of all business owners, generate 54% of National Gross Domestic Product (Small Business 33%; Medium Business 21%), and account for 44% of Australia's working population

In the *United States*, there are 33 million SMEs. They represent 99% of all business owners, generate 45% of GDP, and account for 50% of the working population.

In the *United Kingdom*, there are 5 million SMEs. They represent 99% of business owners, generate 50% of GDP, and account for 45% of the working population.

Those SME statistics also fall comfortably within the statistical range for most of the SME's in other developed economies.

Developing World SMEs

The SME sector also plays a dominant role in the economic development and growth in developing nations. SMEs predominantly support village-based cottage industries and are a significant conduit for citizens transitioning from subsistence living to the cash economy. With funding support from The World Bank, The Asian Development Bank and several other related agencies, SMEs make a significant contribution to all sectors of the supply chain, employment creation and international trade.

John's SME Research

In the 1990s, when I was Head of St. George's Retail Bank, a bright young financier convinced me of the benefits of adding a dedicated small to medium business line of products to what we were then offering. He got the job, and the SME Sector subsequently became a healthy contributor to the bank's business.

After that, I became more aware of the SME sector. I was amazed to learn that one in five households in Australia has an interest in a small business. I soon discovered I could walk through any city or suburban shopping centre, to discover the lion's share of the businesses I passed were indeed SMEs.

As a banker, I visited a vast number of SMEs over my years with St. George and Bendigo Banks, many successful, some still at the breakeven stage, and others who were unable to continue trading. Over time, I observed the clear differences between those doing well and those struggling to survive. Not surprisingly, the major success factors invariably boiled down to the passion, experience and drive of the principals leading those businesses.

Over time, I got to know many successful principals who willingly shared with me information about their business practices, work routines, financials, how they generated revenue, and many other factors that contributed to their ongoing success.

In 2018, I worked up an Excel Spreadsheet of the cumulative performance factors I had by then been observing and recording for several decades. Grading my statistics was a necessarily iterative exercise, given my objective to nail down the common strengths, actions, work disciplines and daily work habits and routines that were most likely to have a positive influence on superior performance outcomes.

From that analysis, I identified seven consistent strengths. The better performing SME principals, those generating consistent year-on-year healthy profitability, had at least some level of competency in each of those seven strengths:

1. *The Foundations*: They had built their business on sound legal building blocks and appropriate trading structures, and they had adequate capital reserves to reach breakeven and expand beyond that.

SME Leadership: The 5 Critical Success Factors

2. *The Finances:* The majority used accounting software, employed competent bookkeepers/accountants and were diligent in tracking their bottom-line performance.

3. *Professional Advice:* They had all retained experienced external accountants to handle their annual tax affairs.

4. *Growing Customers/Generating Revenues:* The most successful principals spent a great deal of their time at the front-line, they had solid pitch statements, and they could elucidate well what was unique about their product offerings.

5. *Time Management:* The best SME principals were at least moderately disciplined about grading their business priorities according to importance.

6. *Continuous Learning and Improvement:* The best of them followed a consistent culture of continuous base line knowledge improvement and could harness that learning by implementing workable strategies to grow their business.

7. *Leadership*: In SMEs, where there is universally a scarcity of human resources and a constant need to make challenging compromises to achieve the best outcomes, all the principals in my higher-performing group were able to demonstrate significant leadership traits as a core strength.

The Traits of the Highly Competent Generalist

Top team executive members in corporations the world over possess unique qualifications, skills and experience related to the specific portfolios and operating divisions they lead. The dynamic when they come together as a Senior Team, is in their confidence that they collectively have *all bases covered* between them in making the vital *whole of business decisions*. That positive dynamic is guided by the quality of their debate, their constantly increasing assimilation of their knowledge of each other's portfolios, and their consequent capacity to evolve into *Highly Competent Generalists* across all those business disciplines.

In my experience, when the most successful senior teams go into debate, they are well-equipped to address the needs of their corporation at large. The CEO is of course the gatekeeper and ultimate decision maker in need, but the best teams tend to navigate differences of opinion well. Their debate is passionate and productive, yet when decision time comes, they willingly unite as a team to support the preferred path forward.

The closest I came to viewing a corporate-style structure at the SME level was with the Cooper Property Group in South-East Queensland. Jeff and Ros Cooper had commenced trading as a micro-SME several decades before, and by the time I came on board as non-executive Chairman in 2007, they had diversified substantially with significant property holdings in the commercial, industrial, retail, office and hospitality markets and with over one hundred staff on board.

My biography *The House that Jeff Built* (Boolarong Press, 2009) tells the story of my friend Jeff Cooper's long battle with Parkinson's Disease, the successful transition of Cooper Property Group's Leadership to Jeff's middle son Andrew, and the highly productive working relationship that developed between Andrew, CEO Graeme Harding and Senior Property Planner Mark Mahaffey. Penning Jeff's biography and stripping down the factors that underpinned the family's extraordinary achievements was the early catalyst for me to start formally logging and categorising the success factors I had been observing elsewhere in the SME sector. I tell more about the Cooper Family's successes in the last chapter of this book: *Inspiring Leadership Tales from the Trenches.*

So, how can the SME Principal transition to become that *Highly Competent Generalist*, armed with the ideal blend of critical skills and capabilities to help them become ultra successful in their business?

This process of knowledge assimilation does, in fact occur, particularly in many larger SMEs, but it invariably takes longer than in the Corporate World. Those who have come out of a senior corporate role prior to going into business for themselves often have a solid head start on the rest. Ditto for well qualified accountants who can rapidly bring to bear their advanced financial skills and capabilities in taking on their new SME challenge.

Franchise Sector Influences

Franchised businesses account for around 4% of Australian SMEs and the relative ratios are not dissimilar elsewhere in the Developed World.

Legendary McDonald's boss Ray Kroc, can be legitimately credited as the father of the *all-systems* style of *turnkey franchising* that became commonplace in the US from the 1950's.

Successful franchised business systems generally come on board with:

> Robust and predictable back office, cost control and financial metrics,
>
> Highly efficient and standardised operating systems, and
>
> Good principal and staff training.

My franchise sector research was well augmented by my decade of front-line exposure to Bendigo Bank's multi-billion dollar mutually structured franchised Banking business, Bendigo Community Bank, and their similarly spirited Community Telco initiatives.

For the SME sector, significant value can be realised by adopting and applying the disciplines that define the best turnkey franchise systems, and these disciplines feature prominently in our *5 Critical Success Factors*.

Sporting Sector Influences

I consciously started drawing parallels between Business and Elite Sports Leadership in 2002 after reading Peter Fitzsimon's excellent biography about Australian Rugby Union World Cup-winning captain John Eales.

Several years later, I became a non-executive director of prominent Australian Think Tank, The Eidos Institute, which had a collaborative working relationship with the *Classic Wallabies*, the association of retired Australian Rugby Union Test Team alumni. I was fascinated to learn how many of them had followed celebrated playing careers with senior leadership appointments in the business world. My *Nine Inspiring Tales from the Trenches* (Chapter 32) includes the story of former champion Wallaby Daniel Herbert's successful transition to CEO of leading Australian Strata Management company, SSKB.

In this book, I have drawn on some of the more obvious transformational learnings between professional sports and business. I've also referenced James Kerr's excellent book, *Legacy*, that distils the unique achievements of the All Blacks, New Zealand's National Rugby Union team, and their 15 tenets of good leadership.

Academic Research

I found extensive validating research from *Columbia University; Harvard Business School; UCLA; MIT's Sloan School of Management; North Western University's Kellogg School of Management; and Case Western University's Weatherhead School of Management*. I also reviewed a number of useful research studies produced by *The OECD; Deloitte; McKinsey; PWC; KPMG*; and several others.

Pulling It All Together

In writing the book, our intention was to deliver a comprehensive practitioner's guide for SME principals and their teams to provide them with the essential *Skills, Strategies*, and *Tactics* they need to learn, then adopt, followed by the clinical *Actions* they will need to take to be highly successful in their business. Our ultimate aim for the SME Leadership cohort is to transform and become our SME version of the Corporate World's *Highly Competent Generalist*.

In pursuit of that quest, we have graded and logically compressed the seven strengths that emerged from my two decades of research into *The 5 Critical Success Factors of SME Leadership*. They are:

1. *The Foundations,*

2. *The Finances,*

3. *The Front-Line,*

4. *Managing Time, and*

5. *Sustainable Collaborative Leadership.*

Critical Success Factors 1, 3, 4 and 5 are predominantly universal capabilities, regardless of where your business trades globally.

Critical Success Factor 2, The Finances, is unique in that Tax and Statutory Compliance Obligations differ from country to country. A core premise of our advice that accompanies Critical Success Factor 2, The Finances, is the importance of retaining a competent, locally skilled contract bookkeeper (part or full-time), or allocating those responsibilities to a staff or family member who has those skills, and also to retain an external Tax Accountant/Advisor to deal with your unique annual higher order Taxation and Statutory Obligations, wherever your business trades.

The accumulated learnings to be gained from universally adopting and following *The 5 Critical Success Factors* is not only for the benefit of the principal or CEO, but also for senior members of any business team, small or large, who are committed to learning and contributing to the success of the venture they work for.

A Salute to the SME Entrepreneur

SME Leadership: The 5 Critical Success Factors champions and celebrates the cause of an intrepid and courageous community of individuals who go into battle every day, working their hardest to keep their heads above water, with a genuine desire to succeed and to make a real difference.

SME's account collectively for 95% PLUS of worldwide businesses, 50% of employment and 40% of overall economic output (GDP). The global economy is therefore highly dependent on the SME Sector for its ongoing survival and success. To be blunt, if the sector were to falter significantly, the impact would be devastating.

Have no doubt that the statistics, the risks, the challenges, the opportunities and the applied learnings that have emerged from our research are just so important to SME's the world over.

In *Burn the Business Plan*, Carl J. Schramm saw three interrelated versions of the successful business entrepreneur, and we're convinced they are relevant to all business leaders regardless of the size of their enterprise.

Entrepreneurs are people who exploit an innovative idea – one they develop, improve, adapt, or copy, to start a profitable, scalable business that satisfies demand for a new or better product.

Entrepreneurs start their business venture intent on making money now, with the expectation that the value of their business will increase over time.

Entrepreneurs begin their journey with a genuine intent of making their business bigger, better, faster, and more profitable.

Each definition implies a genuine intent to create exceptional outcomes. As a vital life-blood component of economic success, the SME sector deserves every bit of support and patronage we can throw their way.

For the SME principal, please know this book has been written especially for you and your team. Most importantly, please embrace and enjoy your learning experience to the fullest!

SME Leadership: The 5 Critical Success Factors

"SMEs are mighty minnows, reflecting the competitive spirit that a market economy needs for efficiency; they provide an outlet for entrepreneurial talents, a wider range of consumer goods and services, a check to monopoly inefficiency, a source of innovation, and a seedbed for new industries; they allow an economy to be more adaptable to structural change through continuous initiatives embodying new technologies, skills, processes or products".

Hashim & Abdullah, 2000, Small & Medium Enterprise in Asian Pacific Countries (Nova Science Publishers Inc., Huntington New York). Ibielski, D. (1997), p193.

Foreword

Small business represents the heart and soul of the global economy, the place where optimism, innovation and hard work exists. To go into a small business may be an act of either courage or naivete, but plenty of people do it.

Life in a small business offers freedom, flexibility and opportunity, but it also comes with huge obligations – to customers, staff, suppliers, the community and, of course, compliance with the law. Trying to make all the decisions and meet all those obligations alone, or with limited support, can be stressful and difficult.

With his thoughtful, well-structured book, John Goddard offers the wisdom of a deeply knowledgeable friend. Working initially in the accounting profession, John built a successful career as a senior career banker and company director. Taking a deep interest in the Small Business Sector over several decades, he developed a statistical framework for understanding and then codifying the critical performance factors in successful SME leadership.

John's *SME Leadership, The 5 Critical Success Factors* offers new insights for every SME Entrepreneur, whether prospective or experienced. He provides a wealth of practical knowledge and guidance and does it in an open and readable style. The book moves seamlessly from the concrete aspects, such as the financial metrics and business ratios, to the more subtle yet critical capabilities of building networks, nurturing, relationships in the community, onboarding customers, generating revenues and also managing your emotions when everything is on the line.

As I read this book, I wished there had been something like it when I started my own small business some years ago. Having been a business regulator (and sometimes de-regulator) as Minister for Finance in the State of Queensland, I later went into my own small business with a genuine interest to know what was on the 'other side.' I soon discovered there was a mountain of baseline knowledge to be had and that being successful elsewhere doesn't guarantee you'll know how to prioritise and get things done when you're dealing with a mountain of pressure coming at you from all directions.

It's that balance which this book so ably provides because to run a business is in part to know the concrete facts but also to gain the important skills, to manage your emotions, to be a good community citizen and to set the right tone with staff. Those traits take a lot of time and a great deal of nuance to learn.

John's *SME Leadership The 5 Critical Success Factors of:* is written with a real generosity of spirit, offering guidance on both hard and soft skills. Its author, John Goddard, is as well placed as anyone I could imagine to be providing this guidance.

I recommend this book and wish the reader well in their challenging and rewarding journey ahead.

Hon. Rachel Nolan
Former Queensland Government Minister for Finance

Prologue

Leaving the safe harbour of secure employment to become a business owner, to pursue a dream, to be their own boss, to create something special is the most exciting yet daunting challenge most SME principals will ever undertake.

During the early stages, they invariably find themselves working longer hours for less money. They have difficulty managing priorities. They frequently suffer from stress and sleep deprivation and feel cut off from the world around them. Time with family and friends all too often becomes a luxury, and the grand vision that brought them into their venture can seem to be a millennium away.

Ian and I have known many entrepreneurs who began their journey as sole traders or micro-SMEs who faced similar challenges, yet went on to build successful businesses, even in tough times.

Please have no doubt that:

- *where there's a serious will,*
- *supported by a well thought out and executed game plan,*
- *with the best possible product offerings,*
- *and yes, peppered with a fair sprinkling of lucky breaks,*
- *success will invariably follow!*

My most important additional proviso is:

- *Be persistent, and*
- *Don't give up*

In a nutshell, this book is about unlocking the keys that will enable you to survive and indeed thrive in the SME world.

About The 5 Critical Success Factors

Brief Synopsis

SME Leadership: The 5 Critical Success Factors offers SME Principals and their senior teams a comprehensive practitioners guide to equip them with the essential skills they need to learn and the critical actions they need to take to be successful.

CRITICAL SUCCESS FACTOR 1: THE FOUNDATIONS

The focus of the Foundation Chapters is about the early Decisions and Actions you should take, i.e., seeking *Professional Advice*, adopting the most appropriate *Trading Structure* for the business, knowing your *Capital* management and sourcing options, and being aware of the Principal's general *Legal Responsibilities and Obligations*.

CRITICAL SUCCESS FACTOR 2: THE FINANCES

The Principal's Financial Responsibilities include getting the important priorities right by:

- Adopting automated, cloud-based bookkeeping software.
- Delegating day-to-day responsibility for managing the books of account to a contract bookkeeper (part or full-time) or a competent, finance-experienced staff or family member. In larger SMEs, an onboard qualified Accountant often manages these functions.
- Retaining an external tax accountant/advisor to deal with the higher order annual taxation obligations.

With those delegated disciplines locked in, the principal's residual financial focus should then chiefly be about:

- Honing your capacity to interpret your financial statements and diagnosing the critical performance challenges, with a view to achieving the best possible financial outcomes for the business,
- Choosing the right financial institution to bank with, understanding the major credit product options, and knowing the vital steps to take in seeking credit, and
- Committing to following the important steps you need to consider when buying or selling an SME.

CRITICAL SUCCESS FACTOR 3: THE FRONT LINE

The most successful SME principals the world over, commit to our *Nine Tenets of Front Line Leadership*:

1. They embrace the essentials of good business planning.

SME Leadership: The 5 Critical Success Factors

2. They know their *Brand* can only ever be as good as their customer's perception of it. Their golden rule is therefore *Don't oversell and underdeliver*, AND *Don't Make Promises they know they can't deliver*.
3. They take the essential steps to protect their *Trade Secrets and Intellectual Property*.
4. They understand the psychology of *Attracting Customers and Closing Sales*.
5. They have very well-crafted *Sales Pitches*.
6. They keep track of their networks and pipeline productivity with *Customer Relationship Management (CRM) Software*.
7. They have a strong *personal commitment to the communities they do business in and with*.
8. They harness the immense potential of *Social Media Marketing*.
9. They constantly challenge themselves with the same recurring question: "*What else can I do to generate the revenues critical to my business surviving and thriving?*"

CRITICAL SUCCESS FACTOR 4: MANAGING TIME

By adopting our *Nine Time and Workflow Management Priorities*, successful principals are able to free up the headspace they need to be able to focus on the critical income-generating, big-picture, front-of-mind business priorities that count.

Those nine priorities are:

1. Locking in a firm commitment to *Continuous Learning*.
2. Tracking their accrued learnings every day in a *Personal Immersion Journal*.
3. Automating and committing to highly productive *Habits and Routines* throughout the business.

SME Leadership: The 5 Critical Success Factors

4. Adopting disciplined *Priorities* in managing *the Front Line, the Finances* and *the Back Office* according to their relative importance.
5. *Delegating and Digitising* all *Back Office Priorities* to the maximum degree possible.
6. Banishing *Zero Value Time Wasters* from the business.
7. Building an *Organisation Structure* that meets and supports the true needs of the business.
8. Committing to and following the fundamentals of sound *Decision Making*.
9. If you are a sole trader, knowing how to manage your time effectively for the best outcomes.

CRITICAL SUCCESS FACTOR 5: SUSTAINABLE COLLABORATIVE LEADERSHIP

Sustainable and Successful 21st-century business leadership is driven by shared values and collaborative work cultures that focus on the power of a productive team and engender a strong sense of collegiate responsibility and *belonging* among each of the team members.

Our six interrelated *Building Blocks of Sustainable Collaborative Leadership* are:

1. Implementing good *Team Empowering Core Values* throughout the business.
2. Knowing the important *Capital Leadership Drivers*
3. Committing to the most productive *Team Leadership Drivers*
4. Knowing *The Important Role of Trust*
5. *Being Consistently Proactive*, and
6. *Accepting Personal Accountability* for all your Actions

Rapid Learning Strategies

We don't apologise for taking a building-block by building-block approach to each of our Critical Success Factors, nor do we presume that many of our readers don't already have a good percentage of those essential skills and capabilities. We do stress however that the 5 Critical Success Factors are interdependent, meaning that to reach peak performance in the business, it's important to make a commitment to master all of them over time.

Given those qualifications, Ian and I drill down here to consider where the most common learning gaps are evident in SME Leaders and their Teams, and the focus of our *Rapid Learning Strategies* have emerged from those findings:

1. *SME Entrepreneurs face up to four Common Learning Challenges, regardless of the size of their business*:
    - Some come up short on the knowledge they need to be able to comprehensively *Analyse their Financial Statements* and know the *Metrics that can Drive the Best Bottom Line Outcomes* (Critical Success Factor 2).
    - Some lack essential expertise in *Front-Line Selling* and struggle to maximise the revenues critical to their business surviving and indeed thriving (Critical Success Factor 3).
    - Most struggle to *Manage their Time* and adequately balance their priorities (Critical Success Factor 4).
    - Finally, many are *Slow Readers* and therefore have difficulty keeping pace with the learning strategies and skills they require for success (Critical Success Factor 4).

2. *The three Logical Follow-on Questions are*:
    - How can our book help you if you are affected by one or a combination of those four challenges?

SME Leadership: The 5 Critical Success Factors

- ➢ When you do purchase the book, how long will it take you to read and fully digest its contents?
- ➢ Is there a logical alternative strategy that will allow you to extract the essential learnings presented in the book's 370 plus pages? i.e., how can you bridge those gaps and learn what you need to know to be successful, A.S.A.P.?

3. *Our four Rapid Learning Strategies*:
    - ➢ This is not a book you should necessarily read from cover to cover in one stretch. Yet it is an immensely valuable reference guide that logically lays out the *Core Skills, Strategies* and *Tactics* you need to learn about and the on point sequential *Actions* you need to take to be successful.
    - ➢ That said, there's a great deal to digest and understand in those learnings. Our consequent recommendation is therefore to treat this book as your *Go to: Long Learning Reference Guide*.
    - ➢ We've consciously chosen not to include a traditional (and too often confusing to navigate) alphabetical index at the end of the book, but have rather chosen to present an extensive, logically laid out *Table of Contents* that will allow you to easily discover relevant subject matter information as you need it.
    - ➢ With those considerations in mind, our recommendation is to adopt and follow the *Quick Start Rapid Learning Guide* we've included in Appendix (i), and to access our complementary *Rapid Learning Toolkit Modules* in Appendix (ii). Our toolkit guides are easily downloadable to book buyers and will provide you with access to the relevant subjects in the book and how to acquire each of the Critical Success Factors A.S.A.P.

Go To: Appendix (i) for our *5 Critical Success Factors Rapid Learning Guide*, Appendix (ii) for how to access our Rapid Learning Toolkit Modules, and Appendix (iii) for more information about the SME Keystone's web platform.

CRITICAL SUCCESS FACTOR 1:

THE FOUNDATIONS

'My golden rule as a property planner has always been to envision and plan before I act! So, if I'm constructing a new building, I first talk to the important stakeholders to be clear on what they want. Then, I prepare a set of basic concept drawings – my golden rule as a property planner is to develop an early sense of what the end product will look like visually and to be satisfied that it's going to meet the client's brief. After that, I draw up a full set of plans, detailed specifications, and the costings needed to build it. Finally, I appoint a reputable builder and track every stage of construction to make sure I get precisely what I asked for. By then, I know I have done the hard yards and that the end product will meet my stakeholders wants! Why do I know this? Because I got my foundations right in the first place and had the good sense to envision and plan before I acted!'

Mark Mahaffey, General Manager and Senior Property Planner, Cooper Property Group.

Why Are You Reading This Book?

I'm guessing your answer will most likely fall somewhere within the following range of possibilities:

- ✓ I'm an existing small business owner, and I'm committed to doing everything I possibly can to be as successful as I can.
- ✓ I'm considering leaving my well-paid job to go into business for myself, but I want to do some solid homework before making the transition.
- ✓ I've been made redundant or have retired from my job and want to explore my next stage options, one of which is to buy or establish a small business.
- ✓ I'm thinking of buying an existing business that is up for sale right now.
- ✓ I'm thinking of buying a turnkey franchise business.
- ✓ I have this amazing *original idea* I believe I can make *millions of bucks* out of!

Bravo to existing SME operators who want to carry out a business health check and are committed to improving their base knowledge, and to those who are considering possible future options. I would encourage each of you to work through this book, undertake the additional research I have suggested and then map out a plan of action.

If you're about to acquire a business that's for sale, I urge you to take the heat out of your current negotiations. Ask for a little more time and do your homework first. If there's pressure to close negotiations, step cautiously. Small businesses can be difficult to sell even in the good times, and there will undoubtedly be plenty of opportunities available for you. The bonus is that the right knowledge will equip you with a sharper negotiating edge.

If you are considering purchasing a turnkey franchise business, the Franchise route could possibly be a good place to start your entrepreneurial journey. You will have the comfort of knowing you are getting a robust business management system with a lot of value-added support. My only caution is to take care, as several of the less robust franchise business systems are under duress, as I write. Do your homework, speak with other franchisees operating in the same sector and check out the numbers to make sure the opportunity is a real one and stands up to scrutiny.

Finally, a few words about that *original idea*! If it's already there now, it will still be there in a few months. Remember, it is your secret until you make the decision to let the cat out of the bag and open the door. So, ditto for undertaking the same pre-research and homework. My only caution? The sheer task of starting a brand new business from scratch with no income certainties to start with, and no idea if the marketplace will be as passionate as you are about it's potential, is a daunting one. In reality, it may well be the toughest gig of all.

Finding the Right Professional Advisors

About now, you may be reading the early chapters of this book and will realise that if you don't already have a good external tax accountant/advisor, it's time to start looking for one. The same accountant will be the ideal person to also advise you on the best trading structure and your capital management plans once you are ready to proceed.

How Many Banks Do I Have to Rob?

You discover you may not have enough capital or *cash in the till* until your business venture reaches breakeven, and you can start breathing again!

It's a common problem for those going into business for the first time, but it also sometimes happens to those who are already trading. Have you got some additional solid savings, a decent nest egg, a golden handshake, a wealthy aunt who loves you to bits, or another source of available capital to invest?

And by the way, in all conscience, I can't say I recommend robbing that bank!

What Are My Legal Obligations?

What responsibilities will I have at law as a business principal, and what are my liabilities if I do the wrong thing or if something else goes wrong? What insurance or other legal protection is available to me to mitigate my risks? Finally, do I need to update my will. AND, while it may well be a sensitive issue, do I need to consider having a prenuptial agreement?

What Else Should I Do?

The Kauffman Institute:

This Kansas City based institute has a focus on promoting, advancing and encouraging entrepreneurship, supporting education, and contributing to American Life generally. Their aim is to *"foster a society of economically independent individuals who are engaged citizens, contributing to the improvement of their communities."*

Some years ago, I took a no-cost subscription to two Kauffman Institute websites that, in my view, are relevant to SME entrepreneurs anywhere in the Developed or Developing World:

Kauffman's Stay Connected Program keeps on giving week after week with regular confidence-building gems about the journey of an SME entrepreneur. Go to: www.kauffman.org home page and click on the *Stay Connected* icon, provide your name, email address, and answer the few quick questions they will ask about your interests – I chose *Education* and *Entrepreneurship.*

Kauffman's Entrepreneurs Program Newsletter provides regular email updates with the latest research and content from Kauffman Entrepreneurs. Go to: www.entrepreneurship.org and provide your email address.

The content that frequently arrives in your mailbox is always an excellent quick-read primer.

Chapter 1: Professional Advice

I first learnt about the Australian taxation system during my Chartered Accounting studies. Australia's company tax rate in the early 1970s was a flat 45%. The top marginal rate for individuals was 0.64c in the dollar for those earning over $20,000! Payroll Tax was a federal levy at a flat 25% of corporate payroll overhead, and several other taxes were well entrenched. But none of it was particularly complex and Federal Tax Legislation ran to a paltry 500 pages.

Capital Gains Tax; Goods and Services Tax; Fringe Benefits Tax; Luxury Car Tax; Transfer Pricing Legislation; the Federal Superannuation Guarantee Levy; Dividend Imputation and Franking Credits; Money Laundering Legislation, and the Higher Education Funding Scheme have all been introduced over the decades since, and they all have an impact on how we manage our tax affairs.

Added to those changes is your core obligation to know about the four tax compliance pillars of *Legislation*; *Lodgement*; *Accurate and Reliable Reporting*; and *On Time Payment*. Australian Taxation legislation now runs to just over 6,000 pages of heavy reading – more than ten times what it was when I first studied tax law!

Today, the Australian Taxation Office's (ATO) tracing technology and capability is well geared to be able to detect income and tax disclosure irregularities in tax returns and to undertake a significantly higher level of targeted predictive corporate and personal tax audits. To their credit, the ATO sends out clear and unequivocal warnings to taxpayers about the types of non-compliance signs they are looking for. But it's not possible for the average SME principal to have gained the knowledge required to go even remotely close to grasping their full disclosure, procedural and compliance obligations.

Those need-to-know challenges and risks are every bit as daunting elsewhere in both the Developed and Developing Worlds. So what's the best way to manage this mountain of knowledge? The obvious answer is you don't have to, provided you appoint a qualified external tax accountant/advisor with deep SME business experience. That professional will guide you in managing your annual business and personal tax affairs and will provide valuable counsel on the performance of your business, regardless of where you operate.

The first ten book chapters are about the business foundations and the finances. An experienced part or full-time bookkeeper will be able to manage all your day-to-day financial transactional and compliance routines, and your external tax accountant/advisor will be your *go-to* advisor on your higher order tax and statutory obligations.

Importance of Retaining an External Tax Accountant

What Does a Competent external Tax Accountant/Advisor bring to the Table?

1. Rolling advice on all your business and personal tax affairs.
2. Preparation and lodgement of annual business and personal tax returns/filings and the other statutory obligations relevant to your country of origin.
3. Provision of advanced taxation planning.
4. Dealing with all Tax Office/IRS communications.
5. Assistance in selection and registration of the most appropriate trading entity for your business.
6. Guidance on selecting cloud-based accounting software and establishing the essential bookkeeping routines and monthly reporting you will need.
7. Advice on the services that can reasonably be outsourced, including bookkeeping, BAS/ sales tax accounting and payrolls.
8. Dealing with tax audit investigations as and when they arise. An initial exploratory audit letter is invariably sent, seeking your responses to questions about specific transactions or about the business generally. A well-handled and full disclosure open response may halt further investigation at that point. A more exhaustive audit may follow if the initial

answers do not satisfy your Tax Office.

Warning: Do not think of taking on this task without your Tax Accountant's guidance.

9. Research & Development (R&D) Grant options may include financial and tax incentives such as export market development, early-stage innovation, accelerating commercialisation, and other available federal, state or local/ municipal government-incentive schemes.
10. Providing guidance on profitability trends, cash flows and month and year-to-date financial performance.
11. Offering guidance on business debt planning and banking negotiations.
12. Updating your will should always start with a chat with your Tax Accountant/Advisor, but you will also need a competent lawyer and financial planner. Your will should achieve the ideal balance between tax minimisation and asset protection but also embraces your preferred business succession plans if you get sick/injured or are unable to continue working.

Tax Accountant/Client Relationships work best for both sides when they are treated respectfully as a *partnership* between the Tax Accountant/Advisor and the SME principal. The accountant will bring to the table their SME experience with businesses of a similar size and look to yours.

In my experience tax accountants want to give useful advice because when their client succeeds, they succeed. Obviously, the principal should respect the time challenges involved and that the accountant also has a business to run.

In my view, there are three separate relationship frameworks to consider:

The first six items on my list are, in a sense, technical *plug-ins* that can easily be put into the general working machinery and operational efficiencies of the average accounting practice. Your accountant will be able to schedule all those activities so the fee you pay reasonably and fairly reflects the value of the work done while not being prohibitive.

Item 7: encompasses your accountant's advice on the best approach to outsourcing bookkeeping, BAS/ sales tax, Payrolls and other services.

Items 8 to 12: these important collateral advice add-ons will require more of your tax accountant's time, expert advice and billable hours, but in my experience, the value you'll gain from seeking that advice is invariably well worth the expense.

Go also to: *Deloitte's: Tax Guides & Country Highlights*

Finding the Right Accountant

Start with a solid shortlist of candidates. Ask for recommendations from friends and associates already in business. Put together a shortlist of several practices to possibly visit. Check their websites to see what you can glean up front, before you pay them a visit, then:

- Confirm they are registered accountants and/or qualified tax agents and what their specific areas of expertise are.
- Do they have clients in the same industry sector as yours? Seek information on the makeup of their client base.
- Ask how they bill for services and get an indication of their fee structure for a business similar to yours.
- Are they willing to give you client testimonials, and would they allow you to speak with one or two of their clients?
- Ask who will be your go-to person at the practice and make sure you meet that person before committing.

When your preferred candidate is ticking all the right boxes, be mindful that this person is going to be a critical part of your inner circle for a long time. Then it's your decision time!

Other Professional Advisors Who May Help

A Commercial Lawyer

While your tax accountant will be your external advisory mainstay, you will occasionally need a competent commercial lawyer. Their services may include advice on estates and wills, partnership or shareholders agreements, certain contracts, protecting intellectual property, resolving disputes, nondisclosure deeds, employment law, debt collection and general disputes. If you don't have someone in mind, ask your accountant for a referral, as lawyers and accountants frequently conjunct on matters that require a combination of tax and legal advice. Also, know that certain areas of the law, such as Industrial Relations or Intellectual Property, require subject matter specialists. Always get an upfront indicative fee quote.

An Insurance Broker

Negotiating your business insurance needs directly is a challenge you should avoid. Insurance is a critical part of protecting your business assets, your employees and your personal corporate law obligations. Qualified brokers understand the insurance market and will negotiate the right small business focussed policies for you at competitive rates. They can also advise on the *self-insurance strategy* of setting appropriate higher excess claim limits vs. lower overall premiums payable in the lower risk asset protection areas of the business.

Have a quick chat with your accountant when annual policy premiums come up. They are well qualified to help you navigate and translate the important Risk Likelihood versus Consequence considerations of your insurance coverage.

NB: Insurance Brokers receive their income from the insurers via the policies they write but are legally bound (and liable!) to give reliable, independent advice.

A Financial Planner

It concerns me the number of business owners I have met over the years who had not adequately planned for their retirement. They too often overlook the potential tax benefits of a well-structured retirement plan strategy to manage their overall personal finances.

A good financial planner will guide you in building a robust personal retirement plan and will recommend the most appropriate investments for you. They will also advise on your personal estate planning and insurance options.

Chapter 2: The Trading Structure

Three similar trading entity options are available in most Developed and Developing World Economies:

Sole Trader,

Partnership, or

Limited Liability Corporation.

You may also consider including a Trust with your Trading Structure that affords you the potential to better manage the collective assets under your control and to better optimise your income distributions.

In this chapter, I provide the specific facts about how each of those structures work in Australia and the liability risks and tax considerations of each option.

If your business trades in another international location, check with your local tax accountant about your specific trading entity obligations and reporting requirements.

Sole Trader

Key facts

This structure is for proprietors who singularly own 100% of the business. You can either trade under your own name (e.g., John Smith), or you may choose to register a business name (e.g., John Smith trading as Smith Business Services).

Set-up costs

There are no establishment fees if you are going to simply trade under your own name. There is a small annual or multiyear fee if you are going to register a separate business name with The Australian Securities and Investment Commission (ASIC).

The pros

Sole trader status is the simplest and cheapest legal framework for the sole proprietor.

The cons

Beware! As a sole trader, you will be trading under your own name, which means, in simple terms, that you and your personal assets (including your home) are totally exposed to any claims that may be made against the business.

Also, sole trader status offers few legitimate tax minimisation options.

Partnership

Key facts

A partnership framework is generally limited from two to 20 partners, although larger numbers are allowed under Australian Corporations Law for defined classes of business (e.g., Professional Practices such as accountants, lawyers and medical practitioners).

Subject to the terms of a partnership agreement, profitability is usually shared in proportion to the cash/capital each partner has injected into the business. The partnership does not incur income tax liability directly. Individual partners lodge their tax returns based on their share of proportionate partnership earnings.

Set-up costs

General establishment costs are not dissimilar to those of a sole trader, but the cost of drafting a partnership agreement (which is a must) will be an added expense.

The pros

The partners pool their unique skills and experience, their assets and their combined capital. The resultant cash injection and pooling of assets may make a partnership a more attractive banking proposition when seeking lending support. There may be some scope for tax minimisation with family-based partnerships, but minimal opportunity generally for non-family partnerships.

The cons

Beware! As per the sole trader framework, general partnerships offer minimal personal liability protection. Each partner is personally liable for all business debts (jointly and severally), regardless of their equity contribution. The obvious onus for anyone considering entering a partnership arrangement is to seek independent professional advice and to ensure you have received full disclosure of your partners' financial position before proceeding.

It is possible for one or more of the partners to take the option of a limited partnership in the business that has the effect of eliminating liability for certain debts and obligations of the business. This alternative may apply to silent investors, for example, who are non-contributing (non-equity) partners who do not get actively involved in day-to-day decision-making.

Other than for some professional partnerships, where there is an argument for allowing limited partnership partners, there may be an even more compelling argument to opt for the formation of a limited liability corporation instead.

Limited Liability Corporation

Key facts

A *Limited Liability Corporation (Pty. Ltd.)* is a privately owned company not listed on any stock exchange. It is a unique legal entity separate from you, its owner, and is capable of trading and entering contracts in its own right. The principal/owners are the shareholders, and they are only legally liable for company debts to the extent of the capital they have invested. A limited liability corporation must have a minimum of one (typically the SME principal) and no more than 50 shareholders.

An *Unlisted Public Company (Ltd)* option allows more shareholders and offers more flexibility if you are raising private capital for the business.

Management of both company options is guided by a constitution that sets out the corporate governance rules, director appointments, meeting protocols and authority to make decisions on behalf of the company and shareholders. Directors of companies are also bound by additional specific responsibilities as laid out in the Corporations Act (Chapter 4).

Set-up costs

Businesses that specialise in company formations have a typical cost range starting as low as $800, and this fee will usually include provision of a full set of company documents. Alternatively, your accountant will attend to all of this for you (always my preference) but will not be offended if you choose to take on these tasks yourself.

The company registration will come with a standard draft constitution that, in my experience, will meet the needs of most SME directors/principals. Alternatively, you may choose to operate under specific *Replaceable Rules*. These rules may specify matters such as dealing with voting rights, negotiable instruments, the appointment of further or alternate directors, the director's remuneration, the appointment or removal of a Managing Director, and so on – your accountant will advise you on *Replaceable Rules*.

You may (in my view should!) also consider having a separate Shareholders Agreement drafted to define the relationship between the shareholders and directors where they are not one and the same.

Other than the initial set-up costs for establishing a Limited Liability or Unlisted Public Company, there are also recurring annual costs and responsibilities to submit an annual updated company return and provide any change of information about the company. There are also additional accounting costs required to produce and lodge the company's annual tax return. The directors (those entitled to a distribution of income) must also lodge their own separate tax returns.

The pros

Directors/principals are not liable for company debts unless they have given personal guarantees, or it can be proven that they have traded while insolvent or have acted negligently.

Given the general differences between Company Tax Rates and the upper tier of the personal tax rates, as well as the treatment of dividends on distributed profit, there may be opportunities to minimise cumulative tax liability, particularly where spousal and family income distribution opportunities present themselves. The additional creation of a family trust and supporting trust deed will undoubtedly add further flexibility but also value to these options.

The cons

Higher ongoing costs and more complex reporting. But, if you are serious about growing a successful business and generating significant revenues over time, the company structural option may well tick the preferred boxes for you. It nearly always does for me.

A Trust

A trust is a legal structure that can hold assets, invest funds and is an efficient vehicle for managing the distribution of income. Trusts are commonly used as a framework to deal with not-for-profit organisations and sometimes more complex family inheritances (usually via *Testamentary Trusts* for each beneficiary), but a *Discretionary Trust* also offers important options for managing business assets and making income distributions.

I could write several chapters on the relative merits of incorporating a Trust framework in your ultimate trading entity decisions, but that formal advice should really come from your tax advisor. Suffice to say, a trust has the potential to maximise flexibility in how your assets are managed, and income is distributed. Trusts efficiently take advantage of the relative tax-free thresholds and personal tax rates of each beneficiary, especially when other family members work in the business.

The set-up and annual recurring costs of including a trust in your business structure are significant and not without complexity, e.g., a separate trust deed is required to define the role of the trust and its relationship with the business and the trust beneficiaries – a separate corporation is easily established to act as the trustee (e.g., a Pty. Ltd. Company) to provide the principal and directors with an extra layer of liability protection.

The benefits and possible tax effectiveness of incorporating a Trust in your business structuring decisions can be significant, but only if the expected income to be generated by the business is expected to be substantial enough to support those additional costs. And let me repeat you absolutely *must* seek professional advice from your Tax Accountant.

The Next Steps?

After drilling through all the pros and cons with your tax accountant, selecting the trading entity structure that is best for you and choosing the business name you prefer, there are several steps required to make it all happen. Your accountant is the best person to advise and assist you with the company/business registration and early tax compliance formalities.

SME Leadership: The 5 Critical Success Factors

Check out the following websites:
- *www.businessname.com.au*
- *www.usa-corporate.com*
- *www.gov.uk.org*

Trademarks:
- *www.ipaustralia.gov.au*
- *www.uspto.gov*
- *www.trademarkdirect.co.uk*

Domain name Registration:
- *www.domain.com*

Social media registration:
- *www.namechk.com*

Chapter 3: Capital

If you aspire to build a *significant business* over time, my instinct to consider doing it under an incorporated Limited Liability (Pty. Ltd.), or an Unlisted Public Company structure (Ltd.), particularly if there will be multiple shareholders investing in the business. But as a matter of course, seek your accountant's wise counsel on those decisions.

In this chapter, my capital and balance sheet observations are relatively similar between limited liability companies, sole traders and partnerships.

Capital Assets

Fixed Capital (or Invested Capital): This is the financial capital you initially put up to bootstrap a new business until it reaches breakeven or to raise additional capital to expand a business. For an SME, that capital is traditionally contributed by the principal and any other early-stage investors/partners in the business. It is categorised as *owners' capital* under the *shareholders' equity* segment of the balance sheet. The actual cash that comes with that investment goes into the business bank account and is classified as a *current asset*.

It's important to achieve clarity about what start-up capital you will need to go ahead with for your SME. Many principals make the mistake of assuming they can build their business on a shoestring, with little or no cash to spare. Please understand this is a potential recipe for disaster with the possibility of eventual business failure. Consult with your accountant about your capital funding needs long before you commit to any new business venture.

Working Capital: Once the business reaches breakeven, where current assets exceed current liabilities and the business can meet its ongoing cash flow needs from net trading surpluses, that source of capital is then known as *Working Capital*.

Financial Institution Funded Assets: This is an alternative source of fixed asset underwriting. Provided there is evidence of a healthy capacity to meet loan repayments from ongoing surplus cash flows (working capital), the business may access lending facilities to purchase or lease a range of possible assets. These assets may include motor vehicles, commercial machinery, manufacturing equipment, office/fit outs, furnishings, and other similar assets. Assets purchased with financial institution funding sit on the balance sheet as fixed assets. Loans related to those purchases are treated as *current or long-term liabilities*, depending on the loan term. Shorter-term *come and go overdraft funding* may also be sourced for the business in a similar way.

Intangible Assets

These assets are not physical in nature. They sit on the balance sheet at a defined value but may be difficult to quantify in terms of realisable value, as their future value may be challengeable. They include items such as goodwill, licensing agreements, patents, copyrights, franchise agreements, and fees.

Intangible assets are listed in the balance sheet when they have been acquired at a specific cost/value. A portion of that value may be amortised (written down) over an agreed number of years.

Social Capital

Social capital is in my view the important glue that allows business teams to work together with shared vision and values to achieve their aspirations and goals. It also incorporates all your stakeholders, including your customers and the community you do business in.

While it's not measurable in finite value and does not appear anywhere on the financial statements, your *social capital* and how well you deploy it could have a significant influence on the ultimate success of your business (more about Social Capital in Chapter 30).

The Initial Seed Funding of the Business

After preparing a robust business plan and constructing conservative profit and loss and cash flow projections, ask your accountant to review those projections. Then, it's time to work out where the vital capital is going to come from to make it all happen.

The starting point depends on your entry point. Are you already in a business, are you purchasing an existing business, or are you starting one from scratch? How much of a cash buffer will you need until you reach breakeven, the point where cash coming in exceeds cash going out? My golden rule is to make sure you over-provide for those preliminary capital needs.

Funding capital may come from one of several sources:

Personal Cash Savings and Reserves: plus, those of any partners you may have in the business.

A Golden Handshake or Severance Package: from a former employer or from any other source of funds you are personally able to access.

Love Money: could be from family or close friends. My general caution is to step carefully in not making unrealistic or unachievable promises about the return of this source of capital.

Bank Funding: Be well prepared before you approach a bank, particularly if it is for early-stage funding of your business idea or if it is to purchase an already trading business. Banks like to see a healthy track record and to know what the financial projections are showing. They will be more open to those who are already in business and who can demonstrate a good trading history with a comfortable capacity to repay. They may also show a more sympathetic ear if you have a solid personal asset position and/or are willing to offer security (Chapter 10).

Angel Investors: are most typically well-cashed-up retirees, willing to invest their capital and their specific expertise in projects where they believe they can add value. Their willingness to invest focuses on their complementary areas of knowledge and experience. They generally prefer to take a directorship and/or be consulted on critical decisions going forward. For further information about connecting with international angel investment sources, go to:

    www.australianinvestmentnetwork.com
    www.angelinvestmentnetwork.co.uk
    www.angelinvestmentnetworks.us

Venture Capitalists (VC): take an equity share in a business that typically has unique intellectual property they want to take to the market and fully develop.

In going for either the Angel or VC path, just having a good idea is rarely enough. You need to be able to back it up with a well-presented, lucid business plan supported by solid financial data, believable projections, an understanding of what your target market will be, and a clear view of where it fits with other possible competitors in the marketplace. You will also need to create a passionate but precise pitch statement, long before you visit any potential investors.

It may sound trite, but if you believe your unique idea has merit, watch several back episodes of *The Shark Tank* (Australian or US versions) or *Dragon's Den* (UK version) where you may pick up some useful tips on working on your investor pitch.

Shareholding Options for a Company

A limited liability company may issue various classes of shares, although, for the typical SME, fully paid *ordinary shares* generally dominate their share register.

The rights and restrictions applying to each class of share distinguish it from other classes. The classes may include *fully paid* or *partially paid shares,* or may relate to *voting rights, employee* or *management share allocations,* and/or *bonus share issues* where no subscription amount is payable.

Finally, *preference shares* grant the shareholders defined rights or preferential treatment over other classes of shareholders. *Redeemable preference shares* are a hybrid debt/equity instrument issued initially as a debenture/loan to the business with the option of full reimbursement or conversion to fixed capital shares at maturity.

NB: If you intend to raise capital via any source other than Ordinary Shares seek specific advice from your accountant.

Shareholding Recording and Reporting Priorities

Share Register: An up-to-date share register should be maintained at the company's registered office containing the name and address of each member, the number of shares held, share classes, and the amount paid and unpaid on the shares. A current copy of the company constitution should also be maintained at the registered office. Any member should reasonably have a right to inspect the share register or the constitution.

Limited liability companies (Pty. Ltd.) are the most typical incorporated structure for SMEs and are required to notify their corporate regulator (ASIC in Australia) when there is a change to member details or shareholding structure. This may include the issue or cancellation of shares or change of directors' details, residential addresses or other biodata. Similar requirements apply to Unlisted Public Companies (Ltd.).

Recording and Reporting Priorities for Partnerships

The following records should be maintained for partnerships:

1. A copy of the partnership agreement. If none exists, then a copy of the certificate of registration. If that does not exist, produce documentary evidence that the partners are carrying on their activities as a partnership.
2. Commencement date of the partnership.
3. Detailed statement of assets and liabilities.
4. Details of each partner's capital account and sources of capital contributed.
5. Details of each partnership bank account, including name and account number, bank and branch, the date the account was opened, the names of persons authorised to operate the account, and the date of those authorisations.
6. The family relationship of the partners and, if the partners are husband and wife, details of the nature and extent of the services rendered by each member.

7. Whether the partners own jointly or in common, any property from which interest, dividends, rents, or royalties are derived.

8. The names in which business contracts are made.

9. Details of services rendered in the production of assessable income by a partner under 18 years old or by a beneficiary under 18 years old in a Trust where the Trustee is a partner. Details must include the nature, extent, and value of the services rendered.

10. Whether the partnership is constituted or conducted such that any partners cannot, of their own will, deal with any part of their share of the partnership income.

Supplementary Private Capital Raisings

You simply *must* seek professional advice before undertaking a supplementary capital raising, particularly if it is to be from investors not already on your share register.

A sensible starting point is a solid discussion with your tax accountant. If it is agreed you should proceed, you will need to also engage a competent commercial lawyer.

While Public Companies in Developed World economies can raise capital from the general public, typical SME limited liability proprietary companies may usually only do so from:

- Existing shareholders or employees.

- Wholesale/ sophisticated investors, who are regarded at law as being capable of making those decisions without the need for independent advice.

- A subsidiary company, or from the public, provided the fundraising does not require a disclosure document or a prospectus.

Beware! I have been intentionally very brief about SME Capital Raisings. Do not, under any circumstances, consider undertaking a Supplementary Capital Raising without first seeking essential legal and taxation advice about the relevant reporting, compliance and capital raising limitations and obligations.

Chapter 4: Legal Responsibilities & Obligations

There are many more similarities than differences in the fusion of global corporate laws and regulations that govern the rules of running a business.

Those similarities have been influenced by the high degree of common/borrowed drafting that has occurred over time, but it's also true that in the 21st Century we increasingly trade and deal in a global economy that is obliged to find ways to accommodate international, cross border business relationships.

Most of the advice that follows is universally applicable wherever your business trades.

Make sure you confer with your tax accountant, who will undoubtedly be your best first port of call on the unique taxation, local governance and compliance obligations you should be aware of.

Corporate Law Directors Compliance

When you become a director of a company, regardless of its size or where it does business, you agree in principle to be responsible and liable for carrying out your defined corporate law obligations. A universal presumption of those laws is that *ignorance is no defence*. In simple terms, this means you are required to reasonably understand and comply with those responsibilities. Saying 'I didn't know!' or 'No-one told me!', is rarely a fall-back defence for non-compliance.

Here is my briefest summary of directors' mainstream responsibilities at law:

- Minimum director qualifications: Directors must be a minimum age, e.g., 18 years in Australia, New Zealand, Canada and the US, and 16 years in the UK. Directors cannot be an undischarged bankrupt or have been convicted of certain offences related to prior directorships.
- Director numbers: Unlisted Limited Liability Companies must have a minimum of one Director in Australia, New Zealand, Canada and the UK, and three Directors in the US.

- The business judgement rule: A director who makes informed, rational and in good faith business judgements on behalf the company, should on balance avoid personal liability arising from making those judgements. In simple terms, the director commits to acting in the best interests of the company.
- Fiduciary responsibility: Directors must exercise their powers and duties with the diligence that a reasonable person would exercise. This requirement implies a sound knowledge of a director's obligations under corporations' law.
- Misappropriation: Where there are multiple directors, any one director may not take any assets, including confidential documents or Intellectual Property (IP), without the agreement of the other directors.
- Financial records: Directors are obliged to ensure all financial records are maintained up to date and that they reflect the true financial state of the company's affairs.
- The conflict-of-interest principle: The Director should disclose to other directors any personal interests that may conflict with the company's best interests and should offer to excuse themselves from debate/decisions that relate to that conflict.
- Solvency and going concern obligations: An insolvent company is one that is unable to pay its debts when they fall due. It's not automatically an offence to reach a point of insolvency, but it is an offence to knowingly continue to trade and enter further commitments while insolvent.
- *Unique Australian director ID protocols*: Directors are required to hold a director ID number as a prerequisite of becoming a company director. Go To: www.abrs.gov.au/director-identification-number

Director Penalty Regimes and Other Liability Risks

The company structural option for a trading enterprise protects directors generally from personal liability for company debts unless a personal guarantee has been granted to lenders or creditors.

However, that level of protection does NOT eliminate the risk of personal prosecution for being in non-compliance of the director's obligations under Corporate Law, OR of a director being enjoined (and being potentially liable) in a lawsuit against the company. Yet it's not all that difficult to comply, provided you do your homework, and you are diligent in carrying out your responsibilities.

There are other universal potential director liability risks, e.g., serious employee injuries occurring where there is evidence of inadequate Workplace Health and Safety (WHS) procedures and controls in the business.

In the case of Australian Corporations Law non-compliance, a Director may be fined up to $200,000 by the Australian Securities and Investment Commission (ASIC) and may be banned from being a Director for a defined period. It doesn't happen very often, but it is a risk. Directors may also be held liable for failure to withhold or remit employee income tax deductions, for company debts incurred while the company is insolvent, or for non-compliance of any of the other Statutory Obligations.

Director Protection Options

Directors Indemnity: A company may indemnify its directors and responsible senior officers against liabilities they incur while they are carrying out their normal duties and responsibilities. (Go to: *DLA Piper Intelligence – How can directors be protected from liability*).

Some companies (including those based in Australia), offer their directors and senior officers the option of a separate *Deed of Access & Indemnity*, which gives them right of access to board and financial documents necessary to properly defend a Liability Action, makes provision for directors and officers legal fees to be paid if they are enjoined in an action against the company, and provides for the option of a minimum level of Directors and Officers Insurance Coverage.

Indemnities cannot cover liability in cases where the director/officer is found to have a personal liability not permitted to be indemnified, such as criminal charges where the director/officer is found guilty, or actions brought by a liquidator where the grounds for making the order are found to be valid, (such as trading while insolvent). The relevant point here is that the law cannot protect you if you wilfully do something inherently wrong, behave dishonestly or deceptively or consciously choose to break the law.

A *Directors and Officers Insurance Policy* is a policy with a reputable insurer maintained in favour of the directors and senior officers of the Company that indemnifies them against certain liabilities for which such an indemnity can be lawfully given. Your Insurance Broker will be able to tell you more about this sort of cover. My caution? Make sure you carefully check exclusions under such cover (e.g., insolvent trading risks are invariable exclusions).

Director / Partner Relationship Management

Shareholder / Partner Agreements: A shareholders/ partners agreement seeks to codify the key roles and responsibilities between the shareholders or partners of a business, where there is more than one shareholder or partner. It is best prepared before a business starts trading.

A shareholders/ partner's agreement will typically cover subjects such as the funding, structure, management and direction of the business, and the specific responsibilities and obligations of each of the parties. It is also designed to deal with the relationship issues that may possibly arise during the life of the business. Properly drafted, the Shareholders/Partners Agreement will help to determine in advance how those issues, particularly the sensitive ones, will be dealt with should they arise, rather than having the parties react after the event.

In some businesses, for example, there is no provision for the death of one of the shareholders or partners, where the remaining spouse may want to take on the interest and an active role in the management of the company. This may not necessarily be in the best interests of the business. This possibility may be avoided with a well-constructed shareholders agreement and adequate succession and estate planning.

If you are currently operating a business or partnership with multiple directors, shareholders, or partners without an agreement in place, you should put a priority on discussing your situation with a commercial lawyer. In most cases, an agreement can be drafted after the event, with the existing structure and operational style of the business used as a starting point.

Who should prepare the shareholders agreement? Do not seriously think of developing a shareholder's agreement under your own steam. Find a competent Corporations Law experienced Commercial Lawyer for this advice. But make sure you also include your Tax Accountant in those deliberations.

Succession

Wills and Estates: This may well be a sensitive subject, but if you have gone into business with a co-partner(s) or co-shareholder/director(s), things have the potential to rapidly go pear-shaped if one of you passes away or suffers a prolonged illness or other affliction while the business is still operational.

Examples may be of a surviving spouse wishing to withdraw from the business and receive a full return of capital or alternatively wanting to take an active role in the day to day running of the business. No offence meant by me (!) but either of these outcomes may have the potential to be disastrous for the prospects of any business and for the remaining partner/director.

A business partnership has some similarities to a marriage/life partnership (!) and there are collateral risks of not planning for all possible contingencies. Ensure you make adequate provision for your shareholding or partnership in a properly drafted will that also includes mirror provisions in your shareholder/partnership agreement. All aspects of this contingency should be actively canvassed between Partners/Directors first, then with a competent commercial lawyer who will help you navigate all the important considerations in the final documents.

One option may be to consider taking out specific insurance/life policies that incorporate an estimate of the assumed future realisable value of the deceased party's capital interest in the business. In this policy, the business pays the premium each year with the beneficiaries receiving the time of death benefit.

Prenuptial Agreements

This is often a sensitive issue and one I have worked on with Estate Lawyers and Accountants several times over the years.

Challenges may emerge with family-based businesses, where spouses and their adult children work in the business and who may ultimately inherit a part, or total shareholding on the death of a parent, or the death of one of the children. Potential circumstances may arise particularly when one of them – a parent or one of the adult children marries or remarries. In these circumstances, the interests of the company and the existing shareholders/beneficiaries should ideally be protected by a Prenuptial Agreement, when the marriage/ life partnership/ de facto relationship comes into being.

A competent Estate Lawyer will be able to take you through the important considerations and options. Also include your accountant in these deliberations as on occasion, preferred tax treatment options may be at odds with recommended estate or asset protection considerations. In fact, please start with your accountant first!

My plea is do not put these deliberations into your *too hard basket*, nor presume it can't possibly happen to me!

CRITICAL SUCCESS FACTOR 2:

THE FINANCES

"Unless you're willing to put in the effort to learn how to read and interpret financial statements, ...you really shouldn't be in business."

Warren Buffet, Chairman, Berkshire Hathaway

The first two financial chapters are about the bookkeeping routines and your financial statutory obligations at law.

It's important to know upfront that those responsibilities will relentlessly weigh you down if you harbour even the slightest thoughts of trying to manage them personally without help.

Our inviolate rules are therefore to:

- Adopt an automated, cloud-based bookkeeping software solution. Monthly subscription options are not significant.
- Depending on the business size, hire a competent contract part or full time bookkeeper OR allocate those responsibilities to a staff or family member who has the requisite knowledge and experience to carry them out well.
- Large SMEs may have an onboard qualified *Accountant* to manage all the Financial responsibilities.

SME Leadership: The 5 Critical Success Factors

- ➤ Regardless of the business size, always retain a qualified external Tax Accountant/Advisor early in your journey to guide you on your annual taxation and other higher order statutory responsibilities – the billable hours shouldn't be substantial.

In the remaining chapters, we have distilled the critical knowledge you will need to:
- ➤ Be able to:
  - interpret the major financial statements,
  - grasp the difference between net profit and net cash flow,
  - learn how to employ financial ratios, benchmarks, trend analyses and some of the other diagnostic tools that will allow you to remedy performance shortcomings, and
  - how to achieve the best overall financial outcomes.
- ➤ Adopt our four-step oversight process to ensure you are adequately managing the major risks your business may be exposed to.
- ➤ Know what to look for in selecting a financial institution to Bank with, while:
  - eliciting the best possible support from your bankers,
  - knowing what credit products you are likely to have access to,
  - knowing the typical loan approval and security conditions, and,
  - knowing how to adopt our four-step process every time you apply for credit.
- ➤ Finally, we lay out the critical steps you need to follow if you are considering buying or selling an SME.

If you commit to doing all of those things well and adopt the no-exceptions good habit of reviewing your critical financial statements monthly and your cash flows daily, you will be well on your way to achieving *financial mastery*!

Chapter 5: The Bookkeeping Basics

Author's Note: Most of the need-to-know information in this chapter about bookkeeping is relevant wherever your business operates from globally. But a good slice of the information in the chapter that follows on Statutory Compliance is unique to Australia's Tax and Statutory Compliance requirements.

Overall, my advice assumes that you will delegate the lion's share of your day to day accounting responsibilities to a locally experienced contract bookkeeper, a finance experienced staff or family member, OR for large SME's, a qualified in house accountant.

I provide the drill-down *mechanics* on how those obligations work in this and the next chapter because to be able to track those delegated responsibilities, you still need to understand and grasp what they encompass.

Wherever your business operates, your external Tax Accountant/Adviser should be your first port of call in providing you with the essential knowledge you need to know, and your experienced local bookkeeper will ensure you are compliant in meeting those obligations.

About Debits, Credits, and Double-Entry Bookkeeping

Leonardo da Vinci's teacher, Franciscan monk and scholar, Luca Pacioli is generally credited with first documenting the rules of *double-entry bookkeeping*.

Under the concept, there are two sets of bookkeeping entries for every complete round transaction: A debit to one or several accounts and a credit to one or several accounts, where the sum of the debits must always equal the sum of the credits.

The major transactional categories that make up a full set of financial statements, are:

Income and Expenses – the components of the profit and loss statement,

Assets, Liabilities, and *Owner's Equity* – the components of the balance sheet.

A Debit Accounting Entry: INCREASES expense or asset accounts, and DECREASES liability, revenue, or equity accounts.

A Credit Accounting Entry: INCREASES liability, revenue and equity accounts, and DECREASES asset or expense accounts.

This double-entry concept and how it works takes a little while to grasp, especially if you haven't done it before. Suffice to say, provided you adopt and use suitable cloud-based accounting software (which is in view an absolute must!), you'll be able to knock over each transaction with a minimum of fuss every time.

The Principle of Accrual Accounting

Again, this is something your qualified book keeper will look after for you, but as a matter of course, you should know the rules

Method of Accounting – Cash or Accrual

Choosing between the cash method and the accrual method of accounting is an important decision for a SME. Each method has its own advantages and disadvantages, depending on the nature of the business, its cash flow, and the important tax considerations. Here's a breakdown of the pros and cons of each method:

Cash Accounting

Pros:

Simplicity: Easy to implement and maintain, as income and expenses are only recorded when cash is actually received or paid. This makes bookkeeping more straightforward for sole traders and micro businesses, especially those with limited transactions.

Better Cash Flow Tracking: Since income and expenses are recorded when cash is exchanged, the cash method provides a clear view of your actual cash on hand. This can help in managing cash flow more effectively.

Tax Timing Flexibility: You only pay GST and income tax when you receive it, not when it's earned. This could help in delaying tax payments if you haven't yet received payment for services or products.

Less Administrative Work: With fewer transactions to track (i.e., only cash transactions), there's generally less paperwork, making it ideal for very small businesses or sole traders.

Cons:

Not Reflective of True Financial Health: The cash method may not give a complete picture of a business's financial situation, as it doesn't account for money that's owed to the business (accounts receivable) or money the business owes (accounts payable).

Inaccurate Profitability in the Short Term: Revenue and expenses may not be matched correctly within the same time period. For example, you could receive a large payment in one period and incur the associated expenses in another, leading to a misleading view of profitability.

Suitability for Larger Businesses: The cash method may not be suitable as your business grows, particularly if you maintain stock/inventory or have a more complex financial structure. In some countries, businesses over a certain size or with inventory must use the accrual method.

Accrual Accounting

Pros:

More Accurate Financial Picture: Income is recorded when it's earned, and expenses are recorded when they're incurred, regardless of when the cash is actually received or paid. This gives a more accurate view of true profitability and financial health, especially over longer periods.

Matching Revenues and Expenses: The accrual method matches revenues with the expenses that relate to them in the same period, providing a clearer picture of a business's true profitability during any given period.

Better for Decision Making: Since it gives a more comprehensive view of financial performance, the accrual method is better for long-term planning and understanding how the business is really performing.

Accrual Method is required Certain businesses: For businesses that maintain inventory or exceed a certain revenue threshold, the accrual method is typically required by tax authorities.

Cons:

It's more Complex: The accrual method requires more effort to maintain, as it involves tracking accounts receivable, accounts payable, and potentially more adjusting entries to match revenues and expenses in the correct period.

It Can Mislead Cash Flow Perception: Because income is recorded when earned and expenses when incurred (regardless of when cash is exchanged), a business may appear profitable on paper while being low on cash. This can create cash flow management challenges.

Increased Administrative Work: The accrual method requires more bookkeeping work, which can increase administrative costs. It may also require the business owner to work closely with an accountant to ensure the accuracy of financial statements.

Tax Liability Mismatch: You may have to pay taxes on income before you actually receive the cash. This can be problematic if your business is experiencing cash flow issues, as you'll need to come up with the cash to pay the tax even though you haven't been paid by clients.

Which method should an SME choose?

The Cash Method is ideal for small businesses or sole traders with simple operations and limited transactions. It's especially good for service-based businesses with few receivables or payables and for businesses that want to keep accounting simple and track cash flow in real-time.

The Accrual Method is suited for businesses that are growing, have inventory/stock, or need a more accurate long-term view of financial performance. It's better for businesses that deal with large receivables or payables and need to match revenue and expenses for proper financial reporting.

Consulting with your expert accountant/tax advisor will help you determine the best approach for your specific business needs.

Here are a couple of examples of accrual transactions:

For a credit sale: the income is booked into the profit and loss account on the day of sale. The owing amount also goes to an accounts receivable account in the debtor's name on the balance sheet. It may be a month or so before the purchaser actually pays for the goods purchased on agreed credit terms.

Stock On-hand: Stock purchased for ultimate sale or as a component of cost of goods sold may be booked to an inventory/stock on-hand asset account on the balance sheet on the day it is purchased. It is only brought to account as a cost of goods sold item in the profit and loss when matched sales for that inventory occur.

The Bookkeeping Software Decisions

I have explained the basis of double-entry bookkeeping, some of the rules of debit and credit transaction accounting, and the accrual versus cash accounting options, and I'm guessing that right about now you are possibly scratching your head and asking the obvious, "How am I going to remember all of this information?"

The short and simple answer is that you don't have to! A good cloud-based accounting software solution will sort out most of the debit and credit transactional allocations automatically and punch out the timely performance reports you need.

There are several robust and reliable bookkeeping software solutions available in Australia and internationally. All have passed the test of time and stand up well to critical analyses. Three of them, Xero, Quick Books, and MYOB, are among the most popular and, importantly, are the ones I have mainly worked with, but there are several other good solutions available in the marketplace.

SME Leadership: The 5 Critical Success Factors

All are 21st-century cloud-based systems and have affordable monthly subscription options. They have overnight direct bank account feed downloads, advanced auto bank reconciliation features, and a multiple of other useful options. The first opening screens of the day are well presented with quick-view *Dashboards* that lay out some of the key performance statistics and graphs of the business. Each software solution accommodates production and printing of a complete range of monthly business performance reports that can be drawn down in their fixed proprietary template formats or as Excel spreadsheets. The Excel option allows you the flexibility of using those spreadsheets as a freehand budget, business performance, or analytical/planning tool.

The good accounting firms are familiar with and have experience using a range of accounting software solutions. I recommend you speak first with your accountant and weigh up the merits of each system you are considering and what specific elements you need for your business. The final decision is yours but seriously consider the option of going with your accountant's recommendation.

Importantly, *do not consider taking the alternative route of managing your books manually.*

I will now take you through some of the basics of uploading your accounting software live in your business, because, as principal, you must know the mechanics of how it all works. But, of course, I am really hoping you will have seen the logic and wisdom of hiring an experienced bookkeeper or allocating those responsibilities to a staff member with those skills because it will allow you more time to focus on the important big picture financial reports you can draw down from the system each month and it will give you more time to spend at your Front-Line generating the revenues that are critical to your business succeeding.

Software-experienced bookkeepers do these transactions in their sleep, they rarely make mistakes, and their fee rates are not prohibitive. A good place to start is to speak with your tax accountant, who may be able to help you find a good bookkeeper.

The Bookkeeping Set-Up Priorities

The Tutorials That Come with Your Bookkeeping Software

These will help your bookkeeper gain a solid feel for how to navigate the system. There will also be someone in your accountant's office who can 'hold your bookkeeper's hand' at this stage.

The Chart of Accounts

This is a preliminary listing of the general ledger accounts you'll need to establish to be able to document all the transactions the business is likely to be doing. Have a preliminary discussion with your accountant first to nut out what they believe you will need for the specific type of business you are in or are about to go into. If the business is in retail, wholesale, manufacturing and/or import/export, you will need to pay significant attention to the trading account presentation, which is the starting point in your profit and loss statement. This will incorporate management of your stock on hand movements and breakdown of all the cost of goods sold items. Specifically, you will need to know what your bottom-line gross margin is on each of the key products you sell.

Your final list of general ledger accounts will fall into the main transactional groupings that have a direct bearing on:

The Profit and Loss Statement: Primarily made up of sales/trading income/ other income, direct cost of goods sold, gross profit, fixed and operational overheads, and net profit before taxation.

The Balance Sheet: Made up of assets, liabilities, and owners' equity.

As your bookkeeper inputs your new general ledger accounts into their various transactional categories, the system will automatically generate the core financial reporting templates you need for the balance sheet, profit and loss, cash flow, accounts receivable, accounts payable, and so on.

When you first review the reporting templates that flow from your chart of accounts, your bookkeeper will have to do some logical reformatting:

The Profit and Loss Statement: incorporates a trading account at the top part of the statement, i.e., sales less direct cost of goods sold equals *gross or trading profit*.

The Fixed and Operational Overheads: the listing that follows the trading account concludes in a *net profit before tax* result. *Fixed and operational overheads* should be logically grouped under a series of key *expense sub-headings*, such as marketing, advertising, and promotion; wages, salaries, and other employee expenses; office expenses; vehicle expenses; bank fees; professional fees; telephone, electricity, and internet ... and so on.

The Balance Sheet: Asset categories are usually found on the top half of the balance sheet and liabilities on the lower half, followed by equity components.

Dealing With Unaccounted for Formation Expenses

This step requires you to bring to account any expenditure you incurred personally prior to the bookkeeping software being implemented. This may include early-stage capital injections, asset/equipment purchases, and other out-of-pocket expenses.

Establishing Your E-Commerce Platforms

The two most popular e-commerce platforms are Square and Shopify. The setup for Square is free, while Shopify charges a monthly fee and offers some additional options. Check out both and make your decision, but for me, Square is a good starting option.

Square's point-of-sale app is downloadable on smartphones and tablets. It enables business owners to manage their shop's finances, staffing, and customer base from the convenience of one screen. You can name and organize your products and put a variety of processes in place to ensure a faster checkout process. Employee training is relatively easy, and the Square 'Dashboard' is designed to help you make better decisions by including several useful metrics at a glance. It accommodates multiple store locations from the same app and allows you to create an e-commerce platform. See: www.forbes.com/advisor/business/software/square-vs-shopify)

The System Feed and Reconciliation Rules with Your Bank

This includes the major trading and any other business bank accounts, business credit card statements, and the card/ merchant EFTPOS, Square, Shopify, and other online selling facilities you will have arranged with your bank. Once these links are set up, you will receive an automatic overnight upload of all transactions for each account up to the close of business the previous day.

An important enhancement is the capacity to embed several transactional 'rules' to enable many of your bank-related transactions to be automatically encoded to their correct destination general ledger accounts with a minimum of fuss. This may include the allocation of account receivable amounts to the client's trade debtor account in the balance sheet. You do need to check the daily bank allocations and transactions to ensure there are no missed transactions. Once the 'reconciliation rules' have been followed each day, you may have several 'unreconciled' items still to clear, but they won't be time-consuming.

Setting up Your Sales Invoice Template

You'll be able to include your masthead/logo in a specially formatted and compliant tax invoice that goes to all customers when a sale occurs.

Once the invoice setup is in place, invoice production becomes seamless. The software system will automatically account for the treatment of goods and services tax (GST) or sales tax. The net sale (excluding tax) is treated as income in the profit and loss account, and the GST/ sales tax component goes to a separate accounts payable account in the balance sheet. The system also distinguishes between cash sales (to the bank account) and credit sales (to accounts receivable items on the balance sheet).

If you are in a business that sells varying stock items with differing profit margins, your software system gives you the capacity to provide further drill-down analyses of sales by department/source item.

Small Business Payrolls

Each of the accounting software options includes an integrated payroll processing capability, allowing an SME to seamlessly manage and reconcile all components of their employees' pay and entitlements (such as sick leave, annual leave, etc.).

Note: Most banks offer efficient and secure payroll portal access to their business clients. A secure formatted pay run file can be uploaded to the bank every pay period that includes each employee's name, net pay, and bank account details.

Treatment of Stock in the Financial Accounts

If you are in a manufacturing, retail, wholesale, or import/ export business, one of the challenges in getting a reliable take on your real trading profit each month revolves around the capacity to be able to reflect an accurate estimate of stock used and other production inputs (i.e., cost of goods sold) in generating that specific month's income.

When purchasing your stock inputs in large volumes that may exceed the current month's stock needs (i.e., in generating monthly income), you will need to 'park' that proportion of unused stock that doesn't relate to the month's profit in an inventory account on the balance sheet. For a trading enterprise, this is traditionally presented in your monthly profit and loss statement in the formula:

Opening Stock + New Stock Purchased – Closing Stock = Stock Consumed in producing the month's sales.

The end-of-month closing stock value would then sit in the balance sheet. If you do not have significant volumes of carry-over stock, your accountant may advise you to bypass this reconciliation approach.

As a subset of your operating profit analyses, if you are selling a range of products with varying profit margins, you may want to produce another trading account that separates each of those product lines. Discuss your bookkeeping options and how to record these transactions with your accountant.

Dealing With Cash / Out-of-Pocket Expenses

The best approach for business cash expenses is to create a petty cash float system. The rules for managing this float need to be rigid:

Give the responsibility to preferably one person in the office and set them up with a lockable cash box. No one else should have access to it.

Start with a reasonable-sized float, prefunded from an initial bank withdrawal. The cash goes in the cash box as your base float.

The float should only be used for genuine cash business expenses. Each time a reimbursement is requested, a tax invoice or payment source cash register receipt must be provided and kept aside in a secure place before the cash is handed over. Ideally, no receipt means no reimbursement!

When the cash float gets low, add up your bundle of receipts into their relevant general ledger expense accounts and make sure you itemise the net expense and the GST component separately for each expense item. The combined totals of the net expenses and GST columns should equal the amount by which the float has diminished. Then bundle up the receipts and staple them together as a payable invoice and reimburse the cash box for the total amount. Credit the bank account and debit the individual expense and the GST accounts.

I confirm again, ad nauseum, that your bookkeeper should manage these transactions for you.

Corporate Credit Card Expenses

There are two scenarios here:

1. A general expenses credit card may be made available to the person who looks after accounts payable to pay for ad hoc business expenses, typically those that require payment on delivery. The supplier's invoices for these transactions should be filed with your accounts-payable invoices.

2. For some businesses, the principal and/or other selected personnel at the principal's discretion may be granted a credit card for defined business expenses. These cards may

be used for items such as motor vehicle fuel, entertainment, and other expenses.

It's the employee's responsibility to retain all tax invoice/cash register receipts every time the card is used. When the monthly credit card statement arrives, it should be reconciled by the employee, with relevant receipts attached to the statement and submitted for approval by the principal.

Preferably, the same person who manages the petty cash system has the responsibility for reimbursing the bank with the monthly amounts owing on the card statement.

'Food for the Table'

One of your objectives of being in business is surely to be able to earn a reasonable income over time – at least enough for you and your family to be able to live on, pay your personal expenses, meet your other obligations, and hopefully to build a nest egg for the future.

One way to account for your personal cash needs is to put yourself 'on the books' as an employee of the business, where the whole transaction (Gross Income less your Income Tax Liability) is accounted for progressively and is automatically included in your Profit and Loss and Cash Flow Accounting. Another option, which you should consult with your tax accountant on, is to take a weekly, fortnightly or monthly drawing advance from the business, which will then be reconciled by your accountant at annual tax time and accounted for in your end of year Tax Return.

Whichever option you choose, you MUST follow the discipline of maintaining a personal annual budget and your bookkeeper MUST always be aware of and account for what you are personally taking out of the business.

The Accounting Software Dashboards

The *Dashboard* that comes with your accounting software is a marvellous innovation where a snapshot of your key financials, bank balances, cash flows, invoices by due dates, and a raft of other useful information appears on the opening screen when you log on each time. The data layouts and graphics are well done and easy to follow. They can also be amended to suit the daily access information needs of the principal. As a matter, of course, the principal should scan the key dashboard financial data at the start of each day.

Accounting Software Community Forums

The best accounting software vendors have excellent interactive *community forums* designed to allow their users to keep up to date with future software enhancements, to review and answer queries about software add-on options, and to exchange views with other users and seek answers to specific questions.

Sales Transactions

Your bookkeeping system will cope with the documentation and record-keeping obligations of all customer sales, provided you are issuing compliant tax invoices. In a cash sale/retail style business, this includes your gross daily takings information, which may include sales data from a cash register, etc. Added to this is a need to set up the necessary information and recording of all EFTPOS and online transactions (Square or Shopify). These transactions will be included with your daily bank statement uploads to your accounting software system. Depending on the reconciliation rules you have established, some of these transactions will automatically be recorded in the sales records and allocated to the same category items in the profit and loss account. Retaining hard copies of all daily EFTPOS batch reports is a good practice.

Yet again, I confirm your bookkeeper should be handling all of these actions for you.

Expense / Overhead Transactions

Retain and file hard copy original invoices/ source documentation of all your purchases generated by purchase order, cash, or credit card. Your accountant will advise you on the minimum required retention periods for these documents that may be required by the tax office as evidence at some time in the future.

What to Outsource

The first order of business is to decide who will maintain the books of account. It may fall initially on the principal's head in the early days, which I consider to be a *very bad idea*, or alternatively to a business or life partner if there are no other employees yet.

The cost of a casual or contract bookkeeper who is skilled and experienced in using the software solution you have chosen is not going to be a significant outlay and pays respect to the principal's precious time limitations. In the early days, you may only need a relatively small number of hours of their time each week.

Also, consider outsourcing your quarterly business activity statement (BAS)/ Sales Tax accounting and reporting responsibilities, at least until your bookkeeping routines are fully operational. Your accountant's office will be able to handle these responsibilities well.

Bookkeeping Routines That Give the Business Oxygen

My best advice is do not let any of the important transactional routines slip to the point of not having any idea of what's happening in your business. Adopt the good habit of recording those important transactions every trading day. The daily bank account upload and reconciliation of movements in accounts receivable and accounts payable are also critical. Keeping on top of all new expenses on the day they occur is important for the same reason.

Meeting your statutory obligations when they fall due, is of paramount importance. Finally, a few words of advice on tracking cash flows. What has happened to date, and what will happen over the coming days, weeks, and months, MUST BE a perpetual top-order priority, particularly when rolling cash flows are tight.

WARNING: Beware the GIGO Principle!

GIGO is, of course, Garbage In = Garbage Out. The golden rule? Do not allow erroneous, fraudulent, factually incorrect, or inappropriate accounting transactions that do not record accurately and reliably what has happened in the business. If you cheat the system to artificially make your performance look better or worse than what it is, for whatever reason, you are only cheating (and kidding!) yourself.

Tax regulators the world over have significant transaction tracking capabilities. As I've mentioned elsewhere, they can keep an eye on indicative trading and expense margins for every industry sector, and any indicative changes to those typical margins are a giveaway that may lead to a TAX AUDIT. Take care. Do the right thing!

Who can access your Online Bookkeeping Software?

In-House Access: the person who does the day-to-day bookkeeping entries and the principal, as a matter of course. If you produce a lot of invoices, you may want to also include the person who has that responsibility.

External Access: your external accountant's office must have full access to your accounting software at tax time.

Manual Journal Entry Protocols

Automated double-entry bookkeeping systems work well and are at their most reliable when manual journal entries are kept to a minimum. Some are vital at tax time, but these are usually for your external accountant's office to deal with.

My strongest recommendation is to limit the authority to approve manual journal entries in the business to only the principal in the early stages of your business operation and/or to an experienced bookkeeper. Check with someone in your accountant's office if you are unsure about these entries.

When the books are out of balance, as reflected in a mismatched trial balance report, the cause is frequently the result of incorrectly processed manual journal entries.

How secure is Confidential Information Stored on Cloud?

The short answer is very secure. Cloud storage systems employ front-line encryption keys with complex algorithms supported by fairly much unbreakable front-end forensic software. The better cloud vendors are secure with a standard failsafe protocol that deploys and stores your data across several unlinked storage platforms. Microsoft continues to make leaps and bounds in securing businesses of all sizes, from small to large. Their Azure cloud platform and its security standards are well-rated.

Virus Protection Software

It's important to grasp the potential exposure and access risks you face with your PCs, tablets, mobiles, and any other devices that connect your business to the online world. Standard stock viruses are often easy to detect with the right software. Your risk exposure analyses must also incorporate *Malicious AI. Bad people* who utilise advanced AI and machine learning techniques have the capacity to move, access, uplift, and destroy your critical data literally at the speed of light.

Most of the well-rated virus protection software packages will protect you from those risks. You'll find several online reviews of the top ten. The ones I know from personal experience are McAfee, Norton, and Total AV, but the others in that top ranking also do the job well. Don't consider for a moment going unprotected! If you are unsure, seek professional advice from someone who knows.

Disaster Recovery

Vital financial, customer, and other peripheral data you store in your technology platforms is an irreplaceable asset if you do not have any backstop capacity to recover it when you have a major crash or lose data, regardless of the cause. Being disciplined about backing up all your data to cloud every day is a must.

Password Security Protocols Across the Whole Business

We all have a good password story to tell. Here's mine: In the early 1990's at St. George Bank, we released a new online lending system that would speed up our capacity to approve loans across the Bank's growing multiple state geographies. To support those systems, tiered lending discretions with two-part access codes were allocated to all our lenders in the bank. From memory, the first was an alpha descriptor that everyone would know, and the second was a numeric code only known to the individual lender.

Because I was running St. George's Retail Bank at the time and because my surname is *Goddard*, our IT head sent a brief note to me advising that my new alpha code was *GOD 1*. I was pretty riled when I barged into the IT floor moments later, but of course, they had already been fore warned by my PA, Di that I was on my way. I was greeted by clapping hands and raucous laughter from the senior IT team at their joke on me!

Here are some 'OMG' examples of what not to do! The UK's *National Cyber Security Centre (NCSC)* researched common passwords, successfully hacked worldwide. The top five were: *123456, 1234546789, qwerty, password, and 111111. I love you, monkey, dragon,* and several swear words were in the top twenty. Password holders' birthdates, birth years, surnames, and Christian names also featured prominently.

NCSC warns against using any of the above and recommends three random linked words of at least 15 characters or more (memorable only to you, not others) in the same password. Since receiving a *'Dear Dad'* lecture from my son Luke about the then simplicity of some of my personal passwords, I now follow NCSC's guidelines and include a combination of upper and lower-case letters, numbers, and symbols in each password.

The rules are pretty basic:

- Keep your passwords safe and well concealed.
- Do not recycle past passwords.
- Avoid using the same passwords over multiple platforms or applications.
- Make sure your passwords do not have any logical associative link to your personal biodata or to the name of your business.
- Have clear and unambiguous confidential staff access guidelines, including a *Non-Disclosure Deed,* which should be signed by all employees.
- When a staff member leaves your employment and has had access to intellectual property or system access password data, make sure you remove their access on the same day.

There's a range of readily available secure password management software applications available that offer unlimited password options on unlimited devices, powerful security breach alerts, dark web monitoring, and full WIFI protection.

They'll give you maximum protection for a monthly fee of around $5 or so. Even some of the free ones, such as Last Pass are pretty good. Seriously consider going this route, as it then becomes one less thing you have to worry about in your busy life. For what it's worth, I'm going through this transition as I write!

Chapter 6: Statutory Obligations

As a business owner you are required to comply at law with your Employee, GST or Sales Tax, Income Tax and other specific statutory reporting requirements. Assuming you've delegated most of those responsibilities to a locally experienced bookkeeper and have retained a Tax Accountant/Advisor to deal with your higher order annual taxation and statutory obligations, you'll be fine, wherever your business trades from.

This chapter focuses primarily on Australian Statutory Obligations, as an example of what those responsibilities may include.

Around the time your company/business is registered, your Tax Accountant will confirm what your specific obligations are, and your bookkeeper will be able to confidently manage most of those day-to-day statutory responsibilities on your behalf.

Australian Employment Law and Obligations

When you employ staff in Australia other than yourself, you will need to be fully conversant with their workplace rights at law.

Go to www.fairwork.gov.au for minimum conditions for Australian employees and for award-specific conditions that depend on the type of business and the industry you are operating (or similar sites for other international locales). Each award lays down minimum pay scales, industry-specific entitlements, and other employment conditions and benefits. As a principal, you need to keep on top of those award components and consequent compliance obligations.

Enterprise Bargaining Agreements

As an alternative to complying with the awards relevant to your industry, the parties also have the option of entering a collective bargaining negotiation with a view to creating an enterprise agreement. Negotiating such agreements is laid out under the Fair Work Act and must include fair representation from the employer, employees, and their bargaining representatives.

An enterprise agreement should be beneficial to both employee and employer, simplifying award compliance where the business is required to deal with staff categories working under different awards, creating more flexibility around the span of work hours, broadening job classifications, and incorporating positive employee productivity initiatives. However, the benefits of taking this course of action will only come when you have enough employees to justify taking this route. To negotiate an enterprise agreement, you will need an appropriately skilled industrial lawyer to guide you through the process.

Workers Compensation Insurance

To ensure all employees are covered and paid if they are injured in the workplace, each state and territory have their own workers' compensation authority office and provides that insurance via a mandatory annual renewable policy. In the first year, you are required to provide an initial payroll budget, updated with the actual payroll spend, at the end of each year. Policy renewal date is variable and is set to the anniversary date of the initial policy commencement.

Payroll Tax

Payroll tax is state-based and payable once total wages exceed defined limits. Limits vary from state to state. Once the business reaches the minimum payroll thresholds, this additional tax impost is payable. Payroll tax rates vary from 4% to 6.85% of the wage bill.

Payroll tax returns must be lodged with state or territory-based revenue offices, and payment of liability must be made at an agreed frequency (monthly, quarterly, or annually).

As a principal, you need to be aware and keep on top of the thresholds and payment/return lodgement obligations and understand what payroll components are included in the requisite calculations.

Tax File Number Declaration

All new employees must complete and sign a tax file number declaration before they receive their first pay. If they are claiming additional eligible tax rebates, they are also required to complete a withholding declaration form. These declarations are then lodged either electronically or by mail with the ATO. You should retain the employer's copies in a secure staff file.

Superannuation

The employer is obliged to add a superannuation guarantee levy amount to an employee's pay, set at 9.50 % at the time of writing, provided the employee's gross pay before tax equals or exceeds $450 per month.

When new employees complete their tax file declaration, provide them with a standard choice form and ask for details of their preferred superannuation fund (name, fund, and membership number). You are obliged to have a default super fund backstop for those employees who do not belong to another fund or haven't provided details by the time you are due to pay the first contribution.

Employee super contributions must be remitted to their fund's bank accounts either monthly or quarterly in arrears (most are paid quarterly) and are due by the 28th day after the end of the month or quarter. To be sure, verify these dates and obligations with your accountant.

Long Service Leave (LSL)

This is an additional perk of employment, peculiar only to Australia and New Zealand. It is regulated by the individual state and territory governments, and they each have differing entitlement periods and amounts payable. It is payable after a qualifying period of employment service has been reached.

Long service leave entitlements accrue progressively with years of service in the payroll records and are catered for in each of the software accounting suites. Discuss with your accountant how you should account for forward LSL entitlements and at what stage the provisions start accruing.

Other Payroll Entitlements

These include annual leave, sick leave, compassionate leave, and any other benefits your employees are entitled to by the specific awards they are paid under.

When properly set up, the payroll component of your bookkeeping system should automatically calculate and keep a running record of these accruals. Individual pay runs account for entitlements taken or used for that pay period.

Setting up Employees in Your Accounting Software's Payroll Module

Pay run cycles are typically weekly, fortnightly, or monthly.

For full and part-time employees, load up their standard pay details with the hours they *usually* work in a regular pay run. That way, all you need to adjust each pay period is any non-standard adjustments such as public holidays, annual leave, sick leave, or overtime, where relevant. For casual employees, gross pay will, of course, vary from pay to pay.

Time Sheets

Standardised pay cycle time sheets with daily start and finish times can be formatted for employees to log in and complete.

Withholding Tax Rates

Ensure that tax withholding calculator tables in your accounting software are automatically updated when changes occur.

Pay Slips

It is an employer's legal obligation to provide payslips to each employee within a day of payday. Check www.fairwork.gov.au for the minimum information that must be included in the pay slip. The payroll modules of Xero and MYOB include a compliant pay slip capability.

Dealing With the Principal / Director's Earnings

The ways to deal with earnings for a sole trader, partner, director of a company, and a beneficiary of a trust vary significantly due to the different tax structures and legal obligations associated with each. Here's a breakdown of the best ways to manage earnings in these different roles:

Sole Traders

As a sole trader, you are personally liable for your business income, and the earnings are taxed as part of your personal income. The key strategies for managing these earnings include the excess of income over expenses is basically the income of a sole trader. Sole traders pay tax on the net income of the business at personal income tax rates.

Partners in a Partnership

In a partnership, income is split between the partners based on the partnership agreement. Each partner is taxed individually on their share of the net income of the partnership.

Partners are taxed on their share of the partnership's profit at their individual marginal tax rates.

The partnership itself doesn't pay tax, but it must lodge a tax return to report income, deductions, and the distribution of profits among partners.

Director of a Company

A director can earn income from a company in various ways, such as through salary, director's fees, dividends, or bonuses. Managing earnings requires careful consideration of tax and cash flow impacts.

As a director, you can receive a salary, which is subject to PAYG withholding tax and provides access to superannuation and other employment benefits.

You can also distribute company profits as dividends, which may be more tax-effective if the company has already paid tax at the corporate rate (25-30%). Dividends may be franked, meaning tax credits are attached to reduce the tax payable by the director/shareholder.

Balance Salary and Dividends: Optimise a mix of salary and dividends to maximize tax efficiency (and minimizing personal tax) while ensuring compliance with company laws.
Directors are taxed on their salary and dividends at personal income tax rates.
The company pays corporate tax on its profits, but when profits are distributed as dividends, shareholders receive a franking credit for any tax already paid by the company.

Beneficiary of a Trust

As a beneficiary of a discretionary or unit trust, you may receive distributions of income or capital from the trust. The tax treatment and management of those distributions depend on the trust deed and the type of income.

Distributions: Trust income is usually distributed to beneficiaries at the end of the financial year. It is essential to ensure distributions are made to beneficiaries in lower tax brackets where possible (income splitting).

Utilise Family Trusts: If the trust is a family trust, distribute income to family members who have lower taxable incomes, thus reducing the overall tax burden on the family.

Deferral of Distributions: If allowed by the trust deed, income can be retained in the trust and distributed in a future year when tax rates might be lower.

Capital Gains Management: If the trust earns capital gains, consider distributing them to beneficiaries who can take advantage of any available capital gains tax (CGT) discounts.

Distribute Franked Dividends: If the trust receives dividend income from shares, the trust can pass on the franking credits to beneficiaries, reducing their tax liability.

Taxation:
Beneficiaries are taxed on trust distributions at their personal income tax rates. If the income is from a trust and includes franked dividends, beneficiaries can claim franking credits.
The trust itself does not pay tax if all income is distributed to beneficiaries, but any undistributed income may be taxed at the highest marginal rate.

Key Issues to Address for All Business Structures

Tax Planning: Working with a tax advisor is essential in all cases to implement tax-efficient strategies, including deductions, superannuation contributions, and timing of distributions.
Record Keeping: Maintain thorough records of income and expenses to ensure accurate reporting and maximize deductions.
Cash Flow Management: Regularly set aside funds for tax obligations, especially if income varies or fluctuates.
Superannuation: Ensure sufficient contributions are made to superannuation accounts to secure retirement savings and benefit from concessional tax rates.

PAYG Instalment Tax and PAYG Withholding Tax

PAYG Instalments are an estimate of your current year's income tax liability, projected from the income you earned and the tax you paid in the previous financial year. You are required to remit these amounts to the ATO in periodical instalment. If your income trends have changed up or down since your last return, your tax accountant will be able to seek an amended assessment of your current year's liability on your behalf.

PAYG Withholding is the tax you deduct from your employees' or contractors' income each pay period. You are required to remit those amounts to the ATO periodically.

Fringe Benefits Tax (FBT)

As the title implies, Australian FBT is a tax payable on the benefits that employees and their families or other beneficiaries receive over and above their normal salary or wages.

The common examples listed by the Australian tax office are:

- Expenses associated with private use of a company-owned vehicle.
- Giving employees a discounted loan.
- Paying for a gym membership.

- Providing entertainment by way of free tickets to concerts.
- Reimbursing an expense incurred by an employee, such as school fees.
- Providing a pre-funded debit card for personal expenditure.
- Giving other benefits under a salary sacrifice arrangement with an employee.
- Additional Fringe Benefit allowances are available to the not-for-profit sector.

FBT is separate from income tax and is calculated on the taxable value of the benefit provided. The employer is required to self-assess and lodge an FBT Return.

You need to have a good understanding of the record-keeping requirements for both employees and the employer. For example, a monthly kilometre return may need to be maintained by employees who garage the car at their personal residence and/or are allowed the private use of their company car.

I have only given the briefest summary of FBT, but there is a lot to know in terms of your obligations. Speak with your tax accountant about these compliance and record-keeping obligations.

Goods and Services Tax (GST)

GST, also known variously as Consumption, Value-Added, or Sales Tax, is a form of indirect taxation levied by 166 of the 193 countries that make up the global economy. At the time of writing, this tax category accounts for over 20% of global taxation revenues.

In Australia, GST is a flat tax of 10% on most goods and service sales and is 15% in New Zealand. The UK general GST Rate is 18%, although that rate varies from 5% to 28%, depending on the category of goods and services on offer.

As consumers, we automatically pay GST or sales tax on most purchases at the point of sale. Businesses pay GST on their purchases and charge GST (on behalf of the Tax Office) on their sales. They are required to provide a business activity statement (BAS), usually on a quarterly basis, summarising the net impact of those transactions (GST charged versus GST paid). Typically, a business collects more GST from sales than it pays out on its purchases and remits the net difference between the two to the ATO as part of their business-activity statement.

At the time of writing, Australian businesses are not required to register for GST if their annual income is less than $75,000, but any invoices they issue must show that GST is not included in the price. They also can't claim GST credits for their business purchases (check the currency of this threshold with your accountant).

Setting up Bookkeeping Software to Cater for GST/Sales Tax

In Australia and New Zealand, there is some complexity involved in allocating bookkeeping system GST tax codes to all income and overhead items, and in catering for the reporting intricacies required of the business activity statement. Your bookkeeper will be able to deal with these responsibilities.

Business Activity Statement (BAS) Lodgement Obligations

Lodging your BAS by the due date is a defined obligation by the law, and you must not miss it. If you do, you are committing an offence, and the fines may be significant.

Late Payment of BAS Obligations

If, for any reason, you are strapped for cash on any of the due dates and unable to meet some or all of the payment obligations, speak to your accountant early about the possibility of applying for a request for time to pay.

Excise Duty and Customs Duty Obligations

Excise duty is a defined tax on specific goods manufactured in Australia, most particularly on alcohol, petroleum, and tobacco products. If you manufacture, produce, or store any of these goods, you may be required to apply for, and hold, an excise licence and to pay excise duty on sales, typically monthly. Likewise, if you import any of these goods, instead of paying excise duty, you may be required to pay an equivalent amount in customs duty.

At the time of writing, craft brewery and distillery SMEs are fashionable start-ups. If you are considering purchasing or buying a business that operates in these sectors, do your homework on the mechanics of accounting to the ATO for and paying excise duty on sales. You will also effectively be taking on bond storage responsibilities and obligations that come with holding stock on hand prior to selling those products.

There are some excellent brewery and distillery inventory tracking software options on the market. It is best to purchase one that includes automatic preparation of your monthly excise duty returns and preferably one that has a direct interface with both your local tax authority and your accounting software. Of the ones I have seen, I like and have worked with US-based *Hooch Ware*.

Tax Time Accounting and Reporting

I cannot stress enough how important it is to engage an external tax accountant to deal with your tax and statutory obligations, wherever your business is based. (see Chapter 9)

Other Statutory Compliance Obligations

Workplace Health and Safety (WHS)

In most international locations, industrial relations legislation sets out defined obligations and responsibilities for managing and mitigating risks that have an impact on the health, safety, or welfare of those people who work in or visit your workplace(s).

Local / State Government Development Compliance

For those businesses operating in the real estate/ vacant land/ development sector, the principal is not necessarily required to hold specific professional qualifications, with the exception of registered building companies and real estate agents, but they will be subject to definite state and local government planning conditions once their development application (DA) has been approved. The conditions precedent included in DAs may run to as much as 100 pages. The developer, in these cases, is obliged to issue any related sub-contract work to appropriately skilled and qualified practitioners.

Local / Municipal Government Licences to Trade as a Business

A license to trade in any type of business at a specific locality invariably requires a local government permit for a defined term to comply with specific trading conditions and to place a copy of the license in a prominent place at the business premises.

Qualification-Specific Licensing, Codes of Practice, and Compliance Obligations

Some categories of business require defined professional qualifications and licensing to be able to operate a private business practice. Examples may include physicians, allied healthcare professionals, pharmacists, solicitors, barristers, accountants/ registered tax agents, financial planners, architects, real estate agencies, electricians, plumbers, and home and commercial builders.

Actions: Go to: www.ablis.gov.au, the Australian business licence and information service. This is an excellent site to help you to discover minimum government licensing, permits, approvals, registrations, codes of practice, standards, and operating guidelines for specific types of businesses.

Chapter 7: The Business Performance Metrics

"Unless you are willing to put in the effort to learn how to read and interpret financial statements, ...you really shouldn't be in business."

Warren Buffet, Chairman, Berkshire Hathaway

With a net worth of well over $100 billion at the time of writing, Warren Buffet is regarded as one of the most successful and astute investors of all time, so he surely knows what he's talking about!

There are three critical financial statements all business principals should commit to getting their heads around, learn to respect, and regularly review as a top priority. They are *The Balance Sheet*, *The Profit and Loss Account* and *The Cash Flow Statement*.

To these three, I like to also add a fourth report called *The Three-Way Cash Flow*. Its value comes from the fact that it combines the other three into one integrated, self-balancing, historical and predictive spreadsheet. It's useful as a planning and budgetary tool and seamlessly accommodates the creation of predictive forward cash flows. The Bankers also like three-way cash flows for the same reasons.

The Balance Sheet

The balance sheet presents a 'big picture' view of the financial position of the business. It provides a summary of *assets*, *liabilities*, and the book value of owners/ shareholders' *net worth* at a defined point in time.

Assets are the things/amounts that the business owns. They include:

Current Assets: short-term liquid assets such as bank balances and cash on hand. Also, items that can be converted into cash in the short term, such as accounts receivable/trade debtors, inventory/stock on hand and prepayments.

Fixed Assets: land, buildings, motor vehicles, sundry equipment and furniture and fittings, after deducting depreciation[1]. The listing of fixed assets may also include an asset revaluation reserve[2].

Depreciation and Asset Revaluations are best accounted for in consultation with your accountant.

Intangible Assets: may sit on the balance sheet at a defined value, but in truth, are more difficult to quantify in terms of actual realisable value. They typically include items such as Goodwill, Patents, Copyrights and Franchise Agreements.

Liabilities are the things/amounts that the business owes.

Current Liabilities: any amounts due for payment within the year. They may include accounts payable/trade creditors, bank and other loans to the business, customer deposits and prepayments, GST/Sales Tax due, PAYG instalments due, income tax due, employment provisions (annual Leave etc.), and other liabilities and short-term obligations.

Long-Term Liabilities: these are the obligations and amounts payable beyond 12 months and may include long-term debt obligations/mortgages (that portion over 12 months), employee obligations extending beyond 12 months (such as Long Service Leave), and deferred tax liabilities.

Owner's Equity/ Net Worth is the net difference between Assets and Liabilities. When total Assets exceed total Liabilities, the business is said to have a *Positive Net Worth*. When Liabilities exceed Assets, the business is said to have a *Negative Net Worth*.

Net Worth: summarises principal/shareholders equity in the following format:

---

[1] Depreciation: As the monetary value of fixed assets decrease over time due to wear and tear, that decreasing value is represented in the financial statements by an annual tax deductible depreciation provision, which effectively projects the remaining productive life of each asset (after the deduction).

2 Asset Revaluation: It is possible to add an Asset Revaluation Reserve to your balance sheet for assets such as land that sit on the balance sheet at original cost but have gone up in value significantly over time.

Share Capital is the amount invested in the business by the Principal/Shareholders as *Fixed Capital*, but it <u>does not</u> include *directors* or *shareholders' loans*.[3]

Retained Earnings is that proportion of annual net profit not distributed to the shareholders/principal at the end of the Financial Year.

Some businesses may also borrow from shareholders via an interest payable fixed term *debenture*, also allocated as a liability (current or long-term, depending on the time frame of the debenture).

The Profit and Loss Statement

This is a summary of the operating income the business has earned over a specific period, less the expenditure it has incurred in achieving that income. When total Income exceeds total Expenses, the outcome is called a *net profit*. When Expenses exceed Income, the outcome is called a *net loss*.

The profit and loss statement is broken up into three main sections.

The Trading Account formula is *Sales and Other Income – Direct Cost of Goods Sold = Trading Profit* (sometimes called *Gross Profit*).

If you are selling a range of products with varying profitability margins, you may want to produce a trading account that separates each of those product lines. A similar argument goes for separating out the components of the cost of goods sold.

If you are in a manufacturing, retail, wholesale or import/export business, one of the challenges in getting a reliable take on real

---

[3] Directors/Shareholders Loans: While Share Capital represents a fixed long term, 'not at call' investment in the business, some shareholders or principals may decide to inject short term business funding needs via a Directors or Shareholders Loan. Such loans do not normally attract interest obligations, are generally treated on Balance Sheet as 'at call' borrowings and are classified as a Current Liability – Directors/Shareholders Loans, not as Share Capital. Conversely, when a director/shareholder borrows money from the business, the amount is classified as a Current Asset – Directors/Shareholders Loans.

Trading Profit each month revolves around the capacity to be able to reflect an accurate estimate of stock used and other costs of goods sold components in generating that specific month's income.

When you are purchasing your stock inputs in large volumes that may exceed the current month's stock needs (i.e., in generating monthly income), you may need to 'park' that proportion of unused stock that doesn't relate to the month's profit into an inventory account on the balance sheet.

Ask your accountant about your stock recording needs and how to record and keep track of them in the books of account. If your carry-forward stocks on hand are not substantial each month, that advice may be to simply include all new stock purchases in the Trading Account as Cost of Goods Sold.

Fixed and Variable Operating Overheads should be logically grouped under a series of key expense subheadings. For example:

- Marketing, Advertising & Promotion
- Wages & Salaries and other associated employee expenses
- Office Expenses
- Vehicle Expenses
- Bank Fees
- Professional Fees
- Telephone, Internet, Electricity and other utilities

An experienced bookkeeper will know how to input the necessary format changes to your accounting software and reallocate each general ledger expenditure item under their relevant new subheadings. If not, your accountant's office will point you in the right direction.

Net Profit Before Tax and Other Adjustments is an automatically calculated result in your Profit and Loss Account, as per the following formula: *Trading Profit – Total Fixed and Variable Operational Overheads = Net Profit Before Tax and Other Adjustments.*

Tax Time Adjustments

For SMEs, these adjustments are not generally included in the Management Accounts. They include provisions for income tax, depreciation, and any other adjustments, which your accountant will include when they lodge your final tax return each financial year.

The Cash Flow Statement

The first logical question you may ask is: What is the difference between *Net Income* and *Net Cash Flow*?

Net Income is revenue brought to account during the reporting period LESS expenses also brought to account for the same period. But as you may recall from Chapter 5, these amounts are generally accounted for by adopting an *accrual basis of accounting*. The income statement, therefore, includes Income items you have not yet been paid for and expenses that you have not yet paid.

Net Cash Flow is the net movement in cash generated or lost during the reporting period. It is measured by taking the cash holdings at the beginning of the reporting period from the cash holdings at the end of that period. The net difference is effectively the net cash flow.

The Difference between Net Income and Net Cash Flow

Expense Accruals are expenses included in your net income statement but not yet paid for. e.g., your trade creditors

Prepaid Expenses are cash payments for costs that have not yet been consumed in earning income, e.g., stock purchases paid for, that relate to future trading income. These items are placed on the balance sheet as Stock on Hand.

Sales made on Credit Terms are in your income statement, but for which payment has not been received, i.e., your trade debtors.

Deferred Revenue: Prepayments and customer deposits for which goods have not yet been sold/delivered. They appear as *prepayments/deposits* on the balance sheet.

Other Balance Sheet Transactions during the reporting period which may affect your *Moving Cash Balances:*

Purchase or sale of fixed assets. For a loss on sale of a fixed asset, where the sale price is less than the written down value (after deducting depreciation), the net difference is recorded on the P & L as a loss on sale. Similarly, where the sale price exceeds the written down value, the net difference is recorded in the P & L as a profit on sale.

Conditional performance bonds paid to local governments, utilities, or others. These sit on the balance sheet as current assets or fixed assets, depending on their term.

Net movement in bank/financial institution loan balances for the period,

Any other cash-impacting transactions that pass through the balance sheet and not the income statement.

The Net Cash Flow is, therefore, the money that flows in and out of the business during the financial reporting period from operations, financing, and investing activities. The cash flow is the lifeline that supports your capacity to fund your short to medium-term obligations.

Cloud-based accounting systems allow you to produce a Cash Flow Statement. It is one of the most important Financial Reports you should review at least weekly, and your Dashboard cash flow summary every day.

Two popular cash flow myths:

1. *Just because the business is profitable, doesn't guarantee you will have adequate cash flows.*

Running short of cash may ultimately lead to insolvency if you don't have a sympathetic banker on your side.

What are the main causes of this sort of cash shortage? It frequently boils down to how much attention you are paying to your *debtors and creditors.*

An example: You specialise in manufacturing a significant component of a popular product for sale in the marketplace. Your wholesale customer who purchases these components from you only offers you standard payment terms of 60 days but sometimes pays closer to 90 days. To further compound this, the suppliers of the raw materials you need to manufacture that component typically demands payment on delivery, or net 7 days.

You are not convinced you have the luxury of walking away from your slow-paying manufacturer, as you may lose the business and a significant portion of your profitability. The answer? Provided your wholesaler is reputable, you can finance the debt obligation from an *invoice financier,* to advance you around 80% of the amount due within a couple of days of writing the invoice rather than having to wait the full 90 days or more. When your supplier ultimately repays the debt, you reimburse the financier with the amount owing to them (Chapter 11).

The debtor financing option is only feasible where you are making a decent enough gross margin from the sale of your products to justify the interest you will have to pay your financier for such a facility. But this is a highly efficient form of financing.

It is so important to keep on top of your trade debtor's ledger. Do not allow customers to slip on their agreed payment terms with you. Remember, when they are slow to pay, you are effectively giving them free overdraft money.

Constant follow-up of your trade debtors and paying creditors when they are due is just so important. Welcome to one of the most important yet least *sexy* tasks of being an SME principal!

2. *Your business is suffering from symptoms of Overtrading:*

In simple terms, this means your business is growing too rapidly. But *hold up*; I hear you say, how could growing too quickly be a problem?

Overtrading is the symptom of growing so fast that you start to lose your grip on the important financial disciplines and drivers of the business, most particularly on your control of operating overheads. The symptoms may include:

> ➤ Exuberant, overoptimistic, and even sometimes manic overhead increases that have not been properly thought through and tend to drive profitability backwards.

> ➤ Ditto for the purchase of plant and equipment, which may be an expensive luxury but not essential for the business at the time of acquisition.

- Ditto for taking on the expense of additional employees too early, where the job could have been done more efficiently with less staff at a lower overall aggregate cost.
- The flow of human resource and customer service challenges that invariably accompany rapid take up and adoption of new equipment, constantly changing procedures and processes, and inadequately trained staff.
- A general drop in customer service standards.

My golden rule? Regularly review all operational overheads, systems and procedures. When Sales are growing at a healthy pace, the temptation to bring on board additional personnel at a moment's notice or to increase other discretionary expenses for little or no bottom-line gain can become a little too easy when cash from new sales is rolling rapidly through your front door. These are the classic symptoms of *overtrading*.

Understand the importance of measuring the *true economic cost* of each new employee who comes on board. That *real cost* could be as much as two to three times greater than the salary you will be paying that new employee. Each time you employ someone; analyse what dollar level of additional net sales you will require to recover the cost of the new employee before the added expense becomes profit neutral and starts to produce net additional income for the business.

An example: a new employee is to start at an annual salary including on costs (superannuation, annual leave, and other non-salary overhead imposts) of $60,000. You know that your Gross Profit Margin in the business is 40% (i.e., every $100,000 of Sales produces a Gross Trading Profit of $40,000), then you can immediately calculate that you'll need an additional $150,000 (i.e., $150K X 40% = $60,000) of annual sales before that additional staff member becomes truly cost neutral to the business.

The real economic cost in this example is, in fact, 2.5 times what the employee is going to be earning. If the Gross profit margin in the business was 30%, the additional income required to reach breakeven would be more like $200K, or 3.3 times the annual salary!

Identical 'what if' analyses should be applied to any increases in discretionary operating expenditure (i.e., those expenses that will not produce an increase in sales/income). Always know your gross profit margin and the real bottom line impact of every net new staff hire or any other net increase in annual discretionary operational expenditure. Make your best guess as to how long it will take to achieve the additional sales you'll need to cover those increases and be satisfied you are doing it for the right reasons and that you can afford to do so.

The Three-Way Cash Flow

The Three-Way Cash Flow is a financial model that amalgamates the balance sheet, profit and loss and cash flow statement rolled into one integrated analytical tool. Because it is populated with real-time data from the other three financial statements and the way in which it self-balances, it has unquestionable financial integrity making it a valuable tool for dealing with advisors, bankers and even potential investors.

Importantly the *three way* transforms the traditional end-of-period cash flow statement into a dynamic forward budget, cash flow and forecasting tool.

How to Produce a Three-Way Cash Flow

I have put together several *three ways* over the years and have worked with accountants in building intricate multiple company/subsidiary interlinked versions. I can confirm that constructing them manually without the use of enabling technology can take many days and is not a job for the faint-hearted.

Thanks to the wonders of the Digital Economy, there are several excellent software packages now available that can do the build in seconds. All the information you need is already locked away in whatever Cloud-based accounting software package you are using, and it makes good sense to find a solution that easily links up with that software.

Xero, MYOB and QuickBooks each come with software options and alliances, that will enable you to knock out your three-way cash flow in a heartbeat. The collateral benefit is it will gives you a reliable and easy to dial up path to dynamic forecasting of future cash flows, building forward budgets, and providing easily accessible tools to combine Key Performance Indicator (KPI) reporting with non-financial goals and metrics. Those software options will also present you with powerful scenario modelling capability, helping you make better business.

This will also enable you to automatically calculate and present the critical *what if* performance ratios in your business. Xero, MYOB and QuickBooks each accommodate seamless integration of both their own proprietorial and third-party technology software solutions. Seek your accountants advice before making these decisions as they may have an alternative solution they prefer.

Trend Ratio Analyses

DO NOT STRESS if you struggle at first with the concept of using financial ratios as an aid to diagnosing performance issues in your business. Over time you will start to recognise how valuable this type of analysis can be.

Xero, MYOB and QuickBooks will allow you the option of including many of them in the *Dashboard* when you log into your software each day.

9

There are 7 financial ratios I traditionally like to rely on:

1. Gross Profit or Gross Margin (GM)

The Formula: Gross Profit ÷ Revenue X100 = GM%.

Extract this ratio from your Profit & Loss Statement both annually and monthly.

What it tells you: The profitability of the business before taking in fixed operational overheads. The higher the percentage, the more that is left over to service your operational overheads.

I've already shown you how to use your Gross Margin to measure the true economic cost of adding new employees, or of increasing discretionary overheads in times of rapid growth. It's a powerful ratio to get your head around.

2. Return on Sales or Operating Margin (OM)

The Formula: Earnings before Interest and Taxes (EBIT) ÷ Revenue X 100 = OM%

What it tells you: an evaluation of operating performance and underlying profitability from day-to-day activities (excluding tax and bank interest).

3. Selected Operational expenses ratios to Revenue.

The Formula: Each Individual Expense Item ÷ Revenue, Times 100 = expense item overhead % to Revenue.

What it tells you: It enables you to extract and be consciously aware of each expense category in your P & L (from largest to smallest) as a percentage of total Revenue. These numbers and their impact on financial performance are also useful when periodically updating your operating budgets.

Operational expense ratios should be measured from those expense category totals.

4. Interest Coverage Multiple

The Formula: Earnings before Interest and Taxes (EBIT) ÷ Interest Expense = the Interest Multiple. Typically, this is measured from a full-year financial statement (i.e., 12 months EBIT and 12 months Interest expense).

What it tells you: It's an important measure of the capacity of the business to meet its loan interest payments. A minimum multiple is often included as a conditional covenant in many bank business loan agreements.

The lower the interest cover multiple, the greater the potential for loan payment default. A multiple of 1.5 or less will be a worry, particularly where the loan requires principal and interest to be paid. Banks sometimes ask for a minimum multiple of around 2 as a defined covenant/condition of the loan.

5. Average Days Overdue

This is a useful statistic if you sell goods on credit terms. It is a measure of how successful you are at ensuring your trade debtors pay their accounts by the due date. Your Dashboard can be easily configured to give you this statistic. Ideally, the Average Days Overdue should be as close to your standard trading terms as possible.

It's a good idea to download a full *Aged Trade Debtors Analyses* at least weekly. It will lay out every outstanding trade debtor on your books by age (i.e., how many days they are outstanding) in the following time frames: Current Month, 30 days, 60 days, 90 days and over. You will know what your standard trading terms on your credit sales are and you should ensure all your customers are paying on time. This is a measure the bankers like to keep an eye on.

6. Stock Turn

The Formula: Cost of Goods Sold (COGS) ÷ Average Inventory (those amounts are extracted from a full year's trading. (NB: Average Inventory = Beginning Inventory + ending inventory ÷ 2; COGS is the total amount for the year).

What it tells you: This ratio is a measure of how efficient the business is in managing its stock holdings in generating sales and how often that stock turns over. The higher the turnover, the better. A lower turnover may be indicative of redundant, impaired, or slow-moving stock. A slow Stock Turn on products that have low-profit margins is a profitability killer!

7. Current or Working Capital Ratio

The Formula: Current Assets ÷ Current Liabilities = Working Capital multiple.

What it tells you: This is a broad financial measure of business liquidity. The higher the multiple of Current Assets to Current Liabilities, the more liquid the business. A ratio of 1.5 to 2 is considered a comfortable buffer for most businesses. Again, the

Bankers may mandate a minimum Working Capital ratio as a covenant of your loan facilities.

Benchmarking your Financial Ratios

Your Accountant

Your tax accountant is the logical first door to knock on. Their business is typically underpinned by many hundreds, if not thousands of clients with rich tax return and industry trend data, also balanced by their own extensive personal experience and observations. They'll be able to point you in the right direction in terms of typical industry sector-by-sector trading and operating margins and what sort of trend ratio norms to aim for.

Access the ATO benchmarks.

It surprises many Australian SME principals when I mention the *Australian Taxation Office* as a helpful source! The ATO publishes extensive small industry benchmarks to assist in the comparison of business performance against potentially similar businesses in each industry sector. The benchmarks are extracted from the aggregated masked income tax returns of over 1.3 million small businesses. It accounts for businesses with varying turnover ranges up to $1.5 million per annum and analyses more than 100 industry categories.

An example of their tax return benchmark indicators include:

- ✓ Typical cost of sales to turnover (excluding labour),
- ✓ Total expenses to turnover,
- ✓ Rent to turnover,
- ✓ Labour to turnover,
- ✓ Motor vehicle expenses to turnover, and so on.

Importantly, the ATO guarantees that the personal information you enter is not recorded by them and will only be used for completing the tool.

Go to: www.ato.gov.au/Business/Small-business-benchmarks for more information on the ATO data base.

How to extract an EBITDA-based valuation of your business

There are three steps:

1. Calculate EBITDA

The Formula: Net Profit After Tax + (Interest + tax + depreciation + amortisation) = $ EBITDA. (These statistics are extracted from annual tax return results. Your accountant will be able to help you with the Depreciation & Amortisation totals).

What it tells you: A measure of underlying profitability. It minimises the non-operating effects of individual businesses in the same marketplace.

2. Calculate Trend EBITDA:

The Formula: Calculate an annual average of three to four years EBITDA.

3. Extract the Valuation:

The Formula: Trend EBITDA x an agreed multiple = $ Valuation.

An EBITDA valuation example: Let us say the business has achieved an average EBITDA of $500,000 extracted from an average of the three to four prior years of trading. Because profitability has been growing year on year, and the business offers quality, in-demand products, your accountant may recommend a multiple of, say, 3 to 5 times average EBITDA.

Based on using an EBITDA multiple of, say 3 times, the business has a valuation of $1,500,000 (i.e., $500,000 X 3), but of course, there is no guarantee you will get that price. If you intend to sell your business, seek advice from your accountant to establish a realistic valuation (there are several other valuation methods) and help you creating vendor presentation for prospective purchasers.

Breakeven Analyses

Breakeven is the trading point at which incoming revenue matches outgoing expenditure. At that point, your business is neither making nor losing money.

Breakeven analyses considers the relationship between discretionary fixed overheads, variable overheads, and total revenue. Fixed overheads are costs that are fixed regardless of revenue levels. Variable overheads are those that are usually related to the direct costs of production and that therefore rise and fall proportionately as revenue rises and falls.

The dynamic of this sort of analysis is in understanding that in most businesses, the quantum of your revenue that exceeds your Breakeven point comes into the financials at a higher profit margin because your fixed costs are already fully covered beyond that point. When you see the resulting yield curve on a graph, it visually demonstrates this effect.

Use This Sort of Analysis:

When you are considering adding an additional employee(s) or further operating expense(s) to the business. Take a hard look at the Breakeven yield curve to satisfy yourself that this additional expense is justified, and to calculate what level of increased sales/revenue you will need to cover that additional expense.

When starting a new business, to determine what level of sales and the price point you need to set to achieve a profit.

To measure the impact on the profitability of introducing new/additional products or services to an existing business.

When you are adding a new distribution option or altering your business model in some other way.

How to Construct a Breakeven Metrics Model

Open a fresh Excel spreadsheet and plot your 3 versions of annual turnover/sales (best, midpoint and worst projections) in side-by-side vertical columns. Then add:

Cost of Goods Sold (COGS): Let's say, for this example, your assumed COGS for each turnover version is 40% of turnover.

Gross Profit: This is the difference between income and COGS, which will in this example be 60% of sales.

Fixed Overheads: These are the essential *bare-bone* costs and should not include income for the principal at this stage.

Breakeven Turnover Assumptions: Remembering that COGS changes proportionately with different sales amounts, whereas operational overheads remain fixed regardless of turnover.

For start-ups and business expansion projects, add the time required (in months) to reach breakeven, the financial capital buffer you need and your base line assumptions about essential operating costs that will vary with different levels of sales.

The Breakeven Formula emerges from linking two equations:

SALES – VARIABLE COSTS (COST OF GOODS SOLD) = GROSS PROFIT
BREAKEVEN IS REACHED WHEN: GROSS PROFIT = FIXED COSTS

These calculations are not a substitute for a full profit projection but do provide a very quick analysis of business viability.

Annual Budget Time

The lazy person's approach to annual budgets is too often to *copy and paste last year's income and expense actuals* (with a small uplift from last year's sales outcome0 and adopt them as this year's budget. I have seen it done too many times!

In their Harvard Business Review editorial *An Agile Approach to Budgeting for Uncertain Times, (August 27, 2020)*, Bain and Company Partners *Rigby, Spits and Berez* proposed a shift from the *traditional command & control budgeting* approach to one based on *Learning, Adapting and Growing*.

This focal shift from *precision* to *strategic success* is underpinned by 7 questions:

1. *What are the outcomes most important for strategic success?*

SME Leadership: The 5 Critical Success Factors

2. *How should our resources be allocated between running the business (operations) versus changing the business (innovations)?*

3. *What should our balance be between incremental innovations versus breakthroughs?*

4. *How much should go to each of our customer segments?*

5. *How much should go to sales and distribution versus operations and product lines?*

6. *Are we using tired legacy technology (or too many manual and outdated processes) that cost a lot to run versus the potential new features and improving architecture could bring?*

7. *What does our optimal mix of resource spend versus what we actually spend look like? And how do we change it to optimise results?*

At budget time, try to answer each of those seven questions objectively, and from there, adopt the principal of *zero-based budgeting,* where you *challenge every income item* and *reset every overhead item* to a *zero-starting-point*. Stress test and justify each in terms of its needs, its costs and how they relate to your capacity to achieve that strategic success.

Budget time also presents you with an opportunity to revisit *all your business supply relationships*, to ensure you are receiving the best possible deal from each of them, and to consider any alternative options.

Make sure you review your budgeted performance versus actuals every month, and don't hesitate to reset those numbers when it is obviously justified. Bain and Company's Rigby, Spits and Berez advise that *setting bold, challenging objectives and then adjusting plans to incorporate valuable lessons learned is the best way to improve.*

Finally, when you prepare your budgets, never stop just at the Profit & Loss. It is imperative that you also project out the effect on cash flows and the balance sheet. Again, *Calxa Software* comes to the fore in delivering an excellent budget construction package that automatically links to your profit and loss, balance sheet and three-way cash flow.

What to Do When Cash Flows Are Stretched to the Limit

In my experience, insolvency rarely happens to a business overnight. It invariably becomes evident gradually over months or even longer. Typical patterns may be:

- Recurring month-on-month *trading losses*.
- Recurring month-on-month cash flow shortages.
- Having to pay creditors well past normal trading terms.
- The business being placed on *cash-only terms* by suppliers.
- A failure to meet federal and state tax obligations by their due dates.
- Reaching the upper limits of or being in default of bank funding lines.
- The balance sheet shifting into negative net worth, where liabilities exceed asset.
- A failure to keep financial records up to date.

Australian Corporate Regulator ASIC recommends a basic four-point action plan if the directors of a business believe they have reached or are getting close to reaching an insolvency position.

- Put a priority on getting your financial records up to date.
- Put a priority on identifying the true financial position, pinpointing the likely causes and putting in place necessary cash flow remediation strategies.
- Seek professional advice from your accountant as soon as you start to see troubling financial performance trends.
- Act with a strong sense of urgency.

My key message is to call your accountant the moment these concerns emerge.

Some of the more obvious remediation strategies may include:

- ➤ Cut overheads that do not add material value to the business.
- ➤ Slash unproductive bureaucracy.
- ➤ Renegotiate one-sided supply agreements when it is clear you are not getting a fair deal.
- ➤ Maximise digital economy solutions that may improve productivity.
- ➤ Negotiate a reduction in hours worked rather than letting employees go, particularly if you are convinced the good times will return.
- ➤ Do not leave it too late to negotiate with creditors for instalment plans to catch up on outstanding commitments, and
- ➤ Talk to your bank early about any short-term assistance you may need.

If it becomes evident your remediation strategies are not improving cash flows, it's important to *understand when your solvency obligations* have reached their legally allowable limits. Your accountant will be able to advise when you are at that point and what your next steps should be.

Dealing with Disasters

Thursday, 28th of December 1989, shortly before 10.30 am, I was sipping a morning coffee while admiring the view from our newly constructed back sundeck at our home in Sydney, when I heard a slight rumble, and the deck beneath me started swaying ever so slightly on its foundations. As I raced in a panic to the phone to call our builder, an incoming call came through from St. George Bank's Head Office to let me know about a significant earthquake that had struck Newcastle only moments before. It was 5.6 on the Richter Scale and was undoubtedly the cause of what I had felt, 160 kilometres away from the epicentre!

SME Leadership: The 5 Critical Success Factors

It was, at that time, one of Australia's worst natural disasters. The epicentre was 15 kilometres from the Newcastle CBD. 13 people lost their lives that day, 160 were injured, and 50,000 buildings were damaged. Several of our bank branches took a hit, and some of our staff members sustained scratches and bruises, but thankfully none of them were seriously hurt. Given my relatively new responsibility of running St. Georges Retail Bank, that phone call marked an abrupt end to my holiday break. Back at work, within an hour, we quickly pulled together our Disaster Recovery Team.

Many large corporations, like St George, have contingent disaster recovery plans ready to go in times of crisis. Our Newcastle team performed supremely well during the weeks and months that followed. They were given all the support they needed from our headquarters team, and we managed to pull through that event well.

I would guess few small businesses have a disaster recovery plan protocol they can draw on in an emergency. The COVID-19 first lockdown in March 2020 qualified as the mother of all crises for many SMEs when their cash registers were sealed, and their doors closed, literally overnight! Hats off to our Federal Government and the each of the States for responding as they did, but the *job keeper*, *job seeker* and other relief packages took some weeks to establish. It's fair to say life was all fear, panic and chaos over that time.

The importance of contingency planning protocols is about being able to inject a solid, measured process of calm, reason and logic and about mobilising necessary support resources wisely when and where they are most needed.

CPA Australia (Certified Public Accountants) updated and got its well-constructed disaster recovery toolkit out in record time in March 2020.

The chapter headings give you a clear picture of their step-by-step plan:

1. What to do immediately following a disaster
2. Taking stock of your business – steps to recovery
3. A post-disaster business plan
4. Financing your post-disaster plans
5. Long-term disaster recovery

6. Preparing business disaster recovery plans

It's a compelling read and a useful guide for dealing with disaster management anywhere in both the Developed and Developing World. The CPA nailed the important things you need to know and sequentially what contingent steps you need to take. Download this Tool Kit and file it away somewhere safe as a handy reference guide for dealing with any crisis that may occur in the future:

Go to: www.cpaaustralia.com.au/disaster-recovery-toolkit

Chapter 8: Risk Management

My early chartered accounting studies included a mandated term of indenture with a respected chartered accounting firm in Sydney's CBD (in my case, a forbear of BDO). I was on *slave wages* (from memory around $25 per week!) but I got plenty of time off to attend lectures, and I studied hard.

The valuable financial education and experience I gained from those years would later serve me well throughout my career, but the obligatory auditing path I was obliged to spend so much of my time on back in those days drove me to distraction.

So, I ultimately transitioned to the world of banking & finance and soon became hooked on the principals of *Credit Risk Management 101*. I came to understand the equation to make good lending decisions was about balancing two principal risk aspects:

> The assumed *likelihood/odds* of a customer defaulting on their payment obligations after first checking out their general occupancy, employment and credit record, their past payment history, their financial capacity to pay, and their asset backing.

> Assessing the *consequences* if that risk did actually eventuate. For example, what if the customer could not or would not pay? Would our security be enough to cover any default? Or would there be any other fall-back options?

> If both *likelihood* and *consequence* were in the low to moderate risk range, you knew you were on relatively safe ground backing the loan deal. The higher the potential consequence, the more conservative was your decision-making.

For those higher-risk deals, you decided to back on a positive gut feel, regardless, the interest margin and ultimate return had to be high enough to justify your willingness to take that increased level of risk. It may well seem cynical, but that was how the mechanics of the Banking and Finance world worked in those early days.

However, there is now a stronger focus also on the general principles of *truth in lending*.

SME Leadership: The 5 Critical Success Factors

Go elsewhere in the business world, and you'll find the same factors at play, *risk likelihood* vs *risk consequence*. At the corporate level, there is also a further consideration invariably thrown into the mix called *risk appetite*.

In larger corporations, the finance and internal audit departments generally have dual carriage of managing and monitoring risk management disciplines across the corporation. The CFO (Chief Financial Officer) typically reports to a Board Risk, Compliance & Governance (or similarly titled) Committee. That committee has responsibility for approving the overall framework for managing financial and nonfinancial risks in affirming the preferred *Risk Appetite* and in certifying to the directors that the corporation is adequately managing its statutory, legal, governance, and other risks and obligations.

In case you have just stopped breathing(!), there's no need to worry because I'm not going to suggest anything like that level of oversight for the SME cohort reading this book. Frankly, you probably have better things to do with your time and less people on board to do them. However, you do need to understand what you can reasonably do to protect your business and yourself from the risks you may face.

My four-step oversight process for managing SME risks is to know and refine your capability to rapidly identify and manage:

- Your Statutory Obligations
- Your Corporations Law Obligations
- Other Risks and Opportunities
- Contingency Planning

Start by opening a new Excel Spreadsheet that should be saved as: *Risk Management* in your Excel save file. For a snapshot on the basics of Excel and how to get started on it, consider taking on one of the easily accessible online tutorials. An easier option may be to scrum down with a colleague who is a skilled Excel practitioner, and you'll learn about the ins and outs of spreadsheeting in no time!

Your Risk Management Spreadsheet will need four separate pages. At the bottom left side of your spreadsheet, right-click over

Page 1 and rename it *Statutory Obligations*, Page 2 *Legal Obligations*, Page 3 *Other Risks/Opportunities* and Page 4 *Contingency Planning*.

Step 1: Statutory Obligations

On page 1, Tax and Statutory Obligations at law are *not-negotiable*, regardless of how insignificant some of them may seem to you. They are subject to sizeable potential fines and enforcement action if you are non-compliant with any of them.

Confirm with your Tax Accountant what your unique Statutory Obligations are and enter each of them down the left-hand vertical column of your spreadsheet. Note whether each one is an *Ongoing, Monthly, Quarterly* or *Annual Obligation*. Then list the 12 months of the year across the top horizontal column.

Diarise a fixed review date at the end of each month. Preferably, this should be included in the same meeting you are reviewing your monthly financial results.

On each review date, cast your eye through the statutory list and place ticks that all deadlines, responsibilities, and remittance obligations have been met. This then becomes an auto-drive process each month without having to rely on what is most probably an already *overloaded* SME principal's memory!

Your bookkeeper can track and keep this list up to date and should be able to verify that all your obligations have been met.

Step 2: Legal Obligations

On page 2 of your spreadsheet, list the following five standard questions that you should briefly ask yourself each month:

Am I aware of my Corporate Law obligations and am I exercising those duties with the diligence that a person with this knowledge should exercise?

Am I making informed, rational decisions, exercising honest business judgment and am I acting in the best interests of the business?

Am I disclosing potential personal conflicts of interest to fellow directors or partners as and when they arise?

Are our accounting records up to date, and do they reflect the true financial position of the business?

Can I certify that the business is meeting its solvency obligations?

Should you monitor this checklist if you are trading as a Partnership or Sole Trader? *Yes,* as a member of a partnership, you should honour the same obligations, in principle, to each other, with no secrets left on the table. As a sole trader, if something goes wrong in the business, a serious insolvency trigger is reached, or you simply take the wrong strategic turn, and it has serious negative financial implications, you and your personal non-business assets may be exposed to possible legal action by creditors, or even others who may be aggrieved or have suffered a financial loss because of the decisions you took.

So, the five questions I have laid out as corporate law obligations all carry with them solid logic in good business management, regardless of your legal structure.

Step 3: Other Risks and Opportunities

On page 3, as a matter of course, you should cast your *wand* over the whole business each month and pull up whenever alarm bells start to ring about possible shortfalls in how you are managing the business.

On the left-hand vertical column of Page 3, place the following subheadings down the page:

Economic/Financial Risks:

These include changing sales and profitability trends, diminishing cash flows, an increase in slow-paying debtors, increasing bad debts, new competitors, and so on.

Reputational Risk considerations:

Are we engaging in any business activities that could be damaging to our good name and reputation? Are any of our staff acting unethically? Are any of our stakeholder relationships at risk?

Operational Risks and Controls:

These include purchasing and procurement systems, inventory/stock control management, accounts receivable and payable disciplines, fixed asset management and protection, inter and intranet security and access controls, sensitive information and documentation controls and accounting software access levels.

People Risks

These risks include culture and staff welfare, performance, new staff inductions, team camaraderie, succession, employment law compliance, safeguarding vulnerable employees, and so on.

Insurance and Underwriting Risks:

Compliance and Continuous Disclosure, loss of income coverage, Directors and Officers coverage.

A good proportion of the operational and back-office systems you use in monitoring and controlling the relative risks above, will be embedded in your accounting software and the timely monthly performance reporting you'll be able to pull down from it.

NB: For each of the operational controls, you should establish a *Staff Procedures and Controls Manual,* which is made available to all staff and describes as briefly as possible what the control policies are. A couple of examples from that Operational Control list may include:

Accounts receivable policies: *Our payment terms on all outgoing customer invoices are Net 14 days after the date of invoice or as otherwise negotiated with the customer. Those payment terms should be included on every invoice.*

Accounts payable policies: *Our normal payment terms for purchases are 30 days or as otherwise negotiated with the supplier.*

IP access levels & controls: *All staff must execute a binding non-disclosure-deed as a condition of employment BEFORE they are allowed to access our customer data base information or any other confidential information.*

Step 4: Contingency Planning

On page 4, this is the time when you take a few moments during your monthly revue to briefly consider what momentous recent

SME Leadership: The 5 Critical Success Factors

events have occurred or may be on the horizon in your part of the universe and the potential impact, positive or negative, you may expect those circumstances to have on your business.

Fortuitously, I initially jotted down my four-step monthly risk review framework for this book in mid-2019, and there was nothing much going on that could have qualified as a serious contingency then.

Yet now, as I am at the final stages of editing this book (early 2025), we continue to deal with the long-term impacts of the COVID-19 Pandemic, Russia's war with Ukraine, and the perpetual challenges continuing to playing out in the Middle East. All of these events which have had a significant effect on global supply chains and on international political and economic exchanges generally. And of course the latest Trump Whithouse Journey also comes significantly into that mix.

Without overdoing it, you need to have up your sleeve workable, but realistic back-up plans you can put in place, rapidly in need, whenever your business is affected in any way by extraordinary events.

Coming back to your Excel spreadsheet, *Contingency Planning*, you are clearly not going to be waiting around for your end-of-month risk review to consider what to do in seriously challenging times or during a full-on crisis. You need to chart out a plan of action and respond to those challenges every day. And at those times, you should very definitely not drop the ball. Towards the end of the previous Chapter, I have made recommendations about how to respond in times of crisis, when the chips are seriously down for you and your business. And I again draw your attention to CPA's excellent Disaster Recovery Toolkit at: www.cpaaustralia.com.au/disaster-recovery-toolkit which will serve as a valuable business crisis management template wherever your business trades.

Workplace Health and Safety (WHS)

WHS should definitely get more than just a tab on a spreadsheet because it carries significant ongoing Statutory Risks and Obligations, depending on your type of business.

The various WHS laws globally and the consequent obligations that accompany them are designed to protect both the physical and psychological safety of your employees. The ultimate responsibility for compliance and the liability of non-compliance sits directly on the SME principal's shoulders.

Many years ago, when I was a State Government appointed non-executive director of Powerlink, Queensland's primary government-owned electricity transmission generator, a contractor's employee had a fall while climbing one of our high transmission electricity towers. From memory, the fall was less than half a metre but was exacerbated by a malfunctioning harness that took a second or so to activate. Pleasingly, our WHS policies were well managed, and the subsequent investigation concluded there was no liability, but there were learnings, as there always are.

Businesses employing people engaged in work-related responsibilities carrying any level of personal injury or exposure risk should have well-documented and effective WHS policies in place. Depending on the nature of your business and what it does, you will almost certainly need help formulating your WHS policies, procedures and monitoring and control systems. My advice is to seek expert advice! Do not try to do it by yourself.

Chapter 9: Tax Time Reporting

In the economic, regulatory and digitised world we do business in, the constraints on the SME Principal's time meeting their tax, statutory, operational and other back-office responsibilities, must be counterbalanced by their capacity to maximise their time at the front line growing the business. Getting those time and priority balances right is the game breaker that will determine how successful you can possibly be.

In Chapter 1, I stressed the importance of having access to expert professional advisors. Frankly, none of those roles is more important than your external Tax Accountant/Advisor, who will help you meet your annual tax time compliance and reporting obligations.

While many international tax codes are levied substantially at Federal Government level, the US differs most substantially in imposing a raft of separate federal, state and municipal government taxes, where separate tax returns may be required at each of each level of Government. Special economic zones such as American Indian Reservations also have unique rights and requirements to deal with. Managing that level of diversity can be confusing and the imperative to seek local expert advice is surely a no-brainer!

What follows, just as an example, is a summary of Australia's Tax Time Reporting Requirements drafted by a couple of tax pros I know, David To and Simon Chun, from the Brisbane Offices of Pitcher Partners, a prominent Australian accounting group.

I thank David and Simon for penning this chapter and I know they support my view that your expert Tax Accountant/Advisor is the only one who can possibly be equipped to give you the vital counsel you will need to meet those obligations wherever you trade.

For a useful summary of nation by nation taxation guidelines, go to _Deloitte's: Tax Guides & Country Highlights_.

Australian Tax Compliance

An independent tax advisor will help the business with all aspects of tax planning, ensure their tax efficiencies are optimised and that all compliance, filing and periodic financial reporting requirements are met.

Expert Insights About Growing Your Business

The best tax and accounting services can advise you on how to maximise your business opportunities and potential. They can provide unique insights to improve your financial position, aid you with in-depth forecasting, and show you how to direct and prioritise your resources to achieve the best possible return on your investment.

With constant changes to taxation and superannuation regulations, as well as dealing with the increasingly challenging requirements of bankers, these complex economic landscapes can be difficult to navigate alone. A good tax advisor will partner with you to overcome those challenges and will help you to mitigate the financial risks and help you grow your business.

You will also be able to source advice on international transactions, cross-border and transfer pricing compliance, unique businesses such as those that deal with customs and excise duty regimes, and generally in gaining access to new market opportunities.

Dealing With Reviews and Disputes

Businesses have come under increasing scrutiny in recent years for the underpayment of tax and for wages and superannuation contribution disputes related to their employee obligations. High-profile cases causing embarrassment and reputational damage have made headlines across multiple industries. The fact is that Federal and State regulators and the Australian Tax Office have access to more data than ever before and are able to utilise sophisticated data mining and *client profiling* techniques.

A dispute with a revenue authority is invariably a stressful and lengthy process. Seeking professional advice at the early stages of such a claim will give you the best chance to achieve a positive outcome.

Your tax advisor will be able to handle the first-stop liaison with the tax office or other revenue authority and will work with you to fully pursue and preserve your rights. They will also be able to help you navigate the complexities of employment taxes, including PAYG withholding, fringe benefits tax, superannuation contributions, payroll tax and Workcover, and to ensure your obligations as an employer are met.

Dealing With Financial Distress and Insolvency

In an uncertain economic landscape, even the more successful businesses can strike troubling times. It's essential to develop an effective protection strategy to prevent these circumstances from escalating beyond your control, but also to ensure that you can secure your assets, family wealth and business legacy should the unexpected occur. Your tax advisor can help you understand and mitigate the impact of financial risks on you, your business and your family.

Other ways your Tax advisor can help:

Payroll tax: Review of annual returns to ensure correct disclosure of taxable wages.

Fringe Benefits Tax: Preparation and lodgement of annual fringe benefits tax returns, as well as advice on benefits to be provided to staff.

BAS Returns: Assistance in the preparation and lodgement of your quarterly Business Activity Statements.

Superannuation contributions: Review of payroll records to ensure the correct amount of superannuation is being paid on payments to employees and assistance in rectifying any non-compliance issues.

PAYG withholding: Review of employer obligations relating to employees and contractors.

Employee share schemes: Advice on implications to both employers and employees regarding employee equity incentives.

Periodical business health checks: A monthly or quarterly collaborative review of the financial statements of the business (as recommended by the author).

Banking Negotiations: Providing support and advice on bank credit submissions.

Valuations: Assistance in producing a valuation of the business.

Purchase and sale of a business: Advice on what to look for in investigating the pros and cons of a purchase. Assistance in preparing a professionally presented business sale document.

Wealth and retirement planning: A plan to protect and grow your assets and reduce your risk exposure.

Estate Planning: Estate planning involves updating your Will and creating a legally sound framework to protect and transition your wealth with a certainty of outcome, financial efficiency and tax effectiveness.

Tax Time Accounting, Reporting, and Lodgement

Income and other sources of taxation represent real cash outflows or inflows depending on the financial performance of the business. Accurately calculating your tax liability and obligations will be influenced by knowing the necessary source data required, why the tax position is what it is, who is required to pay the tax, how much tax must be paid and when the tax is required to be paid.

Entity structuring

The income tax liability of a business is influenced by the legal and financial structure it operates under. Each structure and preferred operating entity will differ according to the individual requirements of the business and the objectives of its owners.

Some of the factors that influence the choice of the preferred operating entity may include tax minimisation objectives, ease of administration, compliance costs, how profits are to be distributed to owners, asset protection and wealth management considerations, succession planning, international expansion or capacity to attract future shareholders.

It's important to understand the tax rates and tax payable at the business entity levels and how business profits are taxed after distribution to the owners of the business.

Tax Rates of Entities

Tax minimisation within a structure may only be the secondary objective and as such the tax payable within the structure will depend on the entities involved. At a high level, it is important to be aware of the relevant tax rates of the entities involved in the structure.

For Individuals, go to:

Individual income tax rates and threshold changes | Australian Taxation Office (ato.gov.au)

For Companies, go to:
Company tax rates | Australian Taxation Office (ato.gov.au)

For Partnerships – the partnership does not pay income tax, which is paid at the partner level. Refer to the company and individual tax rates above.

Discretionary and Unit Trusts do not generally pay income tax except in limited circumstances. The income tax is paid at the beneficiary level. Refer to the company and individual tax rates above.

It is important to grasp that tax may not only be payable by the entity in which the business operates but also when business profits are distributed to the owners of the business.

Tax on Distribution of Business Profits

Company Dividends: The owners of a company are its shareholders. Company profits are distributed to shareholders by way of dividends.

Dividends paid by the company may be franked or unfranked. A franked dividend has an imputation credit attached when paid to shareholders, representing a portion of the income tax already paid at the company level. These credits may be treated by the shareholder as net tax offsets to reduce their personal tax liability. Unused imputation credits may result in a cash refund to the shareholder. The imputation system was designed to alleviate the impact of double taxation.

Unfranked dividends do not include an imputation credit. The shareholder is therefore taxed on the full value of the dividend received with no tax offset available. Unfranked dividends occur when the company has profits available for distribution but for which no income tax has been paid at the company level.

Discretionary Trust Distributions: Generally, income tax is not paid by a discretionary trust, as the net income of the trust is distributed to the trust beneficiaries at the end of each financial year. In accordance with the trust deed, the trustee passes a resolution on June 30 each financial year to determine what proportion of the net income of the trust each trust beneficiary will receive.

Traditionally, all of the net income of the trust is distributed. Any income not distributed to beneficiaries incurs a tax liability at the trustee level – generally at the punitive top marginal income tax rate.

Partnership / Unit Trust Distributions: The owners of a partnership and unit trust are its partners and unit holders, respectively. The profits of partnerships and unit trusts are distributed in accordance with the relevant partnership or unit holder interests. Partnership and unit trust distributions are taxed at the partner/ unit holder level.

Tax Planning

Income tax should be considered a cashflow item and will ultimately impact the working capital of the business. Where a business performs well, the income tax payable by the entity will be significant and the business needs to plan for when the tax payments are due to be paid.

It follows that your accountant or tax advisor will be able to help you determine your tax obligations as the consequences of getting this wrong can result in significant impacts to cashflow and challenges from the Australian Taxation Office.

PAYG Tax Instalments

Be aware that additional tax may need to be paid following lodgement of your income tax return due to your revised PAYG instalment attributes with the Australian Taxation Office.

PAYG instalments represent a prepayment of your income tax for the current year due to the profits generated by the business or profits received based on the previous financial year.

PAYG instalments for each financial year are used to offset the final income tax for the relevant financial year, with any excess payment refunded by the Australian taxation office.

Once you enter the PAYG instalment system, it is incumbent upon you as a taxpayer to be aware of your tax obligations. These can be easily missed and should be referred to your accountant or tax advisor to clarify whether actual payment is required or if the PAYG instalment should be adjusted downward and the amount payable reduced.

Tax Return Lodgement and Payment Dates

On lodgement of your income tax return, the tax payable will be dependent on the entity type, as well as whether a tax agent has already lodged the tax return.

A tax agent registration is required for accountants and tax advisors to perform professional taxation services for a fee.

Tax agents are granted income tax return lodgement and income tax timeframe extensions and concessions via the Australian Taxation Office's lodgement program framework. Tax agent's clients also receive these concessions that can be generous and not available to the general taxpayer. Note tax agent concessions are only available for income tax returns and business activity statements. PAYG instalments are generally required to be paid within 21 days of the period ending on the PAYG instalment.

In most cases, lodgement and payment of any income tax payable following lodgement of the relevant income tax return can be deferred from 6 to 11 months, following financial year-end, depending on the size and type of the entity.

Tax Advisor / Client Relationship

You will need to speak with your tax advisor at least once during the financial year to prepare and lodge your income tax returns and complete other necessary formalities. Full access to accounting records and your chosen accounting software (typically Xero, MYOB or QuickBooks) will be required by your accountant. All management accounts, tax invoices and bank statements should be reconciled on 30 June and be made available.

Some successful SME principals get into the good habit of linking in their accountant by Zoom or Business Skype every two to three months to focus on business performance and strategies. From their depth of experience in dealing with multiple customer's financial affairs over time, and their considerable knowledge of the different industry sectors, the accountant has the capacity to scan the financials and quickly convert them into a useful diagnostic narrative picture of the business. This process shouldn't take more than an hour and the value your advisor can bring to the table is immense.

Chapter 10: Dealing with the Bankers

Dedication: This Banking Chapter and the last three pages of Chapter 15 (Customers and Revenues) are dedicated to an old pal of mine from Westpac Banking Corporation, Michael Robertson, who sadly passed away in late 2024.

Known across the length and breadth of the Brisbane business community as 'Robbo', Michael was a consummate, highly professional Banker, indeed one of the best I have ever known. He was also one of my valued editors of early drafts of this book.

Finding the *Ideal* Banker

Most significant banks and the larger non-bank financiers between them should be able to cater for the broad spectrum of banking needs of the typical SME.

Other than admitting I have a soft spot for the Bendigo, St. George and the Westpac Banking Groups in Australia, because I worked for each of them at formative stages of my career, my best advice in selecting your preferred financial institution(s) is this:

Seek opinions from as many people as you can about their business banking experience, the range of products on offer, the flexibility of credit offerings, the online banking services, the payroll support processes, and so on.

The main difference between lenders is not always evident at first cut. But for me, it invariably boils down to how the bankers deal with what I call the *human equation*. That is, how well they score in terms of old-fashioned customer service… and that aspect is what I particularly likes about my old mate, *Michael Robertson*.

Talk to friends and colleagues already in business. Find out which financial institution they prefer, their likes and dislikes, how much direct access they get to decision-makers.

Your accountant may well be the logical starting point for you as they may have some close banking relationships they can connect you with.

Typical Lending Options

Once you are ready to open your business account with all the standard add-ons and to establish the necessary links with your accounting software, you will need to provide your chosen banker with a certificate of incorporation of the business and give them any of the other source and personal documentation they require.

What will usually follow is a preliminary discussion about your short to medium-term credit needs, and in seeking that support, it's important to be open in disclosing your financial position.

If you are new to your business or only in the early stages of trading, seeking credit may well be a tough ask. You can quite reasonably expect some reluctance from the lenders at this stage, who will emphasise the importance of first establishing a satisfactory trading history with sustainable cash flows.

When you are able to point to a record of successful trading and accumulated cash flows, your credit discussions will be a lot easier.

The typical lending options on offer:

A Corporate Credit Card

A credit card with a sensible limit to cover your client entertainment, motor vehicle and other ongoing business expenses will be relatively easy to get.

Asset and Equipment Financing

Asset Finance is made available to finance any equipment used in the production of income. This may include motor vehicles, machinery, manufacturing plant, furniture, fit outs and other similar assets. These facilities may be offered to release additional cash flow from unencumbered assets in good condition you already own or to acquire new assets.

SMEs with a healthy trading history, acceptable cash flows and evidence of capacity to pay, will often be able to negotiate an overall limit for the purchase of productive assets. These loans are generally easier to qualify for because they are directly secured by the assets being financed.

The optional Asset Finance facilities include Commercial Hire Purchase, Equipment Finance, Finance Leases and Operating Leases. Other than the Operating Lease, they will usually incorporate principal and interest repayments during the loan term with a balloon or residual value payment due when the facility expires.

Your accountant will explain to you how each of these loans is recorded and treated in the profit and loss and balance sheet and the role that depreciation and GST plays with each loan type.

Debt and Invoice Financing and Full-Service Factoring

Debt financing is ideal for profitable businesses that supply goods or services to their customers on trade credit terms.

Explained simply, an Invoice Financier will *purchase* your credit sale invoices up to an agreed financing limit and will deposit into your bank account around 80% of the invoice value, less their charges, within 24 hours of your issuing the invoice, rather than the 30 to 60 days you may normally have to wait for payment.

The remaining 20% or so is held in escrow by the Financier until the final payment is received from your debtor. The credit sale transaction and the consequent debt obligation remain on your books, although the financier will take an *equitable charge* over your balance sheet and effectively owns each receivable until the trade debtor settles the outstanding amounts owing. When the client does pay, you are obliged to pass on to the Financier your net obligation to clear your remaining debt with them.

Debt Financing options may also include the full-service option of the financier managing the collection of the debts for you.

Foreign Exchange and Trade Finance

Australia's SME sector accounts for a significant slice of our international trade transactions.

Trade finance facilities provide working capital cover for import and export transactions. For importers, it includes funding to pay suppliers and allows time for the goods received to be sold and turned into cash. These facilities will usually include hedging support to manage any moving foreign currency exposure from each transaction. For an exporter, the financier provides working capital until the overseas customer pays for the goods or services that have been delivered.

Exporters typically access *export factoring* (a subset of debt finance) and *bill facility* products as the primary means of financing. Their international trade transactions will be supported by a documentary *letter of credit*.

Overdrafts

Overdraft funding is available to assist a business, typically during seasonal or other times when cash flows are stretched. Overdrafts are generally intended as a *Come and Go*, access as you need facility. They sit over your main trading bank account, allowing it to float between positive and negative balances up to the limit of the approved overdraft.

The bank will want to review your moving cash flow trends to be satisfied your business is sustainable in the longer term and that it can manage this type of facility.

An overdraft subset may also include the offer of a once-only *temporary increase limit* via a definite term, usually a maximum period of 90 days.

Pricing of overdrafts is at the high end of the usual lending price scale. They will also usually incorporate a separate line fee which is charged regardless of whether the facility is drawn down or not.

Commercial land and building finance.

Commercial land and construction funding is available to businesses requiring unique standalone headquarters or depot-style locations, most typically for warehousing, manufacturing, heavy vehicle, earthmoving equipment garaging, or extensive storage facilities.

The choice will invariably come down to the alternatives to lease or buy, depending on the market availability of each option. With landlord's commercial leasing yields (annual rent ÷ valuation X 100 = % leasing yield) sometimes running as high as 10% in Australia's Eastern seaboard cities, the argument for buying (versus lease) may be compelling if you have the required asset backing to do so.

Financing these loans is not particularly complex once you know what percentage of the purchase price the financier is willing to fund and what percentage you will have to find up from your own resources. The loan facility is secured by a real property first registered mortgage over the property to be purchased.

The choice to lease or buy is yours to consider. I am sure your accountant can help you in weighing up the relative merits of each option. If the decision is to buy, the principal will need to have solid asset backing and reserves for a financial institution to consider the transaction.

Property Development Financing

Property development loans are structured to cater for the construction of multiple properties on one title.

Small residential developments of up to 4 or 5 townhouses or duplexes are generally treated as residential property development loans. The required approval process is relatively easy, and the interest rate will be lower than it would for a larger, more complex development. Depending on the borrower's experience and track record, there may or may not be a minimum pre-sale condition imposed.

Large property development loans, whether for residential or large commercial property, are more complex for both the developer and financier and require more supervision and oversight. Extensive experience is required to successfully track the migration of property from non-residentially zoned land through to development approval. Developers aim to achieve the highest margin possible on the gap between original land acquisition cost and completed block sale price outcomes. Theoretically, the earlier the entry point, the higher the return.

Many developers (and many financiers!) prefer their starting point to be with *shovel-ready* land with residential zoning, development approval and where the cost to complete is well defined. Land acquisition costs come at a higher per-block price tag but with a lower speculative risk. They are dependent on the developer's capacity to complete and get the development successfully to market.

Regardless of the approval stage, the track record and experience of the developer is the critical success factor in these transactions. Banking these developments is more hands-on than for other lending transactions. Loan funds are typically released in a series of staged settlement amounts. An independent civil engineer, a licensed quantity surveyor appointed by the financier, certifies at each stage that the work done to date is as per the financial assumptions and that the cost remaining to complete the job reconciles with the loan funds yet to be drawn down.

Interest rates are towards the upper end of the loan rate scale. It is rare for the financier to fund developments above 70%. An upfront percentage of committed presales is often required to further mitigate the financing risk.

Other Loan Types

Floor Plan finance facilities are provided to motor vehicle dealers, motorboat and yacht brokers and others to finance their significant rolling stock holding needs. These facilities entail hands-on expertise and supervision by the financier, including the need to conduct regular stock takes. The same financier may also provide finance to the dealer's end purchasers through its motor vehicle/retail finance division.

Some financial institutions provide unique experiential business finance assistance to other specialised types of business, such as *turnkey franchises*.

Peer-to-peer, business-to-business, and broker-introduced business financing are some of the other financial facilities that may be offered.

The disclosure sensitivities and required homework.

Beware of *the pencillers* in your financial institution's back office. These are the credit *genii*, the most astute numbers' people who will take all the information you have given your banker and will process it into a series of lucid, intelligible spreadsheets that lay out your financial history sequentially and will invariably spit out a number of pertinent questions for you to answer. These people are particularly good at what they do in getting to the core of your real story... warts and all! It may initially seem like a naïve approach, but my best advice is simply, be honest and fulsome in what you provide. Otherwise, you put yourself at risk of being caught out by those dreaded *pencillers*! AND be obsessive about following my *Four Standard Steps for Seeking Credit*:

My Four Standard Steps for Seeking Credit

Pray for the best, prepare for the worst, and expect the unexpected. – Gary Busey

My credo for managing the important tasks in my life is to follow my version of Busey's famous quote i.e.: *hope for the best but always plan for the worst*. Haphazardly hoping for good outcomes without seriously committing to putting in the hard yards to get there will often get you a less-than-satisfactory outcome.

You need to plan for all possible contingencies. There is nothing trite or overstated about wearing your commitment and attention to detail as a badge of honour, because in doing so, you are demonstrating the depth of your commitment to the success of your business.

I recommend that you follow my *Four Steps*, without exception, every time you seek credit. Make sure your homework is thorough and complete. Be precise and tick all the boxes. Tidy up any apparent loose ends to give your request the best chance of success.

Those four steps are:

1. Put together all the necessary documentation in a professional, well-presented folder or *e*-submission. Do not leave anything out:
   - Depending on how long you've been trading, up to two years' tax returns. Your bank/financier will have indicated how far back they want you to go in terms of historical performance.
   - Several years of historical profit & loss statements and your most current balance sheet.
   - A cash flow summary for the current year and the next 12 months.

SME Leadership: The 5 Critical Success Factors

- ➢ A schedule listing your current loans and the assets they cover.
- ➢ A *tax portal extraction* for your business that confirms you are up to date with your Taxation obligations. Your accountant will arrange this for you.
- ➢ Personal statements of assets and liabilities for each principal.
- ➢ A brief dot-point snapshot of your current business plan.
- ➢ Finally, prepare a covering letter that summarises the big picture and what you hope to achieve with your planned new borrowings. This letter is your effective *pitch* statement to the financial institution and should preferably not exceed two to three pages.

2. The *Five Cs* is a quick summary used by some lenders to weigh up the relative merits of a lending proposal. How would you score yourself when the banker considers your request?

   Capital: this is about the combination of my business and personal asset position and their overall strength.

   Capacity: do my financials and forward projections support my capacity to repay the additional debt I am seeking? Is my resultant debt-to-income ratio at an acceptable multiple?

   Collateral: where relevant, am I able to provide the security the financial institution is likely to be seeking?

   Character: has my credit history been satisfactory? Do I have a history of paying my commitments by their due date.

   Current Conditions: considers the current state of the economy, interest rates and any other external factors, positive or negative, that may affect business performance. Internally, what is it that makes my request important? Am I growing so fast that I am having to turn away new customers? Am I currently at the upper limit of my available funding lines? Is my problem that I have slow-paying debtors? Or is it that I do not want to dip any further into my personal resources?

3. Ask your Tax Accountant to review your submission and the supporting documentation you intend to provide. Seek their feedback and validate that you have given it *your best shot*. You want to be satisfied that the financials you are including and your narratives about your business plan do a satisfactory job of highlighting your important milestones and that they validate the reasons for your request.

4. Rehearse on your feet (works in front of a mirror!) how you are going to give voice to your proposal with the right tone of confidence when you finally sit opposite the banker. Practice it several times until you are convinced you have it off-pat. Then find someone who is prepared to give you some constructive feedback!

Only then should you make your appointment with the banker!

The Loan Security Options

Some of the loan securities that may be required by a financial institution when they approve your loan are:

Chattel Security: Asset Finance loans usually incorporate a condition that the loan is secured by a registered charge/Bill of Sale over the goods being financed. This gives them a right to repossess and subsequently sell the asset in the event of a payment default.

A Registered First or Second Real Property Mortgage is taken over any real estate that is subject to a loan. This security gives the lender the right to take possession of, and sell the property, if the borrower defaults on their payment obligations.

Personal Guarantees: Personal guarantees are typically taken by financiers when the business is not well established or has an inadequate trading or credit history. Personal Guarantees may also be taken at the other end of the scale from principals of a large business with substantial borrowings and multiple assets. With a personal guarantee, the principals of the business effectively pledge their own assets, and in case of loan default, they agree to repay the debt from personal capital if necessary. The principal is, therefore, effectively a co-borrower on the loan.

A Mortgage Debenture: With a Real Property Mortgage, the lender only has the right to seize the mortgaged asset that the facility secures. A *Mortgage Debenture* on the other hand is effectively an *Equitable Charge* over the entire assets, giving the lender the right to seize the business in the event of default, and to dispose of its assets as a going concern. Mortgage debentures are usually taken as a protective cover over large and diverse borrowing entities with substantive assets.

NB: I have seen Mortgage Debentures imposed on many business borrowers, but only a handful have ever been acted on because foreclosing on this type of security is effectively the first step towards insolvency, that no financial institution wants to force unnecessarily.

A Cross Collateralisation condition: may be included when the borrower has multiple secured loans from one financial institution where the combined secured assets are cross collateralised with each other. It also means the lender gets to choose the order they will sell assets in case of a default.

Mortgage over Directors/Principal's home: this requires little explanation from me other than to say that, in my view, it is a *very bad idea* to agree to this requirement unless you are doing it for an extraordinarily good reason. To counterbalance my negative view, I could tell you about a good number of successful SME principals who have succumbed to this loan condition at some stage and who subsequently went on to build successful businesses. At times, I have also been called in to advise on (and commiserate with) several who lost their homes after agreeing to lock in this punitive form of business security.

Typical Debt Covenants and Conditions Precedent

When you receive your loan approval, it may come with *Conditions Precedent* and other *Loan Covenants*, which basically govern the rules and conditions the borrower is required to follow during the term of the loan:

Financial Performance Ratios: These may include several of the financial performance ratios I have given you in Chapter 7, such as debt to equity, working capital, debtor days overdue, or interest cover.

A Negative Pledge Covenant clause prevents you from pledging any asset (i.e., offering it as security to another financial institution), if doing so would jeopardize your lender's security position with you.

Annual Review Covenants: Most business finance facilities include this covenant on loans that have multiyear terms. It obliges you to update your financial institution on your trading performance and key ratios by the review date, usually the anniversary date of the original loan advance. It's important to treat these reviews seriously and to comply with the condition. A tip – your banker may start to get suspicious if you *drag the chain* in providing requested information for an annual review. The obvious question being: *What have you got to hide?*

Chapter 11: Buying or Selling a SME

"It matters not how straight the gate or how charged with punishments the scroll. I am the master of my fate. I am the Captain of my soul."
Extract from William Ernest Henley's poem Invictus.

There are some serious considerations to address before you decide to buy an existing business or start a new one from scratch, particularly if you are doing it for the first time.

Stress Test Your Motive for Going Into Business

Do you possess the strength of mind to keep going no matter how difficult it may be? Your mindset and personal belief systems should be driven by a willingness to stay the journey, persevere, take consistently positive steps forward and, above all, to do whatever it takes to succeed. If your sole motive for going into business is to build a pot of gold and do it as quickly as possible, I suggest you think again!

As a starting point, you might consider adopting *Carl J. Schramm's* three interrelated narratives for going into business presented in his excellent book *Burn the Business Plan*:

- ➢ *to start a profit-seeking, scalable business that satisfies the demand for a new or a better product,*
- ➢ *to make money, with the expectation that the value of your business will increase over time, and,*
- ➢ *to build a business that is bigger, better, faster, and more profitable than others in your marketplace.*

Now drill a little deeper. What is my Grand Plan? What do I really want to achieve? If it's driven largely by your desire to become your own boss, are you willing:

- ➢ To be *tougher on yourself than any of your former bosses were.*

SME Leadership: The 5 Critical Success Factors

> *To set serious stretch goals.*
> *To ensure you* make them happen.

Finally, are you willing to embrace the spirit of Laozi's famous reflection: *The journey of a thousand miles begins with a single step.* The message? Lock in and brace for the long haul.

About the Business Opportunity & Its Potential to Succeed

Before you start formally constructing a business plan, make sure you have a clear picture of what the business does, or will do. What are my typical products and services? Who is the ideal customer? Who are the most likely suppliers? Who are the competitors? How do I create a true and unique point of difference?

Check out your relevant/comparative industry. Depending on what sector the business is in, arrange for a good and objective mate to join you in visiting similar businesses to test their quality of service and give you a feel for what you are up against.

About that *Opportunity of a Lifetime!*

Is your plan to back an original idea you think will make you *millions of bucks*?

Before taking any further steps, co-opt someone you trust who cares enough about you to be your devil's advocate and also book a session with your accountant.

With a brand-new venture and zero revenue from day one, there are no guarantees the marketplace or your prospective new customers will be as convinced as you are about the potential of what you are about to offer.

Do your homework.

Well, before you get to the stage of looking at potential businesses for sale:

1. Read this book with particularly focus on all the chapters in Critical Success Factors 1, 2 and 3.

2. Check with friends, family and colleagues who are already in their own SMEs and seek their experience and advice.

3. Jot down a fresh CV of your life experiences, your specific skill sets and your strengths and weaknesses. Consider how you may use these capabilities to best effect, and is there an ideal business sector for you?

4. Go online to check out possible business sector opportunities you believe may be worth pursuing:

    - Your preferred industry sector(s).
    - The ideal business size.
    - Geographic considerations – where do you prefer to trade?
    - What cash flow reserves have you got access to?

Consider the lifestyle issues that are important to you and those you care about most. Do you prefer a business that trades 5 days during normal business hours, or a 6 to 7-day retail business? Is your preference for a Retail, Wholesale or Manufacturing business?

5. Research further once you have come up with a short list of potential business sectors that appeal to you.

6. *Count your pennies.* How will you fund your preferred business acquisition? What capital will you need to cover the purchase price, stock inputs and other required expense inputs until you reach the breakeven stage?

7. Find an experienced accountant who has many SME clients operating in multiple business sectors to help you asses the real value of any business you may be considering purchasing. They will help you to analyse the disclosed financials, the real bottom line returns of the business and what the true breakeven position is.

The Due Diligence Stage

Note: Investopedia defines Due Diligence as: *a process or effort to collect and analyse information before making a decision.*

So, you've identified a business you are interested in purchasing. So, what comes next?

1. Ask for a full set of financials, including:
   - Two prior year's *tax returns* and the supporting *profit and loss.*
   - *balance* sheet and cash flow statements for those years.
   - The most up-to-date current year financial management accounts: the profit and loss, balance sheet and cash flow statements, all downloadable from the accounting software the vendor uses.
   - A detailed fixed asset register and an approximation of the average stock on hand at the end of most months.
   - Extract of current-aged debtors and creditors.
   - An aged Stock on Hand reconciliation. Request a breakdown of any slow-moving or redundant stock items.
   - Ask for the vendor's tax accountant to forward to your accountant a current tax portal extraction of the business to confirm they are up to date with all their tax obligations.
   - Discount 100% of any claims of 'undisclosed' cash earnings.

2. Further questions to ask the vendor:
   - Why are they selling?
   - Ask for a copy of their current business plan.
   - Is there evidence of decreasing or increasing turnover trends over the six to twelve months prior to the business going on sale?

Use the business plan template in Chapter 13 to construct your own plan and what you would do post-acquisition if you do acquire the business. It's particularly important to know:
- What the core product offerings are.
- How do they sell – what are the main distribution channels?
- Who are their top competitors?
- What makes their products *stand out from the* crowd (i.e., compared to other competitors)?
- Who are their key team members, and will they all stay post sale?
- Work through a blank SWOT and TOWS analyses with the vendor (explained in Chapter 13) to get a picture of where they see their business Strengths, Weaknesses, Opportunities and Threats.

3. When you have your answers from the vendor:
   - Do your own analyses of what you believe the disclosed financials are telling you.
   - Draw up three basic financial projections from that analyses that reflect what you believe you could achieve in the 12 months following your acquisition: your best case, worst case and the medium case profitability assumptions.
   - Ask your tax accountant to check your assumptions and compare notes. Also, seek advice on the goodwill component of the asking price of the business – quite specifically, is it a fair or overbaked price.

4. Do some mystery shopping. Get some close pals to visit the business and buy something they've got for sale. Then ask for their first and lasting impressions of the buying experience and of the business overall.

The Hard Reflections

Let's assume you have analysed the business data you received from the vendor and have verified with your accountant that your assumptions are reasonable. You've also received sound advice on the asking price and what your *fair value* counteroffer should be if you believe the vendors' price is too high.

Do you now go to the next stage and ask for a draft Sale Contract? This is where you must be as objective as possible:

> Throw away your rose-coloured glasses.

> Find at least one good reason to proceed.

> Find at least one good reason not to proceed.

> Ask do I truly know what I will be buying?

> Ask do *I sense they may be hiding something* from me?

Consider what specific personal qualities you can bring to the table in buying this business and how you think you can grow and expand it beyond its current base.

Know that if you proceed at this penultimate stage, it's *caveat emptor* – let the buyer beware!

On Reaching the Sales Contract Stage

You'll need a Commercial Lawyer to act for you on the business purchase. Ask your accountant for a referral as accountants and lawyers often conjunct on contractual matters.

My advice here is do not consider the possibility of acting for yourself, as you can't possibly have the requisite knowledge you'll need to navigate this critical stage alone.

Matters for Consideration When Negotiating a Business Sale Agreement

The Vendor will produce the draft sale agreement and may ask for an interim deposit of say 10% as a good will sign of your genuine interest. It should be refundable and should be held in *escrow* in a trust account and be subject to satisfactorily meeting any required conditions precedent.

Non-Disclosure Deeds should be executed by both parties.

Beware: if you are purchasing an intact company. You will inherit all *Assets, Liabilities and Contingent Liabilities* of that corporate structure *Lock, Stock and Smoking Barrels*!

Be wary of *Walk In Walk Out Sale Agreements* without a trial period and no vendor finance options offered. Are you expected to take the vendor's word with no additional disclosures or warranties. Some call this the ultimate *closed-eyes deal*. Don't go this way without setting stringent Conditions Precedent.

Your Final Negotiation Should Ideally Include

The option to spend a trial period of, say, two weeks or more that doesn't need to be disclosed to other staff members. It's important to negotiate this *try before you buy* option.

Negotiate a Vendor Finance deal where part of the purchase price is financed via a time-based settlement agreement with the Vendor. This then becomes a test of the Vendor's *bona fides*.

- Full reconciliation of all staff entitlements.
- Full reconciliation of business debtors and creditors.

A *net balance day accounting* of stock on hand, all prepayments and accruals, including rent, rates and other commitments.

Vendor warranties to be offered that may include:

A *no-compete agreement* where the vendor undertakes not to go back into a similar local business for a defined period of time.

Confirm acquired inventories do not include redundant or defective stock.

Agreement on post-sale communications with key customers and suppliers about the sale of the business.

A positive introduction to all staff members.

Purchasing a Turnkey Franchise Business

The positive of taking on a well-regarded Turnkey Franchise business is that you will generally gain access to good principal and staff training, routine and disciplined operating systems, and reliable income/ bottom-line contribution projections.

If considering a franchised business, my standard caution is to do your homework well, visit several franchisees in the sector you are considering investing in and seek an information pack from the relevant franchisor(s). Speak with your accountant and your bank about your tentative plans. The larger banks in Australia often have a dedicated division that specialises in Franchisee Banking and will have a solid knowledge of the sector.

Make sure you seek independent advice and evidence about any specific franchisee/franchisor disputes and/or legal challenges.

Also, follow all the other steps I have suggested in this chapter.

Selling an SME

Over the years, I have occasionally been asked to give my opinion on an SME acquisition opportunity and am invariably underwhelmed at the quality of the data and information provided by the Vendor. It seems to me there's a lost opportunity to step out from the crowd and offer a well-laid-out package of information with a compelling invitation to proceed.

In Chapter 10, Dealing with the Bankers, I suggest a four-step submission framework for seeking credit from a Bank. I recommend you consider following an abridged version of that format if you are contemplating selling your business.

Put together all the necessary documentation in a professional, well-presented *Information Memorandum*. Do not leave anything out. Ask your accountant to review the document. Once you are both happy with it, have the document professionally printed in a smart presentation folder with your business name on the front before making it available to potential purchasers.

CRITICAL SUCCESS FACTOR 3:

THE FRONT LINE

"If you really look closely, most 'overnight' successes took a long time.'

Steve Jobs

'It took 14 years of hard work for Megisti Media to become an 'overnight success'.

John Mangos

Long ago, I lost count of the number of people running their own business who lamented they *could not sell*. Some even viewed front-line selling as being somewhat beneath them. Yet in any business, your greatest assets are surely your buying and spending customers, because without customers, there is NO revenue or business!

I've been fortunate to have been exposed to some masters at the game of selling throughout my working life. A rare few were naturally charming and could literally sell *igloos to Eskimos*, but the majority were engaged, everyday citizens like you and me who

SME Leadership: The 5 Critical Success Factors

made a rock solid commitment to put in the hard yards and who ultimately got the results *we* deserved.

The most successful of them were able to dig deep enough to identify what I have code named my *9 tenets of Good Front Line Leadership*:

1. Successful principals draw on the essentials of *Good Business Planning* but only ever as a starting point. They know their business plan can't be set in stone and must constantly evolve. Their underpinning strategies and tactics are, therefore, constantly responding to what is happening day in, day out, in their marketplace.

2. They understand their *Brand* will only ever be as good as their customer's perception of it. Their two golden rules are, therefore, don't oversell and underdeliver and don't make promises they know they can't live up to.

3. They have taken the essential action to protect the *Trade Secrets and Intellectual Property* that underwrite their unique customer offerings and their well-targeted competitive advantage.

4. They know the psychology of *Attracting Customers*, *Closing Sales* and *Generating Revenues* is primarily about connecting and finding common ground with their potential buyers.

5. To a person, they are competent public speakers. They have developed well-rehearsed, consistent *Narratives And Sales Pitches* about what they do, and are passionate about why their products and services are better than those offered by their competitors.

6. They know that achieving consistently good sales is as much about their well-disciplined processes of building, feeding and qualifying a productive pipeline of future leads, as it is about closing the end sale. They also know the only way to keep track of the productivity of their pipeline and the sales team that is building and driving it, is with competent *Customer Relationship Management (CRM) Software* as their primary pipeline manager.

7. They are *Committed Citizens of the Communities they do Business in* because they know the by-product of that commitment is that community citizens will prefer to do business with them.
8. They promote their business and their brand well through *conventional marketing channels* but have also learnt to harness the immense potential of *Social Media Marketing*.
9. They know from experience that *What counts is not the size of the dog in the fight, but the size of the fight in the dog*. The most successful SME Principals I have known live by the principal of *Carpe Deum, and they Seize their Day* by challenging themselves *Every Day* with the same recurring question: *What else can I do to maximise my sales, revenue streams and profitability*?

If the ability to sell sits in your *too-hard basket*, then dust it off! Ask yourself: *What am I truly in business for*? Perhaps, a more pertinent question for you is: *What finite actions do I need to take to achieve the revenues that are vital to my business surviving and thriving*?

Unless you have solid prior expertise to draw on and have a healthy background in sales and building customer bases, you may need to consider taking on board external professional advice to help you build your productive sales machine and maximise the potential of social media marketing. Be aware those two aspects of sales, *Building the Sales Machine* and promoting your brand using *Social Media Marketing*, are distinctly different skill sets.

Productive management of your time spent at the front line is a critically important skill set. In the chapters that follow, *Dynamic Business Planning, Brand and Positioning*, and *Customers and Revenues* focus on the actions required to create a productive and responsive sales machine. Building *Collaborative Networks, Community Engagement* and seeking guidance from *Mentors and Learning Circles* is about *priming the pump* that will deliver you a constant stream of productive and convertible sales leads.

Chapter 12: Dynamic Business Planning

'Writing a book is not unlike building a house, planning a battle, or painting a picture. The techniques are different, the materials are different, but the principles are the same. The foundations must be laid, the data assembled, and the premises (the key assumptions) must bear the weight of their conclusions. But when finished, it is only a successful presentation of a theme. In battle, the 'other fellow' interferes all the time and keeps upsetting things. The best generals are those who arrive at the results of planning without being tied to the plans.'

Sir Winston Churchill.

Churchill's metaphor of *'the other fellow who interferes and keeps upsetting things'* may be about the opposing team, regardless of whether the action is taking place on the battlefield or the sporting arena, during partisan and bipartisan debate in the hallways and floors of government, or indeed in everyday competition in the world of business. That *other fellow* could even be the effects of a material shift in economic conditions.

The best planning analogy from elite team sport is in the dynamic distinction between set-play attack and defence routines that come out of a team's playbook of their preferred game plan *scenarios,* but also from their video review of their opponents' most recent game strategies. They practice those routines until they can execute them in their sleep. But when live game time comes along, those precise drills work maybe 50% of the time if they are lucky. For the rest of the game, they must respond and play spontaneously to what is unfolding before their eyes in the moment. For high-performance teams, the magic that flows from that spontaneity represents the sum-total of their accumulated learnings and capabilities.

And so it is in the world of business. High-performance business teams that consistently get it right understand their business plan is just a snapshot in time of known data and assumptions. They also know the importance of staying on top of what their competitors and the broader marketplace is doing, and their business planning is underwritten by continually evolving strategies and tactics.

To draw stark examples of uncertainties that will not find their way into any static business plan, the ones for which there is minimal historical precedent to learn from, look no further than the 2019 to 2022 calendar years. Who amongst us could have predicted how devastating the Australian Eastern Seaboard fires would end up being when they first started flickering in September 2019 nor the Californian wild fires that raged in the Northern Hemisphere Summer that followed; what dire impact COVID-19 would have globally when the first outbreak of the virus appeared in barely recognisable numbers in early 2020; or indeed when the Soviet/Ukraine war outbreak came along in early 2022 with its devastating human and infrastructure carnage and its broader international supply chain and economic impacts. *OR* indeed, bouncing forward to early 2025, what about the troubling economic and political uncertainties surrounding the most recent US Presidential election.

In calm or turbulent times, having a business plan is a must. The important distinction is in what you do dynamically with that plan and how you adapt strategically and tactically to a constantly changing world around you. With progressive contextual updates, that plan should incorporate your core purpose and values. It paints the broad canvas for what you intend to do and how you will do it, and it provides the background data for the descriptive narratives you will adopt in promoting the business and selling your products.

My dynamic business planning approach comes in six constantly evolving stages:

A. The First Cut Business Plan.

B. The Plan Stress Tests.

C. The Future Proofing Tools.

D. The Descriptive Narratives.

E. The Projects, Action Plans, Priorities and Timelines, and

F. The Operating Financial Projections.

A: The First Cut Business Plan

Some principals opt to prepare their business plans with no assistance. I'm not convinced that's such a great idea, as it takes away the real benefits that can flow from healthy debate and dialogue. In my view, a minimum of three to four people should ideally participate – the *Principal*, a *Business Partner(s) or Senior Team Members*, a *Mentor/Pal* already in business and a *Professional Advisor*.

Figure 12.1

B: THE BUSINESS PLAN STRESS TESTS

C: FUTURE PROOFING TOOLS

D: THE NARATIVES

E: THE ACTION PLANS

F: THE OPERATING PROJECTIONS

SME Leadership: The 5 Critical Success Factors

1. *Vision:* This is your core purpose, raison d'être, big-picture statement of intent. Let's call it your *grand plan* in how it defines the ideal scope of your business. It's the narrative about who you are and what you aim to achieve. It should include an *expansive* set of goals matched by a punchy description of what it will mean to achieve them.

I have always admired Henry Ford's original vision *to democratise the motor vehicle*. Ford's *Grand Vision* matched that objective well: *when I'm through, everyone will own a car and the horse will have disappeared from our highways.*

Do I hear you say... I'm not a Henry Ford? But who knows. If you are prepared to *put the hard yards in* you may well be one day!

The SME Stakeholders should also get a mention here. At St. George Bank, one of our non-executive directors Len Bleasel, told me how he had recrafted major power company AGL's vision soon after he was appointed CEO. As I recall it, the company had a complex and wordy vision and mission statement few employees could elucidate well, let alone understand. After meeting with a cross-section of stakeholders, Len reframed AGL's then vision to simply incorporate those key stakeholders. The outcome was something like: *AGL aims to be a great company to work for, to be a shareholder in, to be a customer of, and to be a supplier to.* I have no doubt Len's words were far more eloquent than my recollection of them all these years later, but I've never ceased to be impressed by his simple and direct messaging.

2. *Values:* These are the entrenched standards we stand by and should care about deeply. Values are about our core beliefs, the principles that drive how we behave, how we treat and wish to be treated by our staff, our customers and in the broader marketplace. In short, consistent values drive organisational culture and behaviour and reflect how well our actions and outcomes match those values. Dynamic operating strategies and their supporting tactics do and must evolve over time, but core values are the rock-solid foundations. (More about values in Chapter 30).

3. *Products & Customers:* Is yours a new or existing business, and what are your main products and services? Consider any necessary investment in technology and production support

investment to get your product to market. If you are a manufacturer, what collaborative efficiency opportunities are there to link up with your supplier(s) in the production process.

Who is the customer? Are they growing? What are their typical demographics: age, sex, education, occupation, income range, and marital status? Their lifestyle drivers: family status, hobbies, sports? Buying sensitivities: price, quality, big brand preference, unique product features, the ambience of retail presence/locality? To what degree is your product a compelling purchase for them?

Estimate the relative size of the market you will be selling into. How big is it? Is it growing or contracting as a market? What economic factors will influence buying decisions? What digital interruptions are impacting the marketplace for your key product(s).

Finally, what are the key price point metrics, including COGS (Cost of Goods Sold) on each sale, your planned markup and your resultant Gross Margin? This is one of the most important financial ratios to know about in your business!

4. *Distribution Channels:* Where does the business fit in the supply chain hierarchy – as a manufacturer, wholesaler, retailer, reseller, or consulting/ services sector business? Does it sell locally, state-wide and/or nationally and/or does it export goods for overseas sale or import goods (or goods components) for local sale?

Does the business sell its products face to face, telemarketing, online and/or via third-party channels, distributors, collaborators, referrers or introducers. How does the business build its introductory networking relationships?

Today, businesses, both large and small, are responding rapidly to digital technology advances in how they compete for customers and offer additional access options. Those willing to adapt and change their business model to accommodate these advances will reap the benefits. Those who fail to do so could find themselves struggling.

5. *Where are our Major Battlegrounds (The Competitors):* On the Front Line, who are and/or will be *your major competitors*? Check out their price points, what they are good at and what they are not so good at? How do they advertise/promote their business

and/or use social media? Who are the main players and the biggest competitors? What alternative products are offered in the marketplace?

How do our competitors operate, and how do they sell and promote their business? What optional distribution access channels do they offer? How do they treat their customers? Get a feel for their relative strengths and weaknesses, where they source their raw materials from and the drill down on their end pricing. What unique capabilities do they demonstrate? Consider exclusivity features, lower prices, better raw materials costs, after-sales service, etc?

6. *Our Critical Success Factors:* What is your *Sustainable Competitive Advantage* and *Unique Selling Points* (USP's)? What is your *Customer Value Proposition*, (CVP) and what makes your offerings different to your competitors? How are your offerings superior? Focus might be on a combination of specific product features, aspects of *Intellectual Property* (IP), a successful on-point dedicated sales team, superior after-sales service ethics, a good reputation, and a respected brand. It could also be in the way you generate leads, build introductory business networks, convert leads into new sales or even support and advocacy of community need projects within the region(s) you do business in.

What product features or services do you offer that your competitors don't, and how can you positively differentiate your offerings from theirs?

Include any other metrics that may drive successful outcomes for your business, the influencers who will help you along the way and possible partnerships, advocates, business introductory networks and any other potential to actively engage in, and contribute to, successful initiatives or outcomes within the community you do business in.

7. *Workflows & The Team:* In a business planning context this is about how you invest in your Social Capital and build a customer-driven focus, moulding your team to maximise their individual and collective contributions to the business. The undeniable fact is that when you:

> ➢ Invest in good people,

SME Leadership: The 5 Critical Success Factors

- Make a real commitment to building their skills,
- Establish a strong culture of team trust,
- Empower and encourage your team,
- And invest in the community you do business in,

you will almost assuredly achieve good outcomes in return.

8. The Macros: These are the unique external factors that may impact your trading capabilities if you fail to respond to or protect yourself from them. They may include economic settings such as Gross Domestic Product (GDP), inflation, interest rates, unemployment trends, monetary and fiscal policy settings, the prevailing business cycle flows and the incumbent state and federal government responses to them. Other macro factors include changes in government statutes and regulations, evolving industry and demographic trends, or even accelerated technological innovation.

9. The Breakeven Metrics: Open a new spread sheet with three versions of assumed turnover (your first cut *best, worst and mid-range forecast assumptions* and then build a basic Breakeven metrics model around those assumptions.

The model foundation is based on always knowing what your Gross Margin is in the business (NB: Income – Direct Cost of Goods Sold = Gross Profit. Gross Profit ÷ Income X 100 = Gross margin as a %). I explain in Chapter 8 how you can extract the trend Gross Margin and the Breakeven Metrics for your business.

These calculations are not a substitute for full profitability projections, but they do provide a quick analysis of business viability as a starting point.

B: The Plan Stress Tests

SWOT Analyses

The *SWOT* tool (Figure 11.2) emerged in the late 1970s following several years of collaboration between Stanford University's Albert Humphrey and several US corporations looking for a clearer approach to the business side of strategy planning.

Strengths are the things you are particularly good at and do well in and are typically those that give you a point of difference and a distinct competitive advantage. *Weaknesses* are those areas you need to improve on and, over time to transform into strengths. *Opportunities* are the things you are not doing, such as obvious market gaps that, if you adopt them, could give you an additional comparative advantage. *Threats* are the external risks and negative factors largely outside your capacity to control that you need to plan for, and if you fail to do so, that have the potential to threaten your business success.

For each of the four SWOT components, jot down the three to four points that are most relevant to your business. Be as objective as possible in deciding how your business measures up in each dimension.

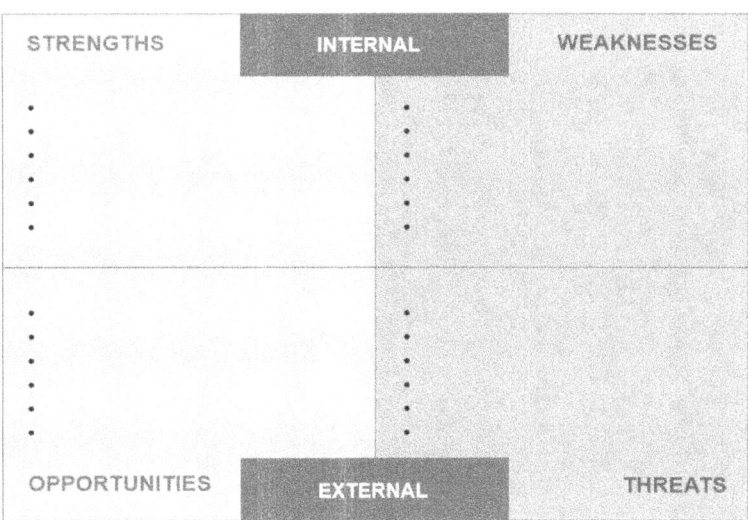

Figure 12.2

TOWS Analyses

TOWS, created by Professor Heinz Weirich at the University of San Francisco, is a more advanced analytical adjunct to SWOT, providing a basis to compare the four SWOT factors against each other. The method provides the key to making productive use of your strengths, to circumvent your weaknesses (and/or converting them into strengths over time), to capitalise and act on your opportunities, and to competently manage/ mitigate your threats.

The four TOWS comparison points are:

- Weaknesses v Threats (WT).
- Weaknesses v Opportunities (WO)
- Strengths v Opportunities (SO)
- Strengths v Threats (ST)

The TOWS matrix process and comparative examples are explained in the TOWS strategy graphic (Figure 12.3).

To maximise value from your SWOT and TOWS analyses, you need to be brutally honest in your analyses. Start by documenting your SWOT and TOWS first, then include your findings and assumptions in your strategy planning review.

Refer to the figure on the following page…

TOWS STRATEGIES

INTERNAL FACTORS

	W WEAKNESSES	**S** STRENGTHS
O OPPORTUNITIES	W + O MINIMISE - MAXIMISE STRATEGY	S + O MAXIMISE - MAXIMISE STRATEGY
T THREATS	W + T MINIMISE - MINIMISE STRATEGY	S + T MAXIMISE - MINIMISE STRATEGY

EXTERNAL FACTORS

STRATEGY FOCUS	ANALYSIS / STRATEGIES
W + T MINI - MINI	Defensive strategies that minimise or reverse weaknesses and mitigate or avoid threats **EXAMPLE:** Cull slow moving stock, cut overheads, refocus business strategies
W + O MINI - MAXI	Adopt strategies to minimise or reverse weaknesses by taking advantage of opportunities **EXAMPLE:** When unique opportunities emerge, act on them
S + O MAXI - MAXI	Adopt strategies that use strengths and maximise opportunities **EXAMPLE:** Leverage / capitalise on your good reputation and brand to launch a new product
S + T MAXI - MINI	Strategies that draw on strengths to minimise / mitigate threats **EXAMPLE:** Leverage / capitalise on your good reputation and service quality to avoid / mitigate threats

Figure 12.3

C: Future Proofing Tools

Commitment to continuous learning and improvement is a constant theme throughout this book. In the context of business planning, it's about your capacity to train your mind to think beyond the boundaries of your own business and to also take a thoughtful look into the future. It's important to lock in *closed-door* private *me time* each month to focus on this sort of thinking. If you do it regularly, I guarantee it will progressively strengthen your capacity to think outside the box.

Here are just a few starters to guide you on your strategic thinking journey:

Sometimes it's all too easy to assume the best possible outcomes for your business without having any realisable backup plans. A good starting point is to challenge the key assumptions in your business plan about the future trading environment over the next 12 months. At budget time, get into the good habit of producing *three financial forecast versions for each trading year, from best to expected to worst case*. Stress test each of those assumptions with alternative realities and consider the possible impact they may have on your business and the strategies you should adopt and what impact each of those realities will have on your operating budgets (both income and expenses).

Always be aware of what is going on in your local marketplace, nationally and internationally, particularly evolving trends and events that could have an impact on your business over time.

Build on your capacity to *look across the valleys*, to be able to identify and react to changing market cycles. Doing it often enough will give you the capacity to positively influence your strategic foresight capabilities, gain a good sense of the best times to roll out new products, make product changes or open an additional outlet.

Your forward viewing capacity should also identify significant business expansion or new/evolving product opportunities ahead of the marketplace and give you the courage to take positive action.

Be diligent about keeping up with *everything happening in your industry sector*. Material changes to consumer demand, new products, shifts in consumer sentiment, pricing, customer service needs, emergence of new raw material suppliers or changes in the cost structure of any of your direct cost of sale inputs. Ensure you know about any new market players, competitive changes or emergence of alternative distribution channels. Know and understand what impact digital interruption and other new innovations are having on your sector, and the impact they may have on how your customers engage with you.

Take every opportunity to be represented at *conferences and networking events* of leaders in your industry sector. Constantly look for any ideas that will improve your source knowledge and your potential to create better outcomes for your business and your customers.

Finally, I urge you to acquire *The Innovators DNA: Mastering the Five Skills of Disruptive Innovators*. (Dyer, Gregersen and Christensen, 2011, Harvard Business Review Press). The authors have uncovered the immense potential of harnessing *Creative Innovation* as a vital skill set. This book is one of my favourites, and its lessons are relatively easy to grasp and follow (see more about Creative Innovation in Chapter 19).

D: The Business Narratives

These are the essential, well-rehearsed narratives you will build about your business and what it does. They should include:

A standard one to two sentence *Elevator Speech*, that is the compact story that you and your customer-facing people use to provide a consistent, quick descriptive explanation about the business and what it does.

The on-point *Pitch Statements* you and your sales team will adopt when meeting with prospective customers and other business lead sources.

A Longer Written Narrative that is used across all your brand marketing, PR, social media and other statements and written communications.

I drill down on how to construct and rehearse these narratives in Chapter 15.

E: The Projects, Priorities and Timelines

Full Action Plans should be produced from the business plan and periodically updated from evolving strategic and tactical responses. These are your Forward Goals and Project Actions that will bring your plan to life. You'll also need separate statements of achievable priorities, who will be responsible for achieving each of them and your best timeline assumptions.

Authors note: In managing multiple projects and the drill-down tasks that support each project, you will need to grade all tasks and jobs required and complete each of your projects within a given timeline. Ideally, you'll need the capability to present them in a graphical layout, that presents a quick summary of tasks allocated to different team members and allows you to track plan performance at every stage. There's a range of project management software options available in the marketplace, but most of the options I've seen are overbaked for the needs of the typical SME principal. Also see readers' access to our *Essential SME Tool Kits* later in the book.

F: The Operating Projections

Assuming you've taken my advice to adopt cloud-based accounting software and have also taken a *Calxa software* subscription, production of your full financials, including balance sheet, profit and loss, and cash flows will be a relatively painless and seamless task for you. If you haven't already done so, I suggest that now might be a good time to look at *a subscription to Calxa*!

In my experience building financial projections, many years out is all too often a wishful act of fiction. As I mentioned earlier, I've learnt the best starting point is to first produce three projections for the coming twelve months – your WORST CASE, BEST CASE and MID-POINT assumptions. Those options consciously oblige you to consider what actions you may need to take under each scenario.

Calxa's software will guide you through the whole process. If you are already in a business or are about to purchase an existing going concern, follow my advice in Chapter 8 of constructing your financial projections on a *zero-based-budget* basis and stress test/re-justify all your fixed operating overhead assumptions.

If yours is a new business not yet trading, you'll need to run full breakeven analyses to estimate the additional capital you will need and importantly to prove that it is indeed a robust and viable proposition.

The case to burn or not to 'burn the business plan.'

While professing his cynicism about the business plan, former Kauffmann Institute CEO Carl J. Schramm makes some surprisingly passionate observations about the importance of planning for business success in his excellent book *Burn the Business Plan*. Summarised below is *my interpretation* of some of Schramm's key observations:

- ✓ *Innovation*: The ability to innovate relates to the breadth of facts at your command. So, the more you know, the more creative you will become.
- ✓ *Mindset*: Success in business requires a dose of *Carpe Deum* – i.e., the will to *Seize the Day,* be courageous enough to embrace every good opportunity and have the strength of mind to stay on the journey and not give up.
- ✓ *Time horizons:* Good business outcomes rarely happen overnight. Give yourself time to get there. Do not set unrealistic timelines.
- ✓ *Sales and Networking:* Your business planning efforts must have a Front-Line focus. Know that sales and new customers are everything and building valuable business networks supported by a competent CRM is a critical adjunct to achieving good sales. The deeper those relationships, the more likely they are to produce opportunities to grow and diversify your business.
- ✓ *The boss*: The buck stops with you. To make good decisions, you need to collaborate and be committed to learning and growing from your mistakes.
- ✓ *Good luck:* Every successful entrepreneur can point to at least one lucky break. Static business plans never mention good luck because it is not a dimension you can conventionally plan for. At the same time, Schramm encourages you to

embrace the well-cited entreaty: *the harder I work, the luckier I get*. The bottom line for Schramm is that regardless of the source, good entrepreneurs make their own luck. Or, as famous comedian Milton Berle once said: *If opportunity doesn't knock, build a door!*

I agree with and support Schramm's conclusions. While I cannot speak personally for him, my deduction is that his book title *Burn the Business Plan* is an evocative metaphor shouting loud and clear that planning for business success must be a dynamic, living, breathing, evolving process. A business plan, with frequent sequential updates needs to be documented and should inform the basis of the narratives you weave in the marketplace about who you are and what you do.

Finally, don't let your business plan become a War & Peace diatribe! Respectfully, I don't have much enthusiasm for reading Business Plans that run to more than fifteen to twenty pages!

Chapter 13: Brand and Positioning

'Google' the word *brand* and too often, you'll find it referring principally to symbols or visual representations, such as a great business name, a logo, a prominent road sign, or a well-known product name. True, those things are all important and have significant value, but the soul and promise behind an enduring brand goes much deeper.

To me, the metaphor for a standout from the crowd brand is an aged bottle of Penfolds Grange Hermitage, an internationally respected Australian dry red wine. The sheer idea of taking that first sip of one of their vintage masterpieces is accompanied by the winemakers promise of something exceptional. For the red wine connoisseur, Grange's reputation precedes it. I know my reds reasonably well, yet in my experience, that first sip outdoes their promise every time.

The Grange metaphor defines what good brand is about - the simple notion that a brand can only ever be as good as the customers perception of it. For that reason, owners of the best brands follow two golden rules. They don't oversell and underdeliver and they don't make promises they are not prepared to live up to.

On becoming the Australian National Rugby League coach, Mal Meninga laid out his four-point blueprint for the Kangaroos brand and what wearing the green and gold Jersey and putting your team and teammates first should look and feel like:

> *Better people make better players: We are inclusive and ensure the team always comes first.*
>
> *We are committed to being the best we can be for our teammates and our country.*
>
> *We love the game, we love the jersey, and we won't let our mates down.*
>
> *We uphold the tradition of the jersey and its values, and we carry the aura of our predecessors since 1908.*

The symbol of the Kangaroos Brand, the aspect you can see and feel and touch, is the *Jersey* and the *Players*. For me, Mal's definition of the Kangaroo brand is also about the transformation that occurs when players actually pull that jersey on, in the knowledge of what and who they are playing for and the proud century-old traditions they represent.

The visual representation of the McDonald's brand is the Golden Arches. The half billion dollars or so they spend globally every year on advertising and marketing and their prominent philanthropic contributions to worthwhile causes such as Ronald McDonald House add voice and substance to their brand. The other critical dimension is the seven documented core promises that empower McDonald's offerings:

> *We place the customer experience at the core of all we do.*
> *We are committed to our people.*
> *We believe in the McDonald's system.*
> *We operate our business ethically.*
> *We give back to our communities.*
> *We grow our business profitably.*
> *We strive continuously to improve.*

You don't have to be a fast-food fan to sense McDonald's delivers well on those core promises and how they feed into their broad target market.

My Core Definition of Brand

> Brand is about the promises we make and our customer's reactions and responses to those promises.
> Brand is about how we position our business to satisfy our customer's needs, wants and preferences.
> By our deeds and actions, Brand is about how we engender customer loyalty and a desire for them to continue doing business with us.
> Brand influences the choices our customers make at every point of contact, powered by how well our actions and outcomes have matched or exceeded our promises.

SME Leadership: The 5 Critical Success Factors

- ➤ The bottom line? Brand strength can only ever be measured through other people's interpretation of it. So, in a very real sense, and in the eyes of the beholder, *perception equals reality*.

- ➤ **What Role Can Brand Play in Small Business?**

The short answer is one hell of a lot, especially when it is done well! Start with a great business name which creates the touch point for what you are selling and around which you can weave a good story. The name should be evocative enough to make customers want to engage with you.

Next comes a good logo and creative graphics to complement the business name.

Ensure your promises are entrenched, deliver every time and ensure you are consistently over-delivering on what you have promised. Finally, your after-sales service must be so outstanding that your customers wouldn't dream of going elsewhere.

How Will I Know if We Are Meeting Our Promises?

Firstly, the critical numbers rarely lie! If you are consistently doing the right thing, you would expect to see an ongoing upward trend in sales, income and hopefully profitability, accompanied by the highest possible customer retention rate and negligible customer loss. That is *The Customer Recycle Challenge* (Figure 13.1).

THE CUSTOMER RECYCLE CHALLENGE

Figure 13.1

But that doesn't mean you can rest on your laurels. You will find a raft of business consultancies around the planet that will happily advise on the strength of your Brand and the things you could be doing better to enhance it. To do the job they will invariably start by sending out a survey to your customers and other key stakeholders, including you and your staff.

This independent process makes sense to larger businesses or corporations but also comes at a high price tag! Consider undertaking your own customer service research by accessing a lower cost online *customer experience* review. With some quick homework you'll find several capable vendors online who can set it up for you.

The golden rule for this type of research? Only undertake it if you are serious about learning from it. Someone in your business needs to have responsibility for tracking the overall service rating trends, directly following up on any negative feedback and responding to innovative ideas from engaged customers. The feedback from these surveys should be shared with all your team.

The Importance of Timely Response to Customer Issues

In a Harvard Review (HBR) editorial dated May 19, 2015, Cynthia J. Grimm considered the importance of timely responses to customer issues.

From her research, Grimm observed that the quality of the customer experience has a direct impact on their loyalty and advocacy. Customers who receive a first contact resolution are nearly twice as likely to buy again from a brand and four times more likely to spread positive word of mouth about it.

How Else Can I Test My Brand Strength

In the January 2019 edition of the Harvard Business Review, Harvard's Emeritus Professor Stephen Greyser and Lund University's Associate Professor Mats Urde, identified eight interrelated prerequisites that underwrite a well-recognised, respected and enduring brand.

Greyser and Urde's *Corporate Brand Entity Matrix* (Figure 13.2) emerged from a decade of global research and engagement with a large number of executives from multiple sectors. Each of the prerequisites in their matrix asks a pertinent question about that element of the organisation's corporate identity and core brand. The questions are presented in four layers:

Internal Elements: are the core mission, vision, values, culture and competencies that drive the business.

External Elements: how the business wants to be perceived by customers and other stakeholders, its value proposition, its outside relationships and its positioning.

Elements that bridge Internal and External aspects: including the organisation's personality, its instinctive ways of communicating and its brand core. What the Brand stands for and the enduring values that underpin its promises to customers.

Brand Core: is at the centre of the Matrix and is the essence of the Brand.

SME Leadership: The 5 Critical Success Factors

A corporation's identity is made up of nine interrelated components. By examining each one and how it relates to the others, an organization can build a stronger brand.

	Value proposition	Relationships	Position
External	What are our key offerings, and how do we want them to appeal to customers and other stakeholders?	What should be the nature of our relationships with key customers and other stakeholders?	What is our intended position in the market and in the hearts and minds of key customers and other stakeholders?
External/internal	**Expression** What is distinctive about the way we communicate and express ourselves and makes it possible to recognize us at a distance?	**Brand core** What do we promise, and what are the core values that sum up what our brand stands for?	**Personality** What combination of human characteristics or qualities forms our corporate character?
Internal	**Mission and vision** What engages us (mission)? What is our direction and inspiration (vision)?	**Culture** What are our attitudes, and how do we work and behave?	**Competences** What are we particularly good at, and what makes us better than the competition?

Figure 13.2

Greyser and Urde's well-tested hypothesis is that when the corporate identity of a business is at its best, each of the eight prerequisite elements will complement, inform and echo the core Brand, resonating with the values of the business and what it stands for. Likewise, the brand core, at its best, will shape the other eight elements.

Periodically test the strength of your brand by objectively asking each of the nine questions at the heart of the *corporate brand entity matrix*. I urge you to include your team in this review.

Chapter 14: Trade Secrets

Trade secrets, trademarks, unique business names, copyright law and patents all fall into that mysterious basket of assets in the business world, some tangible and some intangible that are known as intellectual property, or simply IP.

At the ground floor, Trade Secrets may simply boil down to valuable information and unique selling points (USPs), not publicly known, e.g., those aspects of your business operation that explain why customers prefer and consciously choose to buy from you rather than your competitors. These advantages may include:

➢ Benefits hard to replicate that give your business a demonstrative competitive advantage.

➢ A lower cost of production than your competitors, giving you flexibility in pricing without compromising profitability.

➢ A unique blend of skills, experience, drive, networks, knowledge and passion in your team.

➢ Consistently outstanding after-sales customer service.

➢ Exclusively held distribution rights.

➢ A committed and loyal customer base.

➢ Unique marketing and public relation strategies.

➢ A core product that sits comfortably beyond industry norms in terms of its quality and features.

➢ Unique customer-friendly back-office processes or technical procedures.

➢ Flexible customer supply and access options that may include out-of-hours delivery, easily accessed online purchasing options, or even more direct customer online portal access to your services.

➢ The obvious advantages and valuable lead times that come from being the first in the marketplace to offer a new product.

> OR any other capabilities that may be hard to replicate.

Most of those base-level trade secrets are not formally registrable because, by their very nature, their economic benefit and value to the business comes from the fact that they are not in the public domain, or available to be shared.

Some Trade Secrets may be more formally protected by a possible combination of Copyright, Trademark or Patent, such as:

> New Product Prototypes

> Advantages such as locally sourced products or a demonstrated commitment to environmental sustainability.

> Intelligent and Creative use of commonly available software or digital economy capabilities that make your customer delivery and response times more nimble.

How Do I Protect My Trade Secrets?

Firstly, the act of simply calling it a *Trade Secret* is not enough. The Principal needs to identify and document what needs protection and to demonstrate they have taken specific action to protect those secrets. Tag any descriptive documents in the business that contain information about the Trade Secrets and ensure they are secured under 'Lock and Key'. This also applies to documents in your computer data base such as unique software. It should also include details of your customer base (i.e., they need to be in *restricted access only* files).

Anyone who has access to the Trade Secrets of a business should be asked, without exception, to sign a *non-disclosure deed*. This is an agreement between parties where undertakings are given not to disclose any confidential information that they are made aware of. The Deed may incorporate monetary penalties if a breach occurs and/or injunctive relief to cease actions.

Most specifically, all your employees should be required, without exception, to sign your binding *non-disclosure-deed*, accompanied by periodical team briefings to reinforce employee obligations and to make sure they understand the general 'dos and don'ts' pursuant to those deeds.

There may be circumstances where an external supplier is asked to sign a *non-disclosure deed*, for example where they may be involved in producing a stock input item for the business. Also have deeds signed by prospective purchasers and their advisers if you are considering selling the business.

While you will find plenty of non-disclosure-deed templates online, please know it is so important to get this aspect of your business right. I would urge you to engage an experienced intellectual property lawyer. It is not a complicated document to produce, so your legal fee should not be prohibitive, but the specific legal advice that comes with your final deed is an important part of the process.

Finally, be aware that in having your staff execute deeds of non-disclosure, you may potentially be skirting around the edges of the *Fair Work Act* and the employee's rights at law generally. This particularly applies to circumstances where you may have placed unreasonable conditions in the deed restricting the rights of the employee to seek alternative employment. For example, trying to prevent them from working for a competitor. In hearing dispute cases, judges may rule in favour of the employee if they have the slightest inkling that the deed has been unconscionably or unfairly drafted.

When an employee leaves the business, remind them that their obligations for confidentiality continue after they depart and what the implications are if they break those confidentialities. My advice is to be amicable in those discussions to ensure there is enough respect and goodwill for them to feel honour bound to abide by their signed deed.

Trademarks

You see them every time you drive for any distance, go walking through a major shopping mall, purchase popular brands in a supermarket or hear or see a jingle or advertisement. Highly recognisable signs, words, shapes, logos, phrases, certain food wrappers and songs. Many create an indelible subconscious message every time we see them, saying: *Buy Me!!* Many include product/company names, but those that do not, such as the Apple logo, are no less memorable.

Trademarks may be classified as one of the following:

> A word mark (e.g., McDonald's or KFC).
> A figurative or graphic image (the Apple Logo or the Mercedes Benz 3-pointed star).
> 3-dimensional wrappers and boxes (a Big Mac or KFC wrapper).
> Sound jingles (the famous 20th Century Fox Fanfare).
> Combined Marks (Coca-Cola bottle shapes, Word graphics, and the Coke Jingle).

Requirements for Registration of a Trademark

The examples above are famous international Trademarks, but it is possible to register Trademarks on a smaller local scale. The provisos for doing so are:

> The product and image must be distinctive.
> It must not deceive in terms of quality.
> It must be able to be described simply; and
> It must conform with the law.

How Do I Register a Trademark?

For *National Registration* in most countries, the process is simple and can be done online. The application can take anywhere from three months to a year. Once issued, the Trademark lasts indefinitely for as long as you continue to use and display it.

The current cost of applying for a trademark is $250 in Australia, $275 to $600 in the US, and a broadly similar range of fees if you are registering elsewhere. A concurrent *International Registration* may be achieved using the Madrid Protocol, coordinated by the World Intellectual Property Organisation (WIPO) if you trade internationally.

What's in a Business Name?

Well, as it turns out, quite a lot if the name is evocative and creative enough to make customers want to do business with you. When we see a sign up in lights, a well-known brand name on a package, or a jingle on the radio that includes the business name, it has the potential to evoke an instant triggering of at least one of the human senses.

The McDonald's brand is a graphic example. Backed by their global half-billion-dollar annual advertising spend, the first sight of their world-famous *golden arches* could activate up to three of those senses. The visual is obvious, but it's also linked to the sense triggers of hunger, taste and even aroma long before you get anywhere near the order counter.

An example of a smart business Tagline is the Australian-owned *Coffee Club* franchise group, with their trademarked lines: *I'll meet you at the Coffee Club* OR *Where will I Meet You?* The name and the Tagline send the simplest message that if you want to meet someone for a chat and a decent cup of coffee, the Coffee Club is the only place to go.

So, I hear you ask what's the big deal about finding a special name if it's just for my business and I don't have the *big bucks* to splash around on advertising or grand signage? The one question you cannot answer is: *How big will my business grow?* Or *How big could my business grow with the right name behind it?*

My advice is to give it your best shot up front if you are serious about creating a grand vision for your venture.

Some elements to consider in deciding on that great name are:

It should be memorable, not boring.

There should be a definite link with your main product offering in the business and the core message you want to convey to your customers.

Keep it simple. I could say don't let it be boring, but ... *ho hum* ... Australia's *Coffee Club*? ... and yet it has worked a charm for them.

Try brainstorming with family and friends for their thoughts, but whatever you do, not on social media platforms. Tell them up front that you are still gathering information from multiple sources and ensure they know up-front that you will be the sole decision maker.

Once you have started to lock down some good descriptive words you are comfortable with, open Word on your PC and do some multiple *spins of the thesaurus wheel* to see what alternative words it throws up. You never know; some eye-catching alternatives may literally jump out and grab you.

When you think you're getting close to what you want, check your preferred name at: www.namechk.com for **Website Domains and social media registrations.**

If the name is already taken, you MUST find an alternative one before proceeding. In the 21st century, this is the business name you will trade under, send and receive emails and invoices on, and promote on social media. If any one of them is already taken, go back to the drawing board.

Copyright

A Copyright protects any original work of authorship. To qualify, the work must be written on paper, saved in an electronic file, or preserved in some other tangible and reproduceable format.

Qualified works of authorship include fiction and non-fiction books, songs, movies, literature, paintings, sculptures, photos, diaries, published articles, music, movies, videos, etc., and all are protected under an international copyright protocol.

The copyright protocol protects the originator's moral rights to be considered the author/creator of their work. It also confers financial rights that allow the creator to earn income from their protected works, such as distribution rights, sales royalties, public performances, broadcasts and so on.

Small business examples typically include architectural drawings and plans, software, web content, technology source codes and some published articles about the business. The mere fact that these examples may be treated as copyright, does not mean the principal is in any way obliged to disclose that fact publicly. If the decision is not to disclose with a view to protecting their secrecy and their consequent value to the business, that's fine.

How do I register my Copyright and what is the cost?

Formal Copyright registration is not required by law, but it is recommended that you include your *name, signature and date* OR *your name and the © symbol* beside it on every page of your work (that's what I do).

The general rule for Copyright is that it must be your original work and not copied from another person.

How long does my copyright protection last?

The short answer is until the death of the author, plus a further 70 years.

Patents

A Patent is a document that certifies the rights of authorship and exclusive use of an invention. Patented rights may be granted for any device, substance, method, or process that is new, inventive, and useful. The granting of the patent provides the inventor with the right to commercially exploit the invention for the term of the patent and includes the additional option to license others to use it for an ongoing royalty fee.

There are two principal types of patents:

An Innovation Patent: is a fast and relatively low-cost way to protect an incremental advance on existing technology, rather than a new invention per say. This type of patent is only granted for a maximum of 8 years.

A Standard Patent: involves extensive investigation and expense and must satisfy an exhaustive application process.

For a *Standard Patent* to be granted:

It must involve an inventive, tangible, and useful step forward and must be commercially *useful* in its intended use.

It must involve a device, substance, process, computer hardware or software, or a business process or method. It is, therefore, not possible to patent artistic creations, mathematical models, theories, ideas or mental processes.

It must be new and not have been disclosed to the world prior to the patent application.

There must be a sufficiently clear and complete description of the invention provided with the application, together with all the relevant and critical information, supporting data, drawings and plans, and full technical analyses that backs up the claims made about the processes involved and the realisable outcomes.

There's a two-step process, the initial approval of preliminary patent pending status followed by the later issue of a full patent. The decision also needs to be made about the value of seeking an international patent if you decide to go ahead.

Once you are granted your patent pending status, you can maintain full confidentiality while you further develop the finer details and the commercial viability of your invention. When you receive your full standard patent, which could take several years, your invention, including details of how it works, goes into the public domain. This exposes you to the collateral risk of predators who may try to replicate or reverse engineer your grand idea. With a competent attorney, your patent will usually protect you from that possibility, but not before you've had to outlay huge legal bills in fighting such actions. There may also be additional challenges in becoming aware of such breeches, particularly if they are occurring elsewhere in the international marketplace.

By now, you will have grasped that the process involved in granting a *standard patent* is in fact a very big deal and it could cost you some tens of thousands of dollars in fees over the term of your Patent.

Suffice to say, the inventor needs to consider if the effort required to obtain the patent justifies the time and dollars required to get there. Explore the available protection, as well as the potential risk options with your lawyer if you choose to keep your invention as a Trade Secret solely for your business.

My advice is to find a well-regarded IP lawyer before you even start to consider going the patent course of action. On your first consultation, your lawyer will lay out all the facts, costs and risks you will need to be aware of.

IP Australia has put out a comprehensive document that takes you through the whole process.

Go to: ipaustralia.gov.au and download their summary: *A guide to applying for your patent.*

Chapter 15: Customers & Revenues

Each business SME sector is unique in how it addresses its customer-facing strategies. My intention in this chapter is to lay out the anatomy and building blocks of a best practice sales and customer service machine, presenting a combination of the tools, the skills and the actions you need to adopt and follow to be successful.

Where your business fits in the supply chain hierarchy?

The supply chain traces the network of organisations, manufacturing, production resources, transporting, finances and marketing required to transform initial raw material inputs into final products for end sale. *Supply Chain Management* is about achieving the timely and optimal coordination, management, component costings and control of each of those steps to produce a cost-efficient and saleable end product.

In its simplest iteration, my definition of the *Supply Chain Hierarchy* starts with the relational status of each business in terms of who they principally do business with directly (i.e., to whom do they sell):

- B to C: Business to Customer – i.e., selling to end customers (Retail)

- B to B: Business to Business – i.e., selling to another business (Raw Material Supplier to Manufacturer; Manufacturer to Wholesaler; Consultancy to Business, Agricultural Producer to Retailer; or Wholesaler to Retailer)

- B to I: Business to International Markets – i.e., exporting to overseas Wholesalers or Retailers, and Importing from Overseas Suppliers

- B to G: Business to Government – i.e., selling products or services to Federal/State/Local Government and their related statutory intermediaries.

- B to E: Business to Education – i.e., selling to Schools/Tertiary/University Sectors

B to P: Business to Philanthropy – i.e., selling to NGOs and not for profits

For example, if your business operates principally in the front-end retail segment (B to C), your marketing and sales thrust will be significantly influenced by how effective and successful you are at closing sales at your point of sale. Your external sales focus will be on getting the word out and promoting your offerings to your community of potential customers through the reach and strength of your general marketing, public relations and social media exposure.

If you want to be successful as a retailer, you still have to sell, but it's a unique type of face-to-face selling. Much of it, once you convince members of the public to walk through your door, is about how good and persuasive you and your team are at pitching and closing a sale, creating a flawless service experience and giving them a compelling reason to return the next time. The layout and décor of your business, your commitment to superior customer service, the quality and unique points of differentiation of your product(s) and even the seamless online selling alternatives you can offer for follow-up sales are all important to your odds of success.

For example, if yours is a café or similar style food and beverage outlet, you must be committed to producing a beautifully crafted cup of coffee and a superb plate of well-presented food every time without fail, delivered with exemplary customer service standards.

Put simply, the customer experience in all its dimensions should always be top of mind in any retail business.

If your business sits elsewhere in the supply chain hierarchy, or you work in an advisory or professional services sector, you will be devoting more time *on the road* to building networks, lead prospecting and continually priming your sales machine.

Understanding the Buyers' Viewpoint

The metrics of attracting customers and closing sales is about truly connecting with the other person, looking for common ground and responding to what motivates and drives them.

So it's important to figure out what approach your potential customer will pay the most attention to and how you can present your pitch in a way that satisfies their unique needs. The significant twist is to make sure there is nothing cynical about the way you do it and to ensure your intent is genuine. The early trust you gain by showing the other person you are willing to step into their metaphorical boots is paramount. *Richard Bandler and John Grinder*, the founders of Neuro Linguistic Programming (NLP), updated their UCLA research in the 1970s on three basic methods of perceiving the world around them: Visual, Auditory and Kinaesthetic.

Visuals: tend to understand something better when they can see it and retain information better when it is presented in a visual way.

Auditories: focus on the spoken word. You can spot them because they tend to be better listeners than most.

Kinesthetics: get their information from touch, emotions and gut instinct.

It may surprise you to know that Albert Einstein was a well-known kinaesthetic, who came up with his *Theory of Relativity* by imagining what it would feel like *to ride through the universe on the back of a beam of light!*

Selling to visuals, auditories, or kinesthetics requires you to form early subtle judgements about your potential buyer and which of the three styles they are dominant in. A generation of salespeople have learnt to spot those cues with prospective purchasers and to employ them to successfully close their sale.

Bert Decker's research went much deeper in exploring the concept of *the First Brain.* He explained in layman's terms how the brain operates in an *Autonomic Preconscious State.* Decker's hypothesis was about the importance of making an emotional connection with the other person to discover the triggers that will allow you to make a breakthrough. The motive is not about manipulation or smooth talk, but rather about establishing genuine contact, by connecting successfully with the *Left and Right Brain Hemispheres.* These neural areas process incoming information, compare it to recalled data, and decide if that information is credible and if they are prepared to trust the source. They then exercise their intellect and make their decisions.

SME Leadership: The 5 Critical Success Factors

Following Decker's method triggers a genuine connection that allows you to gain a position of believability and trust with the other person by:

- Using positive body language,
- Varying the pitch, tone and speed of your voice to keep it interesting,
- Looking for feedback to ensure two-way communication occurs,
- Making good use of positive eye contact, and
- Exuding a believable level of warmth and confidence.

Successful salespeople the world over use these cues well and I confess I followed Decker's techniques for many decades. Google: Decker Communications: 40 years of communications lessons and you will find his more recent research. It's well worth the read.

Conventional *Left/Right Brain Thinking* theory assumes that if you are mostly analytical and methodical in your thinking, you are *left brained*. If you are more creative, intuitive or artistic, you are *right brained*. This theory assumes that those two hemispheres of the brain function differently.

Ned Herrmann's Whole Brain® HBDI®

Herrmann's HBDI thinking model concurred with the left/right brain thinking preference approach but went deeper by also incorporating the known visceral, behavioural and emotional responses formed in the *limbic region of the brain* that sits beneath the Cerebral Cortex. From this analysis, two distinct limbic style preferential responses were added to Herrmann's modelling – the stability of *following tradition and order* versus that of *caring and responsiveness*.

In Herrmann's Brain Dominance Instrument HBDI® model (Figure 15.1), he observed four preferences that influence how people put their Whole Brain® to work.

SME Leadership: The 5 Critical Success Factors

A Quadrant: the Left-Brain Rational Analyser with a focal preference for logical thinking, analysing the facts and relying on the numbers first.

B Quadrant: the Limbic Safekeeping Organiser with a focal preference for planning, organising and detailed review.

C Quadrant: the Limbic Feeling Personaliser with a focal preference for the interpersonal, intuitive and expressive self.

D Quadrant: the Right Brain Experimental Visualiser with a focal preference for imaginative big-picture thinking and conceptualising.

OUR FOUR DIFFERENT SELVES

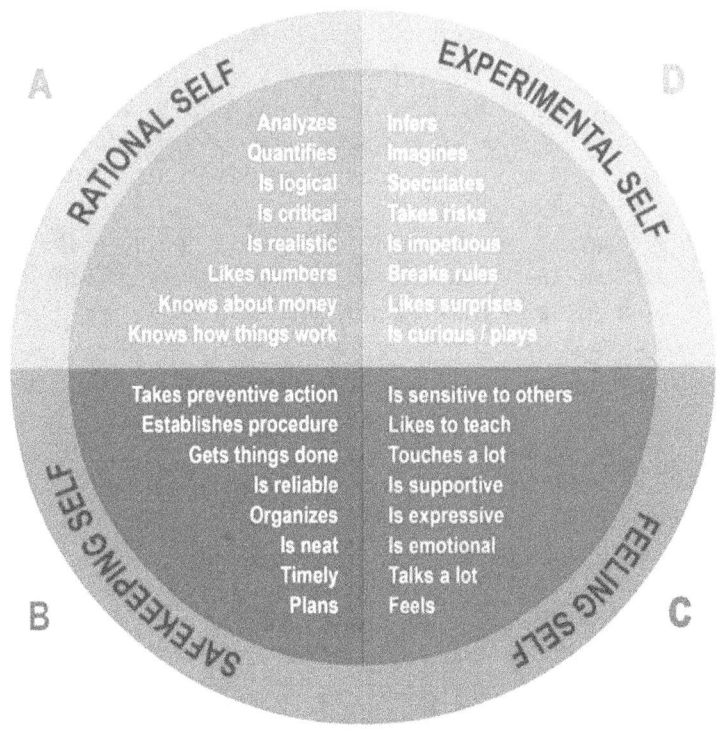

Figure 15.1

SME Leadership: The 5 Critical Success Factors

I'm sure you'll quickly register that the HBDI® also provides a possible key to the typical professions people tend to choose based on their Quadrant dominance and preferences. For example, Accountants tend to be strongly Quadrant A dominant, while teachers/educators tend to be Quadrant C dominant.

While the four thinking styles are our embedded instinctual first preferences, they don't necessarily reflect our competencies. However, dominance does lead to the development of our preferences, which in turn underpins our interests and how we like to put our brain to work. So, we generally become more competent at our preferences over time simply because that is what we like and therefore spend most of our time doing.

Herrmann's HBDI® outcomes may be *Triple Dominant*, *Double Dominant*, *Single Dominant*, or even *Whole Brained* with a reasonably even preference balance across all four Quadrants. In people with a double or triple dominance, their score tends to be a little higher in one of those quadrants.

I first heard about HBDI® on a business trip to the US in 1987, although it took a further visit several years later to check it out in operation. I liked what I saw and on my return to Australia, we initially introduced HBDI at St. George Bank to a small group of senior customer-facing bankers. We saw a healthy uplift in that group's loan and product sales despite the rough early 1990s recession Australia was experiencing. After that, we rolled out HBDI more widely.

Ned Herrmann's HBDI® is a powerful tool for a sales team to help them craft their sales narratives according to their early visual assumptions about a buyer's dominance preference. While you obviously don't have the luxury of being able to formally test your potential buyer, you can quickly learn to spot a person's thinking style dominance, their instinctual way of doing things, how they prefer to interact with others, and how they tend to act and communicate generally. For example, if you find yourself dealing with a person who appears to be strongest in Quadrant A: The Rational Analytical with a tendency to be principally *driven by the numbers*, you may consider going to the facts, figures and evidence of what you are selling earlier in your pitch than you would normally.

I've barely touched the surface of Whole Brain Thinking, the power of HBDI® and how it can be used to good effect in the selling space. Its value in employee development, improving team dynamics and productivity and in supporting strategy development is also immeasurable.

Ned Herrmann and Ann Herrmann-Nehdi's book *Unlocking the Power of Whole Brain Thinking in Organisations, Teams and Individuals* (McGraw Hill, 2015) is, in my view, a must-read for all SME principals. You will gain a solid insight into where your own preferential dominance lies and also how to use it in a sales setting. But I urge you to consider going a step further to explore the option of talking to the people at Herrmann about adopting their easily accessed digital platform technology more formally in your business. (Chapter 27).

CRM Software

CRM software is a cloud-based data management system that allows you and your team to track every touch point in your sales system from initial lead, to sale, order fulfilment, after sales follow up and then to ongoing customer service. CRM Vendor packages come on board with moderately priced fee-per-month options, depending on which access levels and the number of users you require.

The CRM's I've used most are ZOHO (zoho.com) and Salesforce (salesforce.com.au).

Google: Salesforce vs. Zoho: For what it's worth, I lean in favour of ZOHO for the more typical single entity SME, because of its lower cost starting subscription, and it's easier to grasp and understand customer management interface and communication protocols, whereas Salesforce may be the better choice for larger businesses with multiple entity operating divisions and more diverse software and access needs.

Of the CRM's I haven't used, Monday Sales CRM is also highly rated and at face value it looks pretty good to me. Plus I've heard some very good comments from several colleagues who have used it.

Importantly, do your own homework and then choose the CRM that best suits your particular needs.

Look for the following recording and tracking capabilities in your CRM:

- All introductory business networks and sales contacts are recordable and accessible from initial lead, to end sale and after-sales customer service.
- Shared view summaries of all contact communications, including sales visits, phone calls, emails, general communications, and any biodata that may give you a leg up in dealing with unique personalities in your lead pipeline.
- All data is accessible from multiple platforms, including laptop/ desktop, mobiles and tablets.
- The capacity to link up with targeted marketing and social media campaigns.
- The capacity to grade all active leads in your pipeline according to your preferred criteria, e.g., grading likelihood/prospect of a sale proceed.

Tracking sales results using CRM pipeline analytics

Well-constructed team pipeline analytics downloaded from your CRM in spreadsheet format should ideally become the main agenda item for your sales team meetings. This analysis should record the performance outcomes of *each salesperson* in your team across a minimum of five key measures:

- Total new leads generated for the period and current carry-over leads, all graded in terms of their assumed likelihood to proceed to ultimate sale.
- Total sales closed.
- The conversion ratio (i.e., sales to total leads as a percentage).
- Average time in days from initial lead to end sale.
- Sales performance of the team was graded from most successful to least successful.

These measures provide a basis for shared learning and mentoring across the sales team, encouraging debate of known lead and business generation strategies that work and eliminating or modifying those that do not.

This analytic approach provides a precise measure of the overall health of your sales machine. It engenders a competitive environment in which all team members are accountable for and measured by a consistent set of criteria. It also creates a framework for team members to learn from each other and to consciously lift both their individual and collective performance.

Solid evidence is now emerging that high performance sales teams use pipeline turnover metrics from *Leads Generated* all the way through to *Closed Sales* as the principal measure of sales performance and that they tend to produce a higher and more consistent level of end sales compared to teams who do not adopt CRM's.

What then is the important correlation? Pipeline analytics takes the pressure off the traditional hindsight financial measure of budgeted sales results with a more reliable earlier stage focus on being able to decide *what volume of quality leads do I need to achieve the sales results I want*. This new performance measure is increasingly finding that *future results depend proportionately on the quality and quantity of base leads in your CRM*.

Quality Lead Networking

"Cold calling is the punishment you get for not having a quality network."

Michael Robertson, (Westpac Bank, 2020).

Many decades ago, I sustained a torn retina in one of my eyes that required urgent surgery. My optometrist referred me to one of Brisbane's top ophthalmic surgeons. When I visited my optometrist several months after the surgery to pick up a fresh set of specs, I found my surgeon in the waiting room. He admitted with a sort of half grin that he was there doing some business development, something I had naively presumed would be below the average medical specialist's dignity to consider! And yes, more fool me! The surgeon was quite forthcoming in admitting that he blocked out several days of his diary each month to visit optometrists and GPs around the city with the aim of making sure they kept him front of mind for their ophthalmic surgical referrals!

My GP later confirmed it was common practice for specialist surgeons and physicians to maintain regular contact with them for the same *trolling for business* reasons. I got the same feedback from an old friend, one of Sydney's preeminent reconstructive surgeons, who called those periodical GP visits *a fundamental business development 101* imperative for all successful medical specialists.

And this surely is what the principle of quality lead targeting is all about. Quite simply, if you value your time, it's ridiculous to be wasting it by making cold calls to businesses that are least likely to have a need for what you are selling! The logical message is to map out the supply chain of the industry you are principally selling and supplying to and concentrate your lead targeting to potential clients within the same or similar inter-related industries.

Another example is building industry tradespersons (plumbers, electricians, carpenters, plasterers, bricklayers, etc.). If you are in one of those SME categories, your targeting should surely be home builders, kitchen, bathroom, cupboard manufacturers and other similar suppliers who feed into your speciality in your preferred geographic region. Visit a large lighting supplier for example and you will usually see several racks of electrician's business cards on the counter. Ditto for plumbers' business cards in a plumbing supply business.

It would make sense for a tradesperson, hanging up his/her shingle for the first time to try to secure one or more solid building/construction industry-related sub-contract deals to supplement their income in the early stages of being self-employed and building a client base. A favourite tender noticeboard for subcontracting opportunities in the Australian building/construction industry is www.estimateone.com (and similar international websites). It's there principally for builders, suppliers, subcontractors and tradesmen. 1,000 builders in Australia post contract and subcontract jobs to this site regularly.

What other options are there to build on your *quality lead targeting*? One is to go to technology vendors who specialise in providing targeted business data on a fee-per-list basis.

Corelist is a popular international vendor of lead data information. Go to:

- Australia: www.corelist.com.au;
- New Zealand: www.corelist.co.nz;
- US: www.corelist.com;
- UK: www.corelist.co.uk; or
- Canada: www.corelist.ca.

Their data bases are massive, and their downloadable lists come in easy to access Excel spreadsheets. For example, you can access Corelist's 1.5 million Australian or 9.5 million US SMEs – their databases provide further analyses by industry sector.

As I write this chapter, I've just chosen one Australian industry example at random, Cafés. The cost of the list is $75 at 2023 prices. A quick scan of Corelist tells me their data base has 9,000 cafes on it and 80% of those cafés are Eastern Seaboard based. Most are in, or close to, the greater metropolitan areas of Brisbane, Sydney and Melbourne and some of the larger country regional centres. Over 99% of their records include a current address and contact phone number and many include email addresses also. So, if you have a business in any of those city areas that supplies goods, services or systems to the Café sector, you can download a set of possible warm leads that are just a phone call or a visit away.

Another way to source *lead targets* is by going direct to the *Yellow Pages Online*. Off your supply chain analyses, select the industry(s) most likely to have an interest in what you are selling.

Put your thinking cap on and consider what other possible *quality lead-targeting* opportunities you can find.

NB: If you are going to conduct a dedicated email marketing and/or an advanced Social Media campaign, make sure you check out any local Anti-Spam Laws, designed to prevent abuse of email and online marketing.

Digital Lead Sourcing

The global uptake of Social Media has been staggering over the past decade. Here are the pertinent numbers (late 2025):

- There were 5.24 billion regular Social Media users worldwide, representing 62% of the global population.
- Google was the most prominent search engine, processing around 8.5 billion global searches every day and 2 Trillion annually.
- Facebook topped the Social Media Membership Platforms with 3.07 billion users, followed by YouTube 2.5 billion, Instagram 2.7 billion and LinkedIn 1 billion. As I write, Instagram continues to be the fastest growing of these.
- Re social media's *influencer* power 75% of marketers see social media as being an effective means of selling product.
- 71% have had a positive experience with a brand on social media and are likely to continue using that channel.
- 98.5% of social media users access their page via a mobile device.

For more statistical information, go to:

www.oberlo.com/blog/social-media-marketing-statistics

A well-designed social media marketing campaign will offer you an excellent means of generating large lead volumes with the potential for high conversion rates. To get the best outcomes from your social media marketing, you'll need a professionally constructed web site with the capability to provide regular updated product information and to accommodate professionally constructed live voice feed content.

Google's dynamic advertising options have been consistently ahead of the game, incorporating advanced AI (Artificial Intelligence) and the potential to link up with other social media platforms, including Facebook, Instagram, YouTube and LinkedIn. Facebook and Instagram have also recently taken significant steps to further enhance their direct digital marketing AI capabilities.

The challenge for businesses is in keeping up with the rapid evolution of Social Media marketing choices and how to get the best from them. There is a lot to it, and you will undoubtedly need professional advice to make it all happen, but I can assure you the potential rewards are significant.

Planning for Successful Sales Calls

"If you fail to plan, then you are planning to fail."

Benjamin Franklin

I have introduced you to some useful tips that will allow you to gain the best possible insight about the psychology of your potential buyer and how to sell to them. My message is that you need to arm yourself and anyone with a selling role in your business with all the tools and skills you can possibly harness if you are serious about growing your business.

The collateral benefit is that when you adopt the best mix of these tools every time you engage with potential customers, they will soon become spontaneous second-nature traits.

When planning for your sales appointments:

➢ Do your homework thoroughly before each appointment. Gain whatever intelligence you can about the person you are about to visit, the company/business they work for and what it does. Google the business, check it out on Social Media, scan their business web page, and look at recent customer ratings reviews.

➢ Run a LinkedIn scan on the name of the person you will be meeting and if they are listed, jot down whatever information you can garner from that check, including career, background, education and any possible common ground you can find to help you break the ice when you first meet in person.

➢ If your planned sales call is a subsequent follow-up visit, check your CRM before the call to extract a clear picture of what happened on previous visits. Check the notes for insights, clues and cues that may help you. Please know there is nothing remotely professional about not recalling what was discussed on the last visit. Remember, the old maxim 'forearmed is forewarned'.

> Consciously work hard at enhancing your conversational capabilities, but also your capacity to listen well and respond to what the other person is saying.

In her charming book, *The Art of Conversation* (John Wiley, 2018), Judy Apps examines how good conversation is a subtle art. When you converse with someone, you are doing many things simultaneously. Hopefully, you are listening to and hearing what the other person has to say; you are reading the nuances of their voice tone and looking for any clues in their body language. At the same time, you are in a state of readiness to genuinely respond easily and naturally.

Judy Apps' *dance for two metaphor* for good communication is what she calls the *dance of connection* – when two dancers are in sync, they spontaneously comprehend and react to each other's alternative moves and float effortless across the dance floor as though they are one. Good, open two-way conversation is much the same. It's about courteously taking turns and listening, as well as responding with integrity. It is a two-way dialogue, not a monotone, where you share the talking, listen carefully, acknowledging and sharing feedback.

Consciously work towards building a significant repertoire of personal and industry specific stories and short narratives. Make good use of smart metaphors to stress your important points and dig deep for any life examples that can animate your presentations. Back up the stories and narratives you use with solid facts and figures to support your pitch and include testimonials if you have them.

Update your CRM via your mobile phone or iPad link on the details of each sales meeting *while they are still fresh in your mind*. Do the same after any follow-up phone confabs. Focus on the narratives and angles that worked and those that did not and note down any bio or other triggers that may help you on your next, or subsequent visits.

Finally, get into the good habit of running a quick mental *scorecard on how you did after each sale call*. Again, do it before you move on to your next appointment. This is not about flogging yourself or lamenting your shortcomings but rather about underwriting your incremental learning experiences and finetuning your approach to ensure you are the best you can possibly be. So long as you are prepared to be totally honest with yourself, there is only ever one substantial question you need to ask each time: *How could I have done better?*

Creating the Selling Narratives

These are the important and consistent statements and language you use when you promote your business and sell into your marketplace. They include *The Elevator Speech, The Sales Pitch and Accompanying Narratives*, and *the Brand and Positioning Statements*. The first two are the verbal narratives, the ones you and your team use in your face-to-face communications in the marketplace. The third one, the Brand and Positioning Statement, is a well-crafted one to two-page written story about your business and what it does that you will use in your Marketing, PR and Social Media communications.

The Elevator Speech

As the name implies, it's the quick and lucid statement you will deliver in about the time it takes to move up or down one to two floors on an elevator. It should be no longer than 90 seconds and preferably not more than two to three sentences.

The Elevator Speech tells *who you are, what you offer, what problem you solve* (i.e., your value proposition) and *what you and your team bring to the table*. It should be interesting and compelling. The goal is to make a real connection and to leave your target wanting to know more.

This is the narrative you will fall back on at business functions, industry get-togethers, more formal business conferences, social events in your local community and as the quick first-up introduction you draw on in your general networking. After you have delivered your pitch, it's important to know when to pull it up (i.e., to *shut up!*) and allow your listener to respond. Once done, swap business cards 100 % of the time. If the other person hasn't got one with them, get them to jot down their name and contact details on the back of one of your business cards or simply do a screen shot. Aim to update your *CRM* every time while the contact details and what was discussed is still fresh in your mind.

The value proposition part of your elevator speech is where you can demonstrate in a few short and snappy phrases what your true point of difference is to your competitors' offerings. If it's more about your *legendary customer service* capabilities than the product itself, convince the other person how good that service really is, including a brief comment about why your customers like dealing with you so much.

Your customer-facing personnel should be well-drilled in your Elevator Speech. Remember, all your staff are potential brand ambassadors for your business. Spend plenty of time crafting it and as much time, or more again, in rehearsing it before you start using it.

The Sales Pitch and Supporting Narratives

This is about what happens during a live sales call. It may well begin with your standard elevator speech, but what happens after that must be driven by a two-way dialogue. There should always be several narrative variations you can draw on depending on what happens and what questions you are asked.

The priority is to establish a genuine connection and at least some degree of credibility with the other person before earning the legitimate right to move on. I have already given you some cues about this early part of your dialogue. What should then follow is a lot more information than is provided in the traditional elevator speech. This information should flow in bite-sized segments to allow for a genuine two-way discussion. You may or may not have to draw on all your points, but you do need to be well-prepared and confident about what you choose to say and what you decide to hold back on.

Here is an example of how a sales pitch may roll out in six stages. It assumes, and your potential buyer has a reasonable right to expect, that you are an expert on your products and offerings. If you slip up on any significant facts or data, expect your credibility to take a beating. Always be confident, but never arrogant or presumptive. Always keep an eye out for your buyer's cues, interest levels and body language.

1. The basic two-sided introductions and preamble are a good place to start. If you've done your homework well and are

confident in normal day-to-day *biz talk socialising*, it's often better if you don't jump straight to the sales pitch. This intro stage is where you *freelance* a little, identify common ground, talk about something newsy or topical going on in the world around you both.

2. Once you have broken some of that ice, you may decide to kick off with your standard elevator speech, or a separately crafted pitch, but try to keep the business part of your opener to a couple of minutes.

3. Allow time for the other person to tell you a little about what they do and what their specific product needs are.

4. Expand further on what your unique selling point is (additional detail in this part of the pitch is important):

   ➤ What is our core proposition? What is the glue that makes it stick?

   ➤ Why are we different to our competitors?

   ➤ How are we different?

   ➤ What makes our solution a better choice?

   ➤ Why do our clients like us or why do they prefer us?

   ➤ What seamless access options can we provide for future transactions (e.g., online, telephone or portal access for the customer)?

   ➤ How good is our after sales service?

   ➤ Back these statements or answers up with some key facts and figures, i.e., the hard evidence.

5. Assess reactions to what you said and answer questions.

6. If you reach the view that there is not a potential sale on the day, don't give up and make sure you leave the door open for a future meeting. You may also reach the conclusion there is no value in returning!

If your sales target is on a tight time frame and seriously wants you to get on with it, oblige with an appropriate quicker pitch.

Always keep your eye out for those important cues. Spend plenty of time planning for and rehearsing different outcomes and reactions, deciding on your best response/reaction to those scenarios and considering possible questions and answers.

The Brand and Positioning Narrative

This is a shortened well-crafted version of the key components of your business plan and your brand promises – one to two pages that provides the succinct language and touch points contained in your Elevator Speech and Sales Narratives. It's the one you will use in populating the statements, actions and brand promises you will allude to in your Marketing, Public Relations and Social Media programs and in other written communication about what you do.

Remuneration Options for Your Sales Team

One of the easiest Breakeven decisions you should have to make in your business, particularly in the early stages, is in your justification for sales team appointments. Never forget that knowing your Gross Margin is the crucial starting point. To that, you can graft on the base cost of your proposed salesperson(s), say an agreed retainer plus direct oncosts, including the provision of motor vehicle, laptop, mobile, tablet and other expenses where applicable.

From there, you can work out what their breakeven level of sales will need to be. That is the level of sales at which they cover their cost of being on the team and give the business a healthy profit return on top of that. (See Chapter 7 for the Breakeven formula). If they are hired on a retainer plus commission basis, your Gross Margin will give you an indication of what sort of commission you can afford to pay. If their retainer is provided on a full-cost recovery basis, you will be able to potentially offer a higher commission rate.

I know several SME principals who quite happily pay their best salespeople significant commission rates. They do so simply because they run their sales teams as individual profit centres and therefore know precisely what the incremental benefit of each salesperson brings to the core profitability of the business.

The number crunching is perhaps the easiest part of this equation. Seek external professional advice in putting your remuneration scheme together to ascertain what market expectations will be for the position. Recruit the best possible salespeople and be confident they have the capacity to achieve their budgeted sales hurdles, BEFORE you hire them.

Managing the Salesperson's Mindset

Refining and getting your sales narratives right, accessing a good CRM, adopting *smart lead targeting* to track and manage your pipeline, knowing your sales conversion ratios, holding regular sales meetings and following the other cues are essential.

You will also need to effectively manage what I call *sales stage fright*. A consummate salesperson copes well with the ups and downs of what they do. They know from experience how to handle the good times and high points when business is literally flowing effortlessly through the front door, most especially in not letting those high points go to their heads. They also know intuitively not to let the low points, particularly the rejections, convince them that they *cannot do this job anymore.* In my experience, these are the moments where the skilled salesperson manages their emotions well, and the novice tends to falter.

In an SME, *the principal must surely be the driver of the sales machine*. If you have no real sales experience, then you will need to get up to speed rapidly! Depending on what stage your business is at, your early staff hires should be focussed on boosting your capacity to achieve sales and generate revenues.

Unless you are an accredited *genii* at sales and sales training, you may need advice on skilling and motivating your sales team. If that's your situation, consider bringing on board external training contract support. Do your homework, seek references and testimonials, and speak directly with each of those referral sources to know that you are getting what you need. Also, lock in agreed performance hurdles, outcomes and timelines.

Definition of an Accomplished Salesperson

An old pal of mine, Michael Robertson was for many years well known across the length and breadth of the Brisbane business community as *Robbo*. Michael was Queensland State Manager of Trade and Invoice Finance for Westpac Banking Corporation.

I first met Michael in 2008 when I accompanied a client to a Westpac meeting to discuss the annual banking review of his business. The revue discussion went well. Robbo was the lead banker that day and he impressed me. We found a lot of common ground over the years that followed and shared some significant relationships in the Brisbane business community, several of which I referred to Westpac simply because Robbo was there, and I knew he would make sure the Bank looked after them.

Bottom line, Michael Robertson was the best banking relationship manager I ever knew. Yes, as a banker he ticked all the usual competency boxes, he consistently left no stone unturned and was an outstanding networker and business builder. But he was also meticulous about *the little things*. He managed his time impeccably; he never broke promises, and he never failed to return phone calls.

He was a professional in all his business dealings but was also a regular *pain in the 'a'* wherever it really counted. He even changed his voice mail greeting message every morning without fail, a humorous talking point in the Brisbane business community for many years, but also a trait that garnered a great deal of respect.

Michael was a proud first class ambassador for his bank and a well-respected community citizen. For example, he was associated with Ronald McDonald House since 2000, when he was running the Westpac business unit that looked after most of McDonald's Queensland franchisees. Although he moved onto his State Trade Finance leadership role over a decade ago, he continued to be a proud Ronald McDonald House Board Member and a passionate fundraiser and advocate. The bonus for Westpac was that Michael was incredibly well-connected and respected for all of those qualities.

Jim Wills, one of the legendary founding fathers of St. George Building Society before it became a bank, put the view to me in the late 1980s that *a good banker should be famous in his or her own community for all the right reasons*. Michael Robertson wore that tag very well for Westpac, which now owns the St. George Bank business brand.

As an aside, Michael had several favourite quotes that went to the very heart of his character and what made him tick:

> *"Your true character is most measured by how you treat those who can do nothing for you."*

Mother Teresa.

> *"How wonderful it is that nobody need wait a single moment before starting to improve the world."*

Anne Frank.

> *"You make a living by what you get: you make a life by what you give."*

Sir Winston Churchill.

The quote that follows was *Michael Robertson's* own and speaks volumes about how he lived his life!

> *"Do what you say you are going to do, and do not be someone who you are not."*

Michael Roberston.

John's Note: I prefaced the Banking chapter with Michael's sudden passing in November 2024. He is greatly missed and I pay tribute to and salute his humanity, kindness, his irrepressible commitment to initiating and following through on every level, his sense of honour and humility, and his extraordinary personality. I'm honoured to have known him.

Chapter 16: Collaborative Networking

"What a person thinks on his own, without being stimulated by the thoughts and experiences of other people, is even in the best case rather paltry and monotonous."

Albert Einstein on Networking

My father was a classic raconteur and storyteller, who was as comfortable addressing an audience of many hundreds, as he was telling one of his traditional after dinner family gags. Dad had his own weekly radio program in Sydney for many years. He was a master of the spoken word and his sense of timing was always spot on.

Towards the end of my school years, Dad took me aside and told me about his four rules for being successful in life:

1. *Be careful where you put your pen in life and never place your moniker on anything unless you fully understand what you are committing to.*

2. *Always be respectful of and with the opposite sex.*

3. *Be decent, honourable and follow the 'Do unto Others' Golden Rule.*

4. *Never forget the importance of building valuable relationships throughout your working life, both socially and in business. Value those relationships and know that the person you meet today with only pennies to his name could end up being a 'squillionaire' (one of Dad's favourite words!) in the future.*

He then handed over a folded piece of paper with the exact same set of rules written in his neat artist's scribe. I never got around to asking him, but I suspect his father may have given him the same advice.

SME Leadership: The 5 Critical Success Factors

For most of his working life, Dad was an executive with Consolidated Press, the Packer family media empire. Starting out as a commercial artist, he became the youngest Advertising Manager of the Australian Women's Weekly. He could sell advertising copy at the drop of a hat and was a master networker.

Dad also had a role to play in the early establishment of the famous Women's Weekly Kitchen and frequently arrived home from work on Friday evenings with samples of some of the delectable dishes cooked in their Test Kitchens during the week.

What is Networking?

Socially, networking is about meeting people, joining conversations, building mutual relationships, sharing enthusiasm and having some fun along the way.

At a business level, networking is an opportunity to offer your expertise, share your knowledge, learn what others are doing, join the debate on important local issues and keep your finger on the pulse of your marketplace. By doing those things well, you also create an opportunity to write more business and generate more income.

During a phone confab with Scott Elkington, a seasoned networker (in fact one of the best I have ever known!) and my chief collaborator in successfully rolling out Bendigo Bank's Queensland brand and presence, we agreed that if you are naturally outgoing and genuinely enjoy mixing with people in your social life, then you are already halfway along the road to becoming a successful business networker. At its roots, networking is a skill anyone can learn, provided they get the building blocks right.

When we were kicking off Bendigo Bank's Queensland Community Banking program, Scott's first building block credo was always about digging deep until you discovered the single most influential person in each community, i.e., that *go to* person who could just make things happen because of their sheer presence and the high level of trust the community placed in them. This is good advice, and from experience, I can assure you this strategy works.

How to Build a Generic Networking Plan

Regardless of whether your business services an entire state, a capital city, a regional city or town, or even a suburb or large village, the core mechanics of creating your networking plan should be broadly similar. At Bendigo Bank in Queensland, our frontline teams created networking plans across each of those geographic confines and treated each as the unique communities they were.

The starting point comes down to gaining an understanding of the *major network influencers* who drive what happens in their communities. The key *go to* people. Those connective *network influencers* are most typically unearthed from the following sources:

> The *business connections that emerge from your family and friends*, given that one in five households in Australia have an interest in an SME,
>
> Local/Municipal Government *Mayor and Councillors,*
>
> Local/Municipal Government *Economic Development Offices,*
>
> *Resident local Politicians:* State and Federal Government,
>
> Other local *statutory & non-statutory representative organisations*
>
> *Chambers of Commerce, Rotary* and other community service clubs
>
> Locally *resident media connections*
>
> *Universities/schools/colleges*
>
> *Doctors/lawyers/* and other professionals
>
> *Prominent local SMEs*
>
> The *larger locally resident businesses*

Create your plan with initial desk top research and build a *mud map* of *who's who* in your captive community. To be successful, you don't have to necessarily meet every contact or organisation on my source list upfront, but it is important to gain a good grasp of what makes the community tick and, importantly, who specifically are the important influencers who can and will make things happen.

I have learnt from experience to short cut this process in the early stages by getting to specific people and organisations first up. Business connections from Family and Friends, Chambers of Commerce and Community Service Clubs (e.g., Rotary) are often the most valuable initial door openers in any networking plan are the ones you MUST CONTACT if you are serious about becoming well known and building a solid base of local business relationships.

Following on from those sources, early contact with your resident Local Government Representative and State and Federal Politicians who reside in your community should follow.

Make sure you track all your network relationships at every touch point with quality CRM (*Customer Relationship Management Software*).

A Blueprint for Networking at Business Meetings

After I retired from Bendigo Bank, I was non-executive Chairman of the *Cooper Property Group,* a large and successful SME group of companies in the property development game. I became close friends with Cooper Group's patriarch, Jeff Cooper, soon after arriving in Queensland in 2000. Jeff was by instinct a shy and self-effacing man, yet he was rightfully proud of what he had built. He was extraordinarily focussed and driven, and despite his natural reserve, he was an excellent networker.

Ipswich City, about 40 kilometres west of Brisbane, was Jeff's hometown. As a community, it's a very sociable place and you could take your pick of the after-five networking events going on literally every week and month of the year. I went to several of them with Jeff and his wife Ros, and their ritual was always the same. Jeff would start to circle the room in one direction and Ros the other. Even when there were 200 or more people, they didn't stop until they had spoken to every person. When they had completed their rounds, they would then quietly leave, satisfied their mission was complete.

Without fail, the morning after those evenings, Cooper's CEO, Graeme Harding, would receive a bundle of notes from Jeff about the *great opportunities* he had unearthed the night before! I speak elsewhere in the book about Graeme's unique yin and yang collaborations with both Jeff and later with his son Andrew, who succeeded Jeff as the family principal of Coopers.

There are surely several instructive lessons here about good networking – BE SINCERE, BE OBSESSIVE AND NEVER GIVE UP! The best networkers I have ever known have all those traits in droves!

What You Should Carry in Your Networking *Kit Bag*

I agree unquestionably with the advice from my friend Greg Meek, that follows at the end of this chapter about the importance of being sincere, genuine and spontaneous in all your networking endeavours and of not succumbing to the bad habit of being seen to be networking on rote and/or *by the numbers*! So, the list that follows is more about *being prepared and ready* when you open your doors to venture out and grow your business:

Always have a good supply of business cards with you.

Always focus on cementing your personal connection with the other person well BEFORE you get to your pitch and start selling.

Constantly refresh/update your elevator speech and sales pitches. If you are selling something, these short sharp, consistent statements about what you do are a very important initial door opener.

Constantly add to your repertoire of *stories* and use relevant *metaphors*.

Dig deep for any real life examples that have the potential to animate, underwrite and strengthen your presentations.

Back up your stories with solid facts and figures to support your pitch.

Consciously enhance your conversational capabilities and be sincere in all your communications. Create and build trust with the other person. Be attentive, empathic and really listen, process and respond appropriately to what the other person is saying.

If you struggle with everyday socialising, practice upskilling your social interactions with friends and family until you are comfortable.

Read *Judy App's* delightful *Art of Conversation.* Make sure you grasp her *dance for two metaphor* for good communication. This book is a gem!

Stay in touch, be relentless on all follow-up communications.

Having faith and staying on the networking journey will underwrite your good results over time.

To be successful in your networking and business building, you will need access to a good CRM (I like *Salesforce* and *ZOHO*). Update meeting details every day and after every meeting you go to while they are still fresh in your mind.

Author's Collaborative Networking Journey in Queensland

In early 2000, Bendigo Bank acquired First Australian Building Society which was most substantially represented in the Queensland regional cities of Ipswich and Cairns. In short, our brief was to convert the Building Society into a full banking business, and then to take our core offerings state-wide. I tell more in the next chapter about how we successfully achieved those objectives and ultimately became good citizens of all our local communities across our new State.

What follows here is just a few examples of the valuable networks and relationships that helped us join the dots in achieving our objectives:

I was introduced early to Queensland Premier Peter Beattie and John Strano, Peter's senior State Development Director when we were finalising our acquisition of the Building Society. Those two gents went out of their way to make several valuable connections and introductions for us over the years that followed.

SME Leadership: The 5 Critical Success Factors

When I joined *Tattersalls Club Brisbane*, I met Club Chairman, *John Maclean*, and CEO *Greg Meek*, both well-known prominent Queenslanders and highly successful networkers whose relationship diaries still read like a *Who's Who* of Queensland all these years later. At the end of this chapter, I have asked Greg to present his reflections on good networking.

I also struck up a close friendship with *Richard Owen*, who was then the Business Editor at *The Courier Mail*, Queensland's major News Limited owned daily newspaper. Over time we proved ourselves to be good corporate and community citizens of Queensland. The Courier Mail and media at large were generous in the editorials they wrote and televised about the Bank.

I first met *Rachel Nolan* in 2001, around the time she was elected to the Queensland State seat of Ipswich. She subsequently moved up the line to become State Finance Minister. In that role, she drove the multi-billion-dollar privatisations of Queensland's State Rail and various Queensland Port Corporations. Rachel is now a prominent company director and was a great sounding board for me during the writing of this book, given her unique small business sojourn after leaving politics.

State of Origin: For many years, I personally purchased 10 excellent centre line seats to one of the annual Rugby League *State Of Origin* home games at Brisbane's Suncorp Stadium. My son Sam was always there because he loved *State of Origin* with a passion. The remaining eight were all well-connected Queenslanders, all of whom are mentioned at some stage in this book. We invariably had a small wager on the outcome. Sam and I were rudely branded as the *NSW Cockroaches* (which of course we were!) by this group of proud Queenslanders, but it was always in good fun. I make mention of our State of Origin games here for a good reason – taking people to a sporting event where you are going to be together for several hours offers an outstanding networking opportunity in a relaxed and convivial atmosphere.

SME Leadership: The 5 Critical Success Factors

Greg Meek on Networking:

I have been fortunate on my life/business journey to have a diverse range of experience. Commencing my career as a Chartered Accountant with PWC (Price Waterhouse Coopers), I moved on to several senior roles in the banking/funds management industry, ultimately taking on accountability for managing the successful large Industry Superannuation Fund, Sun Super. My career also included terms as CEO of the Brisbane Turf Club, Tattersall's Club, and as Deputy CEO and Queensland Executive Director of CEDA (Committee for Economic Development of Australia).

All these roles presented me with a rich tapestry of relationship building opportunities and the chance to progressively grow my capabilities as a networker. One of my early learnings was that every business professional, no matter how advanced their technical skills, must develop networks if they seriously want to be successful. These days I coach business teams about networking and there are a multitude of tips I provide in those training sessions. I will just give two here:

The Importance of the Personal Touch: Never underestimate the immense power of building personal relationships and learning to communicate in a personal way. This is particularly relevant in the era of social media and electronic communications. Generic communications, often sent to multiple recipients, are impersonal, disengaging and often counter-productive. Just think about how much more powerful a personalised message might be. Remember you are aiming for a result, not to tick a KPI box on a marketing action plan! I recently received a handwritten note from a senior politician thanking me for attending a dinner and commenting on my contribution in terms of the discussion. Can you imagine the effect this had on me? The sheer fact that it was handwritten on parliamentary letterhead in an age of electronic communications, was impactful. That the writer took the time to send and personalise this letter speaks volumes.

Importance of being Genuine: I have attended numerous sessions on networking over the years. Many suggest a rote-style doing it by the numbers approach to relationship building which too often fails to pay respect to the benefits that can accrue from that first connection with the other person. In my experience the best and most rewarding business relationships start very simply with someone showing a real unscripted interest in the other person. This is conducive to building an important and healthy two-way relationship and if you think about it, this applies to both social and business networking.

It was in the CEDA role that I approached John Goddard from Bendigo Bank to sponsor the initial State of the State ....an address by the Premier of the day to be modelled on the US State of the Union.

The Sponsor: John was agreeable to consider the concept and immediately saw the value for Bendigo Bank in linking with the success of the State. After discussing the State of the State over a pleasant lunch, it didn't take John long to see the potential and to agree that Bendigo Bank would be the first sponsor.

The CEDA National Board: Being a State driven event and CEDA being a national think tank, I needed to convince our National Board to endorse the concept. This involved some solid networking with my federal colleagues.

The Premier: I needed to land the Premier and it helped that John already knew him well. I also had a contact in the bunker – the Premier's diary secretary who I'd known during my Suncorp days. She advised me the secret was to pencil it into his diary and when he saw it there, to be ready to deliver my spiel. All I had to do was wait for him to say: 'What is this about?'

Peter Beattie duly did just that. I delivered my pitch along with all the protocol paperwork. I confirmed it would be underwritten by Bendigo Bank, and that it was virtually ready to roll. The rest was history. The State of the State is now the well patronised flagship event on the CEDA annual calendar in Queensland and other States, with attendance at each now invariably well over 1000.

I guess you could sum up the commercial aspects of CEDA's success in matching the vision of government with the business community, a supportive sponsor, and significant branding and profile value to the corporate sector. The networking opportunities alone generated by the 1000 plus corporate audience at each year's State of the State is testament to CEDA's ongoing success.

Chapter 17: Community Engagement

'We make a living by what we get,
We make a life by what we give.'

Sir Winston Churchill.

In their November 2020 HBR editorial, Gabriel Karageorgio and Dominic Selwood wrote about the ancient Greek ideal of *Philotimy*. By origin, *philos* means *friend or love* and *timi* means *honour*. *Philotimy* embraces the principles of decency, dignity, honesty, and altruism and what it means to live your life with integrity. In the business context, they described *Corporate Philotimy* as:

The immutable DNA that determines how a business operates at the cellular level. It is the principle that guides a company's sustainability behaviour and its attitude towards Corporate Social Responsibility, which seeks to align sound Environmental, Social, and Governance metrics (ESG) with Economic sustainability.

Karageorgio and Selwood concluded that society increasingly expects the business community to be sustainable and to build a culture based on looking after their customers, employees and the communities they do business in. These characteristics require an ingrained sense of individual and organisational responsibility and create a positive work culture that translates into higher productivity.

Those who embrace Philotimy do not promise more than they can deliver and they always deliver more than they promise.

PWC's (Price Waterhouse Coopers) 2020 *Global Annual Review*, identified adoption of Corporate Social Responsibility (CSR) metrics as *the growth opportunity of the century*. Companies willing to invest wisely beyond the bottom line are now consistently outperforming their market competitors.

PWC identified four drivers of this change in mindset:

1. *Companies with a culture rooted in empathy, treat their employees well and for that reason they attract and retain the best human capital.*
2. *They are respectful of the communities they do business in. They acknowledge community concerns, increasing engagement and achieving smoother interactions and collaborations.*
3. *Natural compassion for stakeholders inspires them to take better care of the resources they rely on, making their success more sustainable.*
4. *These businesses are managed with transparency and accountability, so that all stakeholders understand the processes and competencies and are able to make better informed decisions.*

Fully embraced, these philosophies encapsulate the essence of *Good Citizenship* and *Corporate Social Responsibility*, supported by a solid commitment to on-the-ground *Collaborative Networking and Community Engagement*.

New *Beyond the Bottom-Line* Perspectives on Capitalism

In the movie *Wall Street*, crooked banker Gordon Gekko arrogantly put to a stockholder meeting his one-sided proposition that: *Capitalism is greed and greed is good.*

In an alternate universe, what if Gekko had been one of the good guys and had instead taken a balanced stakeholder view (hopefully with an alternative last name!):

Is it possible to be virtuous & commercial, liberal and capitalistic, democratic and rich?

Is it possible to do the right thing and create good business outcomes without compromising either?

The answer must surely be a resounding *yes*, depending on how you perceive, react and respond to the world around you.

SME Leadership: The 5 Critical Success Factors

The stories that follow, and the ones in the preceding chapter on the basics of good collaborative networking, put a strong case for redefining critical business stakeholders to incorporate the broader business community or sector you do business with and in. Genuine community engagement and the networking disciplines that underpin it are about joining the debate, providing workable solutions to local problems, and lending your moral and intellectual support to matters of importance at the heart of your community.

The collateral financial benefit you gain from committing to and driving those collaborations well is in the opportunity to:

> Contribute to debate on matters of importance in your community,
>
> Meet people and form new professional relationships
>
> Share information about your own business and what it does and create and identify added business opportunities.

Restating the obvious, the automatic two-way benefits that emerge from doing those things well, honestly and with an open heart is that you will be *doing the right thing while also creating great business outcomes, without compromising either.*

Engaging Your Local Community

In 2000, my family and I moved to the idyllic semi-rural/hobby farming community of Samford Valley, about 25 kilometres from of Brisbane City. Once settled, I asked around and soon discovered one of the most important *go to* people there was Bob Millar, the resident Morton Bay Region Councillor.

I arranged an early intro to Bob and over a coffee one morning, I was able to draw a relational *mud map* of all the important local connective communities and their leaders in the Samford Valley region. Bob and I would go on to become good friends and co-directors on a Bendigo Community Bank Board.

I first met Peter Dutton in 2001, soon after he was first elected to the Federal Seat of Dickson, a geographically large electorate that covers a good number of suburbs North West of Brisbane including Samford Valley, where Peter and I both lived with our families.

SME Leadership: The 5 Critical Success Factors

By the end of 2001 Bendigo had completed all of the legal aspects of our acquisition of First Australian Building Society and had carried out vital renovations, including rebranding each of the Building Society branches we had acquired the year before. Peter Dutton was most generous in joining me and my team in officiating at the relaunch of a number of those sites.

I have invited Bob Millar to tell the story of his engagement and networking journey in the Samford Valley region, where community successes have been substantially underwritten by the SME business sector.

My Community – Bob Millar, OAM.

Over three decades ago, a young family from suburban Brisbane made the decision to move to the nearby semi-rural and hobby farming community centred around the village of Samford, around 25 km north of Brisbane city. The primary motivation for our move was to give my three young children an opportunity to grow up in a social environment like that enjoyed by my wife and me in our youth, and for me to find interests and opportunities beyond the complex and often mind-sapping environment of big city banking!

In 1986, I joined the Samford Bush Fire Brigade (later known as the Samford Rural Fire Brigade) which gave me an opportunity to serve the community in a voluntary emergency services role, but also to engage with a group of men and women who were similarly motivated to serve their community.

Little did I know that this first foray as a volunteer firefighter in the socially inclusive environment of the Samford Valley would continue to this day and include a quarter of a century as the Brigade's Chairman.

What followed over the succeeding years became for me a blur of various roles within groups focused on community service or on boards whose culture was to help grow and strengthen the social capital of their community.

Joining Rotary in 1991 gave me the opportunity to participate in an organisation whose global foundation in the early 1900s was based on the principal of 'service before self'. It brought together people from diverse backgrounds, either as business owners or senior management, who had the capacity to leverage their positions to drive positive change for the benefit of the community and its best interests.

The Samford community continues to be the beneficiary of the investment made by these persistent men and women over the Club's 40-year history. Rotary was also the catalyst for the establishment of the first business networking group which subsequently morphed into our local Chamber of Commerce, advocating for the more than one thousand small to medium enterprise businesses based in and around Samford Valley.

By the turn of the century, my collective contributions had been such that some in our community felt I could be of even greater value as a local government representative. Like my father, Clarrie Millar AM, who had entered Federal Parliament one-quarter of a century earlier as the Federal member for Wide Bay, I was a reluctant starter, but with a narrow election win in March 2000, I began a 16-year stint as a councillor for the Pine Rivers Shire, that in the 2008 Local Government Amalgamations became Moreton Bay Regional Council. In my time on the council, I served the needs of more than 35,000 constituents and 80 plus community and business organisations in what is Australia's third largest local government authority.

With the catchphrase 'working with the community', I committed my time in local government to championing the role of the small businesses who were creating employment opportunities for a large percentage of our regional population, but also by encouraging them to reinvest in the communities from which they drew much of their business success.

Through this journey, I was approached by the author, who was then Chief Operating Officer of Bendigo Bank in Queensland, to join the board of Pine Rivers Community Finance Ltd., which held the Bank's Brendale Branch.

There started another career as a volunteer director (including two years as its chairman). In that time, we saw the company and its second branch in Samford Valley, grow into a significant local employer and provider of Bank services during a time when most of the other Banks had withdrawn.

I referred earlier to businesses reinvesting in their community. I can proudly report that the Community Bank, of which I remain a director, has done that in spades, by not only supporting the banking needs of its business and personal customers, but also in rewarding its community shareholders through dividends and by its direct investment of more than $800,000 in community need projects since establishment.

Samford Rural Fire Brigade, Rotary, Chamber of Commerce, Bendigo Community Bank and many other community service roles, together with the challenges of also being the local councillor, Bob Millar exemplifies what commitment to community is all about. And for his dedication, Bob was awarded an Order of Australia Medal (OAM) early 2022, presented to him by the Governor of Queensland.

From my view, Bob has been and continues to be a 'true blue' local legend of his community.

John's Community Engagement Learnings

The stories that follow are memorable ones for me as they demonstrate how much can be achieved in any community individually and collaboratively as part of a team.

The PNG Development Bank

Working for the World Bank and Asian Development Bank funded Papua New Guinea Development Bank (PNGDB) from the late 1970s to the mid-1980s was, for me, a life-changing experience. What I saw when I arrived was a remarkably committed and passionate team of professionals who had created a range of ground-breaking managed credit initiatives. These projects underwrote a defined pathway for PNG citizens to acquire their own rural or commercial small holder SME businesses. It was, for many of them, the important first step in transitioning from subsistence living to the cash economy.

Joining the PNDB team was my first real experience of collaborative community engagement supported by a level of corporate social responsibility that was mind-numbing in the strength, clarity and resolve of its vision – a concept pretty much unheard of in the 1970's!. We all felt proud that every day we were doing good things for our borrowers, the communities they lived in, and for the PNG economy at large.

The bank's coffee, cocoa, rubber and oil palm smallholder agricultural schemes produced economically sustainable outcomes for the rural economy. Our core agricultural projects entailed the acquisition of substantial arable land developments throughout regional PNG, conducting successful negotiations with village elders, creating a unique *Native Title* smallholder ownership structure and subdividing each large development into many hundreds of two-hectare lots. Mini-economic communities were established at the centre of each development with a range of essential services, including basic shopping, schooling for children and expert advisory support for the projects. This was community collaboration at its best at every level.

Our retail, commercial and industrial locally owned entity initiatives included a trade store ownership scheme, where our team acquired foreign-owned trade stores and then provided unique funding and legal structures for PNG citizens to manage and ultimately own those businesses.

The critical success factors for the bank were in our process-by-process SME design templates that literally left nothing to chance, well supported in the field by the bank's close collaborations with the PNG Government's primary, secondary and fishery industry extension and advisory agencies in every business sector we funded.

Our trade store acquisition initiative, known in Pidgin English as the *Stret Pasin Stoa Scheme*, was a good example of the bank's modus operandi. Successful indigenous participants were required to first graduate from our trade store training school in Port Moresby before being allocated a store to start trading. Each venture was incorporated as a Limited Liability Company for which the Bank held a majority shareholding until the operators could demonstrate a successful trading history and prove they were capable of going it alone. We were operating in a pre-digital economy era, yet our financial performance tracking was always reliable and timely, and our leadership mentoring was world-class.

SME Leadership: The 5 Critical Success Factors

After six years in PNG, Leslie and I decided it was time to return to Australia, where I joined the Senior Team at St. George Building Society in Sydney.

I will forever carry fond memories and many valuable learnings from my time at the PNGDB.

St. George Bank's Rent-Buy Scheme

One of my most satisfying St. George engagement collaborations was in the late 1980s, when we rolled out our innovative *Rent-Buy* Scheme that gave several thousand lifetime renters the opportunity to become homeowners for the first time.

Our vision was based on selecting low-income long-term renters with stable employment and credit histories, but who had zero capacity to raise the deposit gap required to finance and buy their own home. Our aim was to give applicants a newly constructed home (3 to 4 bedrooms), to set the rental level as low as possible, and to add an additional savings component that would eventually build towards a minimum deposit, while ensuring their combined weekly financial commitment would still be sustainable.

At St. George, we were fully committed to trialling the scheme, but knew our significant challenge would be in finding the other partners necessary to make it happen. Fergus Macpherson, who headed up Landcom, the NSW State Landbank, had a brief from the government to progressively feed low-priced land allotments into the marketplace to help first-home buyers, particularly in the Western Suburbs of Sydney. Fergus loved the idea of Rent-Buy and bought in immediately, as did his other State Government colleagues. Several large Sydney building companies agreed to participate in a series of round tables with us, but they were initially what I could only describe as *lukewarm* about the idea.

After several days of discussion and number crunching around a well-used whiteboard, the enthusiasm of our builder representatives grew rapidly, to the point where one of them finally slapped his hand on the table and said (my recollection): *Just imagine what we can achieve brand wise by turning the impossible dream of home ownership into reality for these people!*

From that moment on we became a proud collaborative community collective that others progressively joined, focussing on bringing *Rent-Buy* to life. We also agreed unanimously that the income we could generate from the scheme would simply be a by-product of doing *something intrinsically good*. From there solutions flowed rapidly and hurdles quickly vanished:

Landcom agreed to provide up to 4,000 minimally priced blocks of land in Sydney's West on a *turnkey* basis, with settlement not required until each home was fully constructed.

Our builders each offered a small range of basic but appealing project home design options also at a moderate discount, and again on a *turnkey* contract basis with settlement on completion.

We wanted these people to take pride in their new homes and to treat them as traditional homeowners would. Fergus was happy to spread his entire land allocation on a mixed tenure basis, where Rent- Buy participants and traditional homeowners would be mixed in each subdivision across many of his Western Suburbs land offerings. We all took pride in that decision.

Paved driveways, fencing, and basic grass turfing were included, but the Rent Buy participants were required to establish and maintain their gardens.

We included a *pride of ownership* covenant in their contractual agreements to ensure they maintained and treated their properties as if they were traditional homeowners from day one.

Many SME operators progressively joined our community of generous suppliers by paring their fees to the bone, as did several large appliance and furniture suppliers.

We negotiated support from federal, state and local governments, including exemptions from stamp duty and capital gains tax at purchase conversion time. The councils also pared their routine planning and approval fees to the bone.

Two of our long-standing St. George loans officers managed the pre-vetting of applicants and coordinated the Rent-Buy loan and savings components of the scheme superbly and did so with pride.

From memory, we enrolled not far short of 2,000 participants, a good number of whom were prior Housing Commission tenants. As luck would have it, the Sydney housing market was on a significant positive upswing trend over those first couple of years and a good percentage of our Rent-Buy tenants were able to convert to standard home loans within two years from a combination of their cumulative savings and the healthy gains in their home value.

SME Leadership: The 5 Critical Success Factors

To a person, everyone who had a role to play in Rent-Buy's success felt that warm glow that invariably comes from doing something good!

Banca Monte Dei Paschi di Siena

In 1997, when Bendigo Bank acquired the Australasian operations of Italian Bank, *Banca Monte Dei Paschi di Sienna*, I took on the role of CEO of that business which was subsequently renamed *Cassa Commerciale Australia Ltd*. My focus over the years that followed was on bedding down and integrating the business into the Bendigo Bank group, ensuring our client base, mostly Italian/Australian businesses, stayed the journey and for the business to continue on a healthy growth path. As Bendigo Bank was then only represented in Victoria at that time and *Cassa* had offices in all the State Capitals, this new business was also able to support the Bank in its early National expansion plans.

It was important for *Cassa* to be accepted by our new community of banking customers, over half of whom were medium SMEs, and for them to understand what Bendigo Bank could bring to the table. Two things that helped us on that journey were invitations to join the Italian Chamber of Commerce in Sydney and for me to be offered a seat on the late Lady Mary Fairfax's Opera Foundation Australia Board. The Italian Chamber in Sydney was a Community Engagement 101 *no-brainer* for us, and we successfully collaborated with the chambers in all the state capitals. Pleasingly, Bendigo Bank was warmly accepted by the business community in each capital and many more doors opened for us.

My Opera Foundation Australia board appointment came with a slight sting in the tail. The foundation's brief was to provide scholarships to promising young Australian singers to study, fully funded for six months with some of the great international opera companies, including those in Italy. After accepting the appointment, I learnt at my first board meeting that funding for the Foundation's Italian Opera Award had been struggling for several years and I was offered the challenge of fixing it. A charming smile and nod from the good Lady herself and how could I possibly say *no* – touché Lady Mary!

Over the following days, I put a call out to some old friends from my St. George Bank days and Ferdie Dominelli, Ford Motor Company's major Sydney Southern Suburbs dealer principal, responded. Ferdie was one of the best salesmen and networkers I ever knew and he happily joined my crusade. With him as my running mate, we rapidly restored the Italian Opera Award scholarship coffers. We hosted several grand gala fundraising auction dinners in Sydney over those years, generously bankrolled by the Italian business community and kindly MC'd by my friend John Mangos.

Historically, the Australian Italian Community has been generous in their support of community causes. They were as surprised as Ferdi and I about the lack of funding for the Italian Opera Award and took great pride in stepping up to the plate.

Several months after I moved on to my next assignment for Bendigo Bank, I was honoured in the New South Wales June 2000 Italian National Day Celebrations with an award presented to me by the Italian Ambassador to Australia, for my *contribution to the Italian Australian Business Community*. I offered to share my award plaque with Ferdie Dominelli, but he wouldn't have a bar of it! He reminded me of the fun we had shared, but also the deep satisfaction we both felt in what we had achieved with the opera award funding. Pleasingly, Ferdie was honoured with a full Italian Knighthood several years after that.

Our Italian Chamber and Opera Foundation participation presented good business opportunities and the respect we garnered as good community citizens. It is, after all, what meaningful community engagement in business can generate.

First Australian Building Society

In early 2000 I headed up the Bendigo Bank team that drove the acquisition of the Queensland-based First Australian Building Society. With a third of the Bank's post-acquisition shareholders residing in Queensland, we received an unequivocal brief from Group Managing Director Rob Hunt to roll out our unique style of regional and community banking and to legitimise our reputation as good citizens of our new State.

My collaborator in chief was Scott Elkington, who arrived from Bendigo in early 2001. Scott was a gem in everything he took on. He was successful in marshalling our branch troops to fully embrace our community-building initiatives, rapidly establishing community banking beachheads from Cairns in the north all the way to the QLD/NSW border in the south. Our team's accomplishments over the years that followed were an excellent case study in Engaged Citizenship and when he returned to Victoria, Scott would ultimately take the spirit our community engagement model nationwide, delivering multiple positive outcomes for the Bank in building it's Community Banking Network.

We doubled our Queensland branches to 80-plus locations throughout the State. Most of the new sites were community-owned franchises and the shareholders and representative boards were heavily laced with SME principals. Additionally we launched the community bank inspired South-East Queensland Community Telco, modelled after the bank's first community Telco in Bendigo. I proudly chaired SEQ Telco for several years after I retired from the Bank.

Bendigo Bank sponsored the 'Lead on Youth Development Program' that gave over 1,000 young teenagers in South-East Queensland an opportunity to engage with the business community, learn new skills and connect with potential employers.

We provided early stage banking operations and a school savings incentive program to remote indigenous communities in Far North Queensland. Noel Pearson and his Cape York Institute gave us a great deal of support in establishing those initiatives.

I also joined respected indigenous academic and University of Queensland Deputy Vice-Chancellor, Cindy Shannon and several others in establishing the Queensland and Torres Strait Islander Foundation (QATSIF). With Cindy as Chairperson, the State provided significant seed funding from which the foundation would go on to build a highly successful further education scholarship scheme for promising young Indigenous scholars.

I joined several other not-for-profit boards during those years, including the *Bremer TAFE*, prominent Australian think-tank *The Eidos Institute*, The *Ipswich Arts Foundation* and *Careflight Queensland*. The state government also invited me to join the board of *Powerlink Queensland*, the State's major electricity transmitter. All those appointments gave us access to additional valuable connections that opened doors to collateral opportunities for our banking business.

Building the vital networks and being an active and engaged citizen of the community you do business in, creates the opportunity to simultaneously *do some good* and *grow your business*, provided you are willing to put in the hard yards to open those doors and make it all happen.

Chapter 18: Mentors & Learning Circles

Several valuable mentors have guided me throughout my banking career. Two of the most significant ones for me were *St. George Bank's Jim Sweeney and Bendigo Bank's Rob Hunt*.

St. George Bank's Jim Sweeney

Jim was the most gifted public speaker I worked for during my corporate years. He was also a natural salesman who could effortlessly sell virtually any proposition at the drop of a hat, his only condition being that he had to first believe in it.

When Jim was appointed CEO of St. George in 1989, I inherited his old office and prior job. The first day I sat behind that desk, I found a large envelope addressed to me in Jim's neat italic scrawl. The note inside wished me luck in my new job of running St. George's Retail Bank and signalled some *homework* he wanted me to undertake. Also inside the envelope was a portable Dictaphone and a master key which opened the line of cupboards spanning the entire back wall of the large office. On opening them, I discovered dozens of thick manilla folders containing many of the speeches Jim had given over the years, plus sales pitches for every one of our products then on offer.

I pulled out a couple of the speech files and observed a consistent pattern. Three to four progressively updated hand-written drafts of each speech were followed by a final typed version that included multiple pause breaks where Jim would stop to give his listeners a few seconds to ponder a key point before he started speaking again. A small cassette tape sat on top of the final draft of each speech. I listened to five minutes of the first tape. It was of Jim practising his delivery, experimenting with alternative word and phrase options, and even testing changes to the pitch and tone of his voice to stress important points he wanted to make. His obvious strategy was to practice each speech until it was as good as he could possibly get it. I'm sure it won't surprise you that one of Jim's favourite quotes from those days was St. Jerome's: *Good, better, best, never let it rest, 'til your good is better and your better best.*

I checked a couple of Jim's sales pitches and found a similar pattern with multiple shorter drafts and a final tape recording of each one. They bought out the unique aspects and selling points of each of our products and had the same common tail about our legendary brand of customer service, driven largely by our unique and egalitarian building society roots and values.

I looked up sometime later to see Jim leaning against my new doorway, wearing his traditional trademark grin. He chuckled, wagged his finger at me and said (my recollection): "And you thought I just popped those speeches out naturally, didn't you, Goddard! Well, let me tell you, son, there's no such thing as a natural-born salesman or public speaker – you need to know that self-belief, hard work, and persistence win out every time, provided you're prepared to put in the hard yards. Assuming, of course, you want it badly enough." Jim winked and left without another word.

Over the following 12 months, Jim made sure I took on a good number of regular public speaking engagements, internally and externally, and he kept track of my progress. He edited my early speeches and even had me present some of them to him first. And yes, he was the toughest of task masters! After that I joined Jim and our senior media boss in taking on my fair share of our TV and press interviews.

The penultimate moment for me came at one of our quarterly *executive leadership meetings* held in the main auditorium of the St. George Leagues Club in Kogarah, not far from our Sydney corporate headquarters. Between our branch and head office management teams, there were around 1,000 people seated in the auditorium that day. Jim preceded my presentation with his usual flawless performance without a note in sight. When he came off stage and as we passed each other behind the curtains, he snatched my speech notes and refused point blank to return them! Under my breath, I let him know quietly what a *bastard* he was, and seconds later, the auditorium erupted in laughter! I had, of course, forgotten my lapel mike was already switched on! Jim gave me a pat and then a nudge on the back, assuring me: *It's time, JG. I know you'll be fine*! Of course, I was because I had no choice not to be!

Too often in the corporate world, people are given senior managerial posts without any serious prior leadership experience or vital training, on the assumption that because they were outstanding in their prior role, they would automatically become *natural leaders*.

Jim knew my public speaking wasn't up to scratch when he appointed me, and so he made it his mission to remedy that weakness. Over the years, he taught me how to become a better networker (and salesperson!) and he opened many doors for me in Sydney's senior business community. Jim sponsored my attendance at a life-changing residential executive development program at Columbia University's Business School in New York City, an international inter-university executive development program a year later, banking conferences in London, Cape Town, the Channel Islands and Tokyo, and an excellent media training program in Sydney.

My learning journey was enhanced by the fact that I was in the role Jim had carried out so capably for many years before he was appointed CEO.

Bendigo Bank's Rob Hunt

I first met Rob in the wake of the Farrow/Pyramid Building Society Group collapse in 1990. As incoming chair of the Victorian Building Societies Association, Rob was working around the clock to rescue the reputation of the industry he had so honourably served.

At the behest of our St. George board, I took our senior lending and legal team to Geelong, Victoria, in May 1990, initially to investigate if we could help Farrow's Societies get through the crisis. We quickly formed the view the job was beyond us and returned to Sydney with a recommendation to batten down the hatches for what was likely to come.

The subsequent multi-billion-dollar Pyramid collapse and the financial instability it caused led to St. George Building Society's decision to convert to a bank in 1992. Bendigo's board made the same decision to convert soon after.

Rob Hunt's abiding conviction was to respect the unique heritage that came with the regional Victoria turf he had inherited. Australian banks at the time were exiting country branches at an alarming rate. Around 3,000 bank branches closed in the final decade of the 20th century alone, and communities outside the capital cities were rapidly bleeding capital.

Bendigo Bank's solution emerged from the need to bring back banking services to those communities. Rob's *back-to-the-future* strategy was about forming co-operatively spirited ventures in the regions, which would honour the bank's building society's origins. Following the model he developed, 200 or more local citizens in each community, many of them SME principals, agreed to collectively put up the required capital to start their new banking venture. They pledged their personal banking patronage and undertook to go out and convince others in their community to do likewise. The cooperative shareholding structure was mutual, with voting rights per shareholder rather than being based on the amount each had invested.

An unlisted public company was formed in each community with its own local board of directors to raise the capital required and to manage and champion the day-to-day banking business. Constitutional rules of each community company mandated that a healthy percentage of the profits of their banking venture would be pledged to support community need projects. Bendigo Bank ensured all regulatory obligations were met and revenue earnings were shared between the bank and the local community company.

The staggering results that followed tell the story. From a standing start in 1998, Bendigo's network of community-owned banking franchises would ultimately grow over the following two plus decades to more than 300 sites Australia-wide, with consolidated balance sheet footings of over $20 billion.

And here's the *rub*, to date, those community-owned businesses, all of which were effectively franchised SMEs, have collectively invested well over *a quarter of a billion dollars of their accumulated profits back into local community need projects*.

I worked for Rob Hunt from 1995 to 2008, initially in providing my business partners and my support to the team that drove Bendigo's Banking Conversion. From 1997 I became CEO of the bank's newly acquired Italian banking business (Banca Monte de Pasche de Sienna Australia), and for my final eight years based in Brisbane, taking our major Queensland acquisition there state-wide. Pretty much every time Rob and I spoke, I listened assiduously and jotted down multiple pages of notes from his collective wisdom and learnings, which allowed me and my team to constantly refresh the community messaging we were providing in our Queensland

SME Leadership: The 5 Critical Success Factors

speaking engagements and media briefings. As it turned out, the Queenslanders loved Rob Hunt's grand vision and embraced the ultimate contribution we were able to make in our new state.

In creating his unique, mutually spirited, locally-owned community banking model and empowering local shareholders to underwrite and secure their sustainability, Rob's initiatives and outcomes went far beyond just banking by discovering broader pathways to aggregate buyer demand, including the bank-sponsored Community Telco initiatives; enhancing regional and community capital raising options, including rebooting the original Bendigo Stock Exchange; investing more broadly in the Not for Profit sector in building its Community Sector Banking business; and in supporting programs that encouraged Young People to remain in the regions of their birth to ultimately become productive, committed and proud citizens of those regions.

Those collaborative initiatives were also good for the Bank's bottom line. I'll quote here from a speech Rob Hunt gave over those early years:

> *It's been clear to us for some time that as the world becomes global people are acting more tribally. There's evidence everywhere that this is beginning to occur, and recent world events have heightened the importance of "local community" and "belonging".*
>
> *The fact is that product, price and feature can be replicated in a heartbeat and convenience is available from everyone. What will set us apart will be matters of the heart, and issues of trust and relevance to each customer and to each community's aspirations.*
>
> *Finally, we've rapidly learnt that "Doing the right thing" and "creating great business outcomes" – are not mutually exclusive.*

Mentors can do a great deal for anyone who seriously aspires to be successful in their business endeavour, provided they have the skills and experience you need.

These people have the capacity to:
- Impart their personal skills and knowledge,
- Pass on the benefit of their overall life experience,
- Give on-the-job feedback and advice,
- Give you a gentle nudge to step up the pace when you need it, and
- Improve your overall self-confidence.

Jim Sweeney and Rob Hunt each gifted me with critical slices of knowledge and support I needed at different times. Interestingly they were pretty much polar opposites of each other. Jim was a seat-of-the-pants front-line salesman, which afforded me the opportunity to learn from one of the best in building on those particular capabilities.

But for me, Rob Hunt was and still is an intellectual titan, and I am frankly yet to meet his match in the business world. In creating the vision for his Community Banking franchise and the substantial collateral initiatives that flowed from it, Rob embraced the core 'raison d'être' of Corporate Social Responsibility (CSR) long before many in the business world had any idea what CSR truly meant, or how it could add incremental bottom-line value to their businesses.

Being on board for the ride at Bendigo Bank during Rob Hunt's time was, for me, the most satisfying learning journey of my working life and was quite the grandest way I could have imagined to serve out my banking career. For that endowment, I will be eternally grateful to Rob.

Building Collaborative Learning Circles

While *Mentorship* is about garnering one-way career guidance, support and feedback, *Collaborative Learning Circles* offer a broader opportunity to augment your learnings by tapping into the strategic networking and community relationships you build throughout your life.

The old saying: *It's not what you know, but who you know that counts,* has always been a misnomer to me.

In business talk, it should undoubtedly have been: ***It's a combination of what you know AND who you know that truly counts!***

Collaborative networking unleashes a significant set of opportunities to unlock the potential behind both those *what* and *who* dimensions. It's that place where you meet people, join conversations, build mutual enduring relationships and:

- Offer your expertise,
- Share your knowledge,
- Learn from what others are doing well,
- Actively contribute to the debate on important local issues,
- Keep your finger on the pulse of your marketplace,
- Discover wonderful incremental business writing opportunities.

By engaging in those complementary *give-and-take* activities, you'll soon become a part of something quite special. In the spirit of what we call *Traditional Down-Under Aussie Mateship*, it's about driving collegiate relationships to their fullest potential. From there, you'll find pathways not only to guide you in growing your business but also to join valuable *learning circles* to allow you to *gain and share those two-way business smarts* that invariably emerge from those relationships and connections.

The obvious starting point is to tap into the knowledge of family, friends, colleagues and associates who are already in business. Given that one in five Australian households has an interest in a small business, you will undoubtedly know several people who are already on their SME journey and are willing to give you sage advice.

From there, embrace the collaborative networking and community engagement logistics I have laid out in chapters 16 to 18. The first important step must be, of course, your willingness to be brave enough to *open the door and step out*!

What's a good example of this from me?? In building my learning circle for this book, I collaborated with numerous colleagues and friends who were individually and collectively able to bring to the table their unique knowledge and skills. They included successful SME principals, senior bankers, prominent accountants, former elite sportsmen, academics and educators, a respected former News Ltd Business Editor, a former state Finance Minister, several Australian technology vendors and several US-based corporations with global offerings to the SME Sector. My colleague and co-writer, Ian Hulbert, who is CEO of *SME Keystone Leadership*, has also been a valued friend, supporter and adviser through this journey.

If you haven't done so already, start building those collaborative networks and learning circles and enjoy the far-reaching benefits you will undoubtedly gain from them.

CRITICAL SUCCESS FACTOR 4:

MANAGING TIME

'Time is a sort of river of passing events and strong is its current; no sooner is a thing bought to sight than it is swept by and another takes its place, and this too will be swept away'.

Marcus Aurelias on Managing Time, 170 BC.

'Who can define the difference between the long and the short term! Especially when our affairs seem to be in crisis, we feel most compelled to give our first attention to the urgent present, rather than the important future.'

Dwight D. Eisenhower, Former US President.

'I must govern the clock, not be governed by it.'

Golda Meir, Prime Minister of Israel, 1973

Critical Success Factor 4 lays out the time and workflow management priorities that are the productive breeding ground for achieving superior performance. They are to:

1. Make a commitment to *life-long learning* and *continuous improvement,*
2. Track and learn from your daily reflections in a *Personal Immersion Journal,*
3. Automate, maximise and institutionalise *productive habits and routines,* throughout the business.
4. Follow highly disciplined *priorities* in managing *the front line and the finances,*
5. *Delegate, automate and digitise* all *back-office priorities* to the maximum degree possible,
6. Put a total ban on the *zero-value time wasters,*
7. Mandate the *time management and workflow efficiencies and actions* that will underwrite your best possible outcomes:
   - Hire an *experienced bookkeeper/accountant* to manage all *transactions, cash flows, statutory obligations* and *financial reporting.*
   - Retain an external *tax accountant* to advise on your higher order tax obligations.
   - Place your principal's financial focus on the critical *performance metrics.*
   - Maximise your time at the front-line *acquiring customers and generating revenue.*
   - Establish the optimum *structural settings* that will enable you to maximise the benefits of those decisions.

By committing to those priorities, you will learn how to:
- Turn hard work into smart work.
- Better control of every aspect of your work life.

- Gain back many valuable hours each week by institutionalising and automating productive work habits and routines.
- Place your priority on the income generating, big picture, growth and future-proofing business priorities that count.

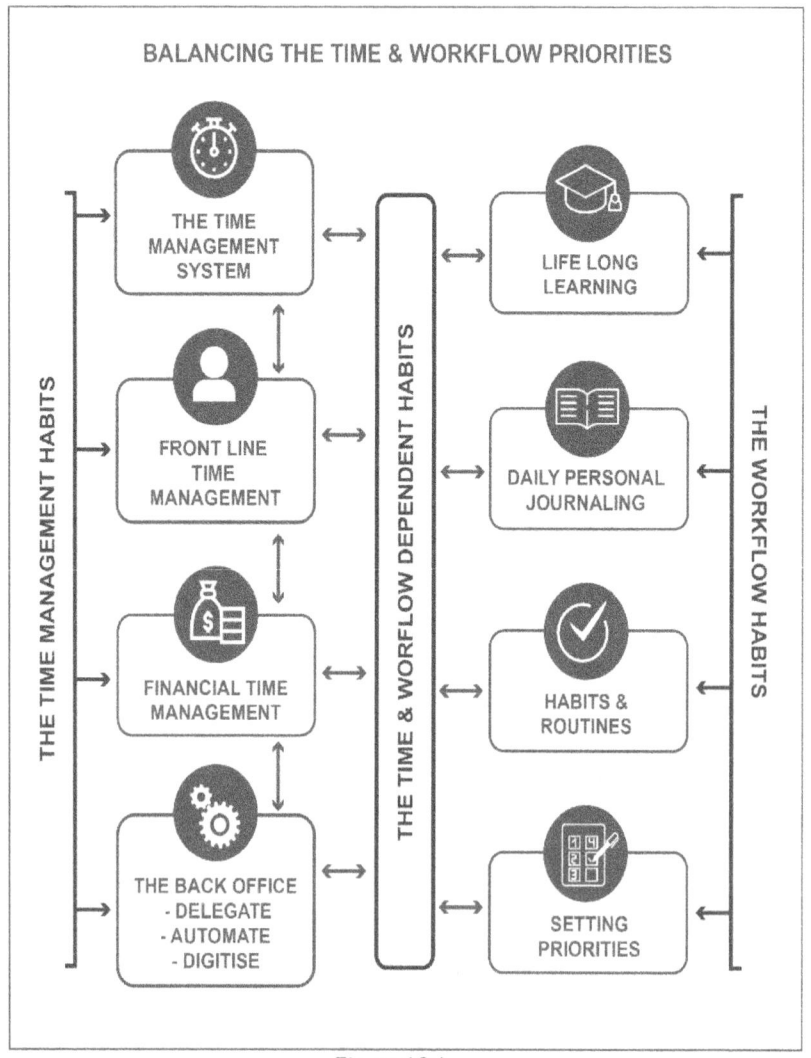

Figure 18.1

Chapter 19: Continuous Learning

*"Good, better, best, never let it rest,
'Till your good is better, and your better best."*

St. Jerome, Catholic Priest & Bible Translator 420 AD

"The first step in the acquisition of wisdom is silence, the second listening, the third memory, the fourth practice, and the fifth teaching others."

Solomon ibn Gabirol, 11th Century Jewish Philosopher

Your personal commitment to continuously accumulate new knowledge and skills throughout your life and a genuine willingness to pass those learnings onto others will undoubtedly have a positive influence on your ultimate successes, but only if you are committed to fully embracing this critical dimension.

In the words of American social and moral philosopher Eric Hoffer: *In times of change it's the learners who inherit the future. Those who have finished learning find themselves only equipped to live in a world that no longer exists.*

Continuous Learning – A Starting Point

A commitment to lifelong learning is the most essential building block that will accelerate and enhance your capacity to accumulate the *skills* and tap into the *valuable ongoing ideas, intelligence and business smarts* you'll need to be successful in your business. The most logical place to start is to:

- ➢ Cultivate and be committed to *productive reading habits,*
- ➢ Make good use of instant *digital learning* opportunities,
- ➢ Build and learn from your *personal and business networks,*

> *Observe and replicate* the things that others in the business world are doing particularly well, and

> Learn from respected *Mentors and Advisors*.

Cultivating Productive Reading Habits

A strong personal commitment to productive reading habits has been a significant contributor to my learning journey throughout my adult life.

When I graduated from high school, I was reading at a laboriously slow 200 words a minute. At the behest of Sir Keith Yorston, a valued occasional mentor at the Australian Accountancy College during my Chartered Accounting studies, I enrolled in one of the early night courses in speed reading and was able to more than double my speed in the first month alone. Today I read and comfortably digest at least 500 to 600 words a minute and 800 to 900 words when I'm pressed for time.

Speed reading is a purely mechanical skill literally *anyone* can learn. It's about harnessing an alternative way to read. You'll rapidly learn to stop mentally sub-vocalising every word (which is the agonising enemy of the slow reader), then you'll progress from reading single words to sentences and finally short paragraphs at a glance. Bottom line, your comprehension improves because you will have removed the extreme boredom of focussing on singular words and phrases.

You'll find an easy-to-follow chapter on how to master speed reading in Jim Kwik's marvellous book, *Limitless: Upgrade your Brain, Learn Anything Faster and Unlock your Exceptional Life* (Hay House Publishers, 2020). Or go to our Appendix ii) for details of how to download our Essentials Toolkit Rapid Learning Guide: *How to effectively Double Your Reading Speed in 10 days.*

Following the good habit of reading a quality daily *newspaper(s)* will keep you up to date on what's happening in the world and in your own industry sector. It complements your general knowledge, supports the business decisions you make, improves your networking capabilities and makes you much more interesting in the relationships you nurture. My only caution? Beware the risk of assuming the validity of one-sided unvalidated news, particularly those stories that emerge from social media sources.

I read my *newspapers* online first up every morning. My Australian favourite is *The Sydney Morning Herald/Melbourne Age* (same masthead). My favourite journalist is Ross Gittins, although I enjoy following a tribe of other respected scribes at the Herald.

I also scan The Australian Financial Review and The Wall Street Journal and download what's happened in the overnight financial markets. I start each story by rapidly scanning several paragraphs to give me the gist of what's covered and then only fully read those items that interest me most. I'll admit to taking a little longer on my favourite sporting pages!

Although I'm an avid *e-book* fan and have amassed a significant Kindle library over the years, I tend to purchase soft back versions of *my favourite business books* and *biographies about serial high achievers* – the ones I know I'll want to pick up more often for some in the moment inspiration. Before committing to buy a book, I peruse the jacket blurbs, introduction, foreword, testimonials and contents table. Nowadays, it takes me two and a half to three hours to read the average 400-page book or an hour if I'm really in a hurry.

If you had the opportunity to browse my home library, you'd find my favourite titles with dog-eared page corners, circled quotes, pencilled margin notes and even yellow *post it* notes flagging ideas I particularly like.

Tapping into Digital Learning opportunities

While I don't rely on social media to source my news reports because of the one-sided biases that too easily distort the core message, I acknowledge that, at the time of writing, *Google Search* is my core search engine of choice for accessing *raw data*. As a writer, **Google Search** opens the door for me to the generally reliable *instant data and information* I'm seeking progressively during my writing sessions.

Google's data base of information from respected academic and other sources is vast. Its organic search results are based only on their relevance to and match with your search request and are generally well supported by the *source notes* that accompany most downloads. The circa 10 billion searches that are carried out on *Google Search* each day tells a story in its own right about Googles broad credibility and value.

For deeper drill-down research, I'm a fan of several AI apps, including *Microsoft Co Pilot, Chat GPT, Google Gemini, and Perplexity AI*, because of their capacity to address more detailed on-point analysis that also allows *voiced based conversational capacity* with *Question and Answer* type queries and more *contextualised on point responses*.

At time of writing, Perplexity is my favourite app, but make sure you check them all out – most offer a free limited access or free trial option, with a fee of around $20 per month thereafter.

Learning from Business Networks

In the context of continuous learning, networking is the social interaction of building mutual relationships with other people in business, joining debate on important local issues and keeping your finger on the pulse of your marketplace.

Joining a local Chambers of Commerce or community service clubs such as Rotary is the logical place to start your networking journey.

The collegiality of sharing stories with like-minded business leaders will open the door to many opportunities. You'll be able to learn from a broad spectrum of business endeavours. Some members will be in relatively new start-ups, others more established, and you'll undoubtedly meet some people who are in a similar line of business to yours. Good networking habits also reinforce that you are not alone! (Chapter 16).

Learning by Observing

One of the satisfying benefits I gained during my 4 decades as a banker was the opportunity to visit vast numbers of businesses. During my career, I saw factories and manufacturing plants of varying sizes; retailers across every sector; hotels, restaurants, cafés and similar hospitality venues; service and consulting enterprises; land development and construction sites; large and small agricultural enterprises; and many more. I also visited business incubator hubs sponsored by Universities, State Governments and others, and had the opportunity as a banker to finance some quite novel ways of doing business.

Out of those exposures, I developed a radar system I call my ***Importance, Value, Worth Barometer.*** Every time I visit a business; I turn over a consistent series of nine questions in my mind:

- How do they compare with others I've seen in a similar industry sector?
- Do they seem to be going well?
- What are they doing that is clearly outstanding?
- Are they innovative and fresh in their approach?
- What could they be doing better?
- Do they understand the core metrics that drive their financial outcomes?
- Do they work well as a team?
- Do they promote their business well?
- How disciplined is the principal about managing time?

While I don't ask those nine questions verbatim, they reflect the consistent patterns I'm looking for. From a networking strategy I learnt many decades ago, I pose broad open-ended questions designed to get the principal talking. I then draw my own conclusions from what they tell me and from what I can see in front of me.

I drew heavily on those observational strategies in building the data base and assumptions underpinning my *5 Critical Success Factors*.

Observing is a powerful adjunct to continuous learning because you are witnessing first-hand what works and what doesn't. Always keep your eyes open when you pass or visit another business. When you sight something special being done well, aim to replicate some of those good practices or ideas.

Learning from Mentors and Advisors

I would not have achieved a fraction of what I did during my career without the valuable guidance I got from some very special mentors and professional advisors. At various times they helped me clarify and focus on my goals, sharpen my vision and always encouraged me to dig deeper. I have spoken about two of those mentors in Chapter 18.

The Driving Power of Mindset in Continuous Learning

"I didn't fail 1000 times. The light bulb was just an invention with 1000 steps. Our greatest weakness lies in giving up. The most certain way to succeed is always to try just one more time."

Thomas A. Edison, Circa 1879.

The research laboratory Edison founded in Menlo Park, New Jersey in 1876 became well known as the *invention factory* because Edison and his team were constantly bringing to life a stream of groundbreaking creations. Edison could afford to fund projects like the light bulb that had a longer gestation because of the steadily flowing royalties he was generating.

Unless you are fortunate enough to be a Thomas Edison, consider new projects with an anticipated long lead time very carefully. Before you commit, be satisfied you'll be able to go the distance and get the positive outcomes you are seeking.

The 7 Stages of Learning and Self-Awareness

The role instinctive self-awareness plays in life-long learning is a valuable foundation for achieving outstanding outcomes.

Let's start by considering traditional *Stages of Learning Theory* that transitions through four steps:

1. *I'm* **unconsciously incompetent**: I don't yet know what I don't know.

2. *I'm* **consciously incompetent**: I know what I don't know and am willing to learn more about it.

3. *I'm* **consciously skilled**: I can do it, but I still need to check off each step every time.

4. *I'm* **unconsciously skilled**: I can do it intuitively and competently on auto drive without having to think too much about each progressive step.

Please know there's a significant continuous learning risk in pulling up at stage 4. That's why I've added three additional stages that will harness your *Creative Intelligence* and your capacity to cultivate deeper insights Those additional stages are: *Creative Ideation, Creative Innovation,* and *Spontaneous Instinctive Thought.*

I call this expanded hierarchy: *The 7 Stages of Learning & Self Awareness*:

5. **Creative Ideation** provides a systemic pathway for connecting the visual, concrete and abstract components of the thought cycle. In *Ideation, The Birth and Death of Ideas,* (John Wiley and Sons, 2004), authors Graham and Bachmann identified nine dimensions of Creative Ideation:

Basic problem-solving: someone has a problem and finds the most logical solution.

Derivative ideas: improving something that already exists.

Symbiotic ideas: combining a string of ideas to create a singular new idea.

Revolutionary ideas: a transition from traditional thinking to new perspectives.

Serendipitous discovery: Totally new concepts and ideas.

Targeted essential innovation when it's needed: e.g., the quest for a COVID-19 vaccine.

Technology-assisted discovery: widening options using technology and/or AI.

Artistic innovation: puts aside practicality with no constraints.

Philosophical ideas: living and evolving deeply within the mind of the creator.

Try consciously engaging your analytical thinking capacity by running your slide rule over each one of those nine dimensions whenever you are seeking a solution to any problem or are creatively considering other possibilities or alternative ways of doing business.

6. Creative Innovation In the business world, Creative Innovation is the process of transforming new/original ideas into products and services that create additional incremental value for the business. What makes one person more creative than the next? As Principal/CEO, the real question is *how can I become more innovative?* How can I find *more innovative people* for my business?

In their groundbreaking book *The Innovators DNA* (Harvard Business Review Press, 2011), Dyer, Gregersen and Christensen put innovation under the microscope and examined how the most innovative CEOs came up with the unique ideas their businesses were built on. From that research the authors identified *5 principle discovery skills* that explain how disruptive innovators think differently from most other leaders:

Associating: This is the capacity to successfully identify and connect *seemingly unrelated questions*, problems, or ideas from different fields. e.g., Pierre Omidyar successfully launched eBay in 1996 after linking three seemingly unconnected dots:

- o His obsession with creating a more efficient Twenty First Century marketplace,
- o His fiancés obsession with trying to source hard-to-find *Pez Dispensers*(!!), and
- o The ineffectiveness of traditional pre-digital local classified advertising in sourcing such items.

Questioning: In the 1970's, the legendary Peter Drucker described the power of asking provocative questions: He said: *The important and difficult job is not to find the right answers. It is indeed to ask the right questions*:

- o The right questions are: *Why? Why Not?* and *What If?*
- o Always *deal with opposites* positively!

- Always *embrace constraints*!

Observing: Innovators source ideas by closely *scrutinising what staff, customers, suppliers and their competitors are doing*? If they see something they automatically ask *why do they do that*, and *how can they/we do it better?*

Experimenting: Innovators are not afraid of failure. They actively try out new ideas by creating prototypes. Jeff Bezos online bookstore didn't stay where it was after its launch. It morphed into an online discount bookstore AND THEN an immense range of other products. Bezos in fact institutionalised fearless innovative thinking at Amazon: *I encourage our employees to go down blind alleys and experiment.*

Networking: Innovators go out of their way to meet people with ideas and perspectives *different* to their own. They also build networks of *willing testers.*

The authors of *The Innovators DNA* suggest that Creative Innovation is not a genetic disposition but rather a learnable and scalable, active endeavour. If you want to be a successful Innovator, a good place to start is to *set aside 15 to 30 minutes of every day writing down questions that challenge the status quo in your business and elsewhere in your marketplace.*

7. **Spontaneous Instinctive Thought** is a dynamic means of discovery that combines the sum total of your combined professional knowledge and life experience with an in-the-moment instinctive opportunity. An 'outside-the-box' response often has the potential to be a welcome slice of spontaneous magic.

Here's my favourite example of *Spontaneous Instinctive Thought* from the world of elite sport. When he was 30 metres or so from the touch down line, former champion Australian Rugby League Half Back, Johnathon Thurston occasionally pulled up to a *dead stop*, with ball in both hands, then looked in every direction, deciding what his next move would be. Yet here's the rub – opposition players also froze because they feared he was about to pull off one of his freakishly instinctive moves! In not tackling him in the moment, they were in fact allowing Thurston the breathing space he required to do what they feared he would do! In rapid time, Jonathon then went *with what his gut was telling him*. A touch down by Thurston or one of his nearby mind reading disciples invariably followed! Newcastle's favourite son, Andrew Johns often did the same thing with his pinpoint in-the-moment tactical kicking. You'll occasionally see similar examples of Spontaneous Instinctive thought in Rugby Union, Australian Rules and American Football.

An act of *Spontaneous Instinctive Thought* in the business world may occur when you come up with a novel idea that has emerged from an intuitive thought flash you've had about a unique or different way of doing business. That momentary flash has emerged from something you've heard, read, seen, observed from afar, or perhaps even dreamt about. You draw on your deep knowledge and experience to convert that idea into a workable solution. You realise the potential to score, while your opponents are yet to even know that opportunity exists. Being first to market, you'll gain a *first past-the-post* advantage over your competitors.

THE STAGES OF LEARNING & SELF AWARENESS

1. UNCONSCIOUS INCOMPETENCE
I don't know what I don't know

2. CONSCIOUS INCOMPETENCE
I know what I don't know and am interested in learning more about it

3. CONSCIOUSLY SKILLED
I can do it, but I still need to consciously consider every step every time

4. UNCONSCIOUSLY SKILLED
I can do it intuitively and competently without having to consciously think about each step

5. CREATIVE IDEATION
Exploring the visual, concrete and abstract aspects of the thought cycle

6. CREATIVE INNOVATION
Transforming original ideas into products/services that create additional value for the business

7. SPONTANEOUS INSTINCTIVE THOUGHT
Explore possibilities that combine your life experiences with an in-the-moment instinctive idea

Figure 19.1

Continuous Learning and the Team

If you want to create a culture of continuous learning across your business, the steps may be easier than you think. Encourage your team to observe how things are done in your business and in similar businesses elsewhere. Let them in on some of the valuable *tips and tricks* I've included in this chapter. Urge them to speak up when they have a good idea. When they emerge, workshop those ideas in round-table discussions giving everyone an opportunity to contribute. Celebrate collective achievements and give positive feedback when they present themselves.

A Continuous Learning Checklist for the SME Team:

Embrace/live by the overwhelming truism that *success leaves clues:*

- Read a quality daily newspaper every day – ideally on line!
- *e*-subscribe to industry magazines relevant to your sector.
- Consider subscribing to the *Harvard Business Review* (HBR) – their articles are gems, most run to ten pages or less, and they are easy to learn from.
- Read books about skills, habits, strategies and good tactics in business and check out some of the valuable tomes in my bibliography.
- Read and learn from biographies about serial high achievers from all walks of life.
- Learn by observing and replicating what others do well.
- Embrace the unique learning capabilities of adopting all of my *7 Stages of Learning and Self Awareness.*
- Dig deep to tap into your capacity to acquire, assimilate and act on new ideas.
- Embrace the spirit of Solomon Ibn Gabirol's *pay it forward* strategy, by placing a high priority on the acquisition of wisdom. Promote a culture of continuous learning across your team by committing to follow Gabirol's five steps:
    - First and Second steps: *Silence*, then *Listening*,
    - Third step: *Memory*,
    - Fourth step: *Practice*, and
    - Fifth step: *Pay it Forward i.e., Teach Others.*

Chapter 20: Daily Personal Journaling

In 1987, I joined a residential executive leadership program at Columbia University's Graduate School of Business at their upstate New York, Hariman House campus. There were 40 or so of us on the program. During our evening down time, several admitted to maintaining a daily personal journal that extended beyond the realms of the traditional diary in recording their progressive personal learnings, but also importantly in using their journal to track the efficiency of their daily work plans and outcomes.

I liked the idea, so back in Sydney I purchased my first A4 spiral-bound notebook. Over several decades, I filled over 100 of those notebooks until I more recently transitioned to a digital version. Over time I called those reflections my *Personal Immersion Journal* as they progressively morphed into my daily *deep dive into the voice of my conscience*, guiding me to add clarity and substance to my values, visions, goals and actions, and to constantly challenging me to do better. I added further insights after reading biographies of some great thinkers in history who were daily journalers.

I record my Personal Immersion Journal notes twice daily, first up in the morning while planning out my business day and at the end of the day to emotionally sign-off from work. A quarter of an hour each time is all you need once it becomes an entrenched habit. Start with immediate trigger words, thoughts, feelings and ideas that come to mind and allow them to flow freely. They will undoubtedly help you energise and engage your inner creativity.

The Nuts and Bolts of my Morning Journal

- ✓ *My Learnings:* What *New Insights* have I gained in the past 24 hours? How can I improve my personal and business outcomes by adopting some of those learnings?
- ✓ *Yesterday:* Review how my team and I did with each of yesterday's appointments. *How could we have done better?*
- ✓ *Today:* Mentally rehearse today's planned tasks with a view to underwriting the best possible outcomes, i.e., what do I want to achieve

- ✓ *My Emotions*: Affirm that I have been consistent in positively managing my emotions with my team, our customers and in my dealings in the business community at large.
- ✓ *The Big Picture*: Take a brief *helicopter view* of my domain. Revalidate my values & goals. Are they stretch goals? Or are your aspirations a little light on? Which one's need tweaking?
- ✓ *Events and Trends*: Jot down events/trends that have recently impacted our business and its trading performance, positive or negative. How did we respond? What were our learnings?
- ✓ *Kindness to Others:* Get into the good habit of consciously *bringing light and joy to at least one person* every day and soak up the positive energy those acts of kindness generate for you! Jot down a few words about yesterday's kindness interactions.
- ✓ *My Dashboard*: Finally, scan our accounting software *dashboard*. Focus on new income, cash flows, debtors, creditors and any other critical financial data that's important to us. Note any required follow-up actions with our bookkeeper.

End of Day Journal Sign-Off

This is a formal *shutdown routine,* which supports your sign-off from work with a focus on shifting your mindset to the non-work priorities that count at home. (see end of Chapter 21).

Less Formal Journal Entries During the Day

Note down any fresh ideas, inspirations or showstoppers as they come to you. Because I'm obsessive by nature, those ideas become negative interrupters if I allow them to percolate in my mind for too long at critical times when I need to remain focussed. Capturing a brief note in your journal, in the moment, allows you to compartmentalise it and get back to what you were doing. Revisit the idea during your scheduled quiet time.

My early journal notes were long and verbose, sometimes running to many pages, but over time they became explicit and concise, with a focus on descriptive words and brief phrases rather than long sentences and longer paragraphs. The memories flood back from those short notes, even when scanning my notes years later.

Chapter 21: Habits & Routines

The movie *Groundhog Day* showcases a narcissistic TV weatherman, forced by a strange twist of fate to relive a day of his life over and over again. The lead character's self-improvement emerges progressively from his predicament of waking each morning to realise he's still living in yesterday and that he's the only one this is happening to. His first instinct is to exploit his unique knowledge for his own exclusive benefit. But after a week or so, he quite miraculously gains a conscience and sees his character flaws for what they truly are through the eyes of others rather than through his own distorted prism. He then jettisons his selfish bad habits and replaces them with desirable new ones.

The allegory of the movie is the daily grind many of us experience: the same old job, the same old people and the same ingrained old habits. The hidden message is that if we persist in doing the same things tomorrow, as we did today and yesterday, then nothing will change.

Do you sometimes feel like you are locked in a time warp in your own version of Groundhog Day in which you can't shake off the flawed habits preventing you from taking positive steps forward?

Defining Habits, Routines & Paradigms

Habits are skills, acquired patterns of behaviour, customary practices and simple ways of doing things that become ingrained over time. They are actions we habitually carry out without having to consciously think about the individual steps required to make them happen. Statistically our regular habits account for around 40% of our daily actions.

Routines are ways of doing things in a particular order, typically made up of a string of linked common-purpose habits.

Definite cues trigger our habitual behaviour. Passing a café near the office at the same time each day triggers the subliminal message I must have my morning coffee now! The wafting aroma seductively lures you into the shop. The barista automatically starts brewing your preference before you even place your order. Taking your first sip as you leave, you give the barista your customary thumbs-up nod of approval.

When you are driving on a road you know well, you'll generally be doing it as a routine without an overabundance of conscious decision-making, other than constantly watching the road in front of you and occasionally scanning your dashboard. When the traffic slows, you approach traffic lights, go through a roundabout, or turn a corner, your brain consciously re-engages at a higher level because you have to make defined discretionary decisions – i.e., do I slow down, do I break, do I stop, do I turn?

Paradigms: Paradigms are logical patterns, methodologies and ways of getting things done. In the business world, Paradigms are generally about finding the most efficient ways to get things done.

Being strict about locking down good work habits and routines is the only way I can be sure my most important jobs will get done and that I'll be able to block out the lower value tasks and distractions that are of little value to me or my business.

Those work disciplines are underwritten by my willingness to modify my critical work habits, routines, and effective ways of getting things done when it becomes evident that they are not working as well as I would have liked and not allowing me to get the best possible outcomes.

Am I obsessive about following those disciplines, but also constantly committed to reviewing their effectiveness? That's a definite YES and for that reason the system works well for me.

Discarding Poor Habits

The best way I know to lock in good habits is to automate them to their fullest, so I no longer need to think too much about them. The solution to managing poor habits is then surely to find a way to make them nigh on impossible to keep doing.

I like Tony Robbins Neuro Linguistic Programming (NLP) inspired version of Success Conditioning he calls Neuro Associative Conditioning. In Personal Power 2 The Driving Force (Anthony Robbins, 1996, Robbins International), Tony advises that to eliminate habits that hinder your capacity to succeed, take three steps:

1. Get leverage on yourself:

   Three levels of responsibility are required. You must firmly face the fact in resolving that:

   Something must change.
   I must change it.
   I know I can change it.

2. Interrupt your current patterns of association, and

3. Condition a new empowering association.

Eliminating poor habits and replacing them with better ones takes time, but Robbin's method works well if you stick with it. This is how his disciplines work for me:

- Find a conscious trigger to interrupt the behaviour you need to change or get rid of,
- Create a believable alternative narrative every time without fail,
- Constantly reinforce your new habit until it becomes your new norm. Any thought, emotion or behaviour that positively supports the new habit is fine.
- Reward yourself by linking pleasure to your new choice. Do it for every step you take to jettison the bad habit.
- This strategy helps to keep you accountable.

Automating Good Habits

> *"We are what we repeatedly do. Excellence, then, is not an act, but a habit."*
> **Aristotle, 335 B.C.**

If we accept Aristotle's proposition, then what form should the ideal combination of habits and routines take in our business and in our private lives? How can we efficiently carry out the less important but still essential tasks in a way that frees up our capacity to be able to focus on the more important ones?

You can develop your own auto-drive routines by consciously scheduling every facet of your day. Automate and/or delegate the lower value tasks that still must be done, eliminate the zero value time wasters, and adopt a disciplined diary management routine to keep track of every job and task.

What follows is Ian's and my nuts-and-bolts system of programming our day. When I am disciplined about following the system, my days are productive, I get the most important things done, and I take positive steps forward. When I let any of those routines slip, I only get a fraction of the work done.

So, the absolute critical first rule is to:

PROGRAM YOUR DAY.

Start by breaking your day into scheduled blocks of time: before work, during the workday, and the end of your workday.

It will take you a while to adjust to tracking every aspect of your day, but if you stick with it, it will eventually become an entrenched set of habits and routines that allow you the time to lock in and focus on your most important tasks and priorities.

Before Work Habits and Routines

Wake up: preferably at the same time each workday morning, so it becomes a habit. When I'm writing, it's 5 am for me because I know I am at my most productive in those early hours while the rest of the house still sleeps!

Exercise: Have a brief workout or take a brisk walk for a healthy start to engage your brain and get you going.

Read your preferred morning paper online: and check what happened overnight in the international markets.

Map out your workday: Sit in your favourite quiet zone at home with your *Personal Immersion Journal* and a printout of your e diary from yesterday plus today's diarised commitments. Jot down your achievements and learnings from yesterday's tasks, map out what you need to achieve today and make any necessary changes to today's planned tasks. Then work through the remaining journal review tasks summarised at the end of Chapter 19.

Finally, scan your accounting software dashboard financial summary: check if any follow-up action is required.

Workday Habits

Email Disciplines:

Like Google and Facebook, email can be a devastating productivity killer, but only if you allow it to control your life. Try these suggestions:

Check your mailbox a maximum of three times a day:

- ✓ First up in the office, check for any changes to meeting arrangements and clear and respond to new emails that have arrived since yesterday.
- ✓ After lunch, clear any urgent matters or requests and review and respond to new emails.
- ✓ Before leaving the office, clear new emails and note any required changes to the following day's meetings.

Leave your email screen out of view at other times. If anyone has an urgent issue to raise with you by email, they can call or text you to let you know it has been sent or is on the way.

Take at least one action with every new email you open:

- ✓ If it's only for information, archive or bin it.
- ✓ If it's something that requires further thought, copy it to a follow-up file and reply to the sender that you need time to consider it.
- ✓ If it needs input from someone else, send it to that person.
- ✓ Do not copy someone else's sensitive message to a third party without their permission.
- ✓ Send all email replies with caution, particularly with emails sent to a distribution list.

Too many people I know let their inboxes swell to 100 or more unresolved issues. Procrastination is invariably the problem, but the owners of those mailboxes are also allowing themselves to suffer the extreme boredom that comes from rereading the same messages over and again without acting.

Even worse, it's a mind-numbing waste of your valuable time!

Before you send an email reply, proofread the message, double-check your intended recipients and think twice before hitting the send button. I've learnt from experience no email is ever guaranteed to be truly confidential because you have zero control over what your email recipients will do with it. So, presume the worst. What you write today could surface in tomorrow's newspaper!

Make sure you lock in a standard Private and Confidential Disclaimer to all your outward emails to sit below your signature line. You'll find plenty of examples online. Here's a very basic disclaimer:

This message is confidential. If you are not the person to whom it was addressed, please let me know, do not divulge the contents to any other person and delete the message from your mailbox.

As a final check before sending an email, ask yourself, do I really need to send it, or would a personal phone call or even a face-to-face meeting be better?

Texts in Business

Texting is a sensible and efficient way of communicating to let someone know you are running late for an appointment, that an imminent or urgent email is on its way, to share contact details, or when you haven't got time for the customary niceties that accompany a phone call, or face to face communication. Be clear, succinct and unambiguous in your text messages. I'll admit I sometimes send a lengthy text message, but in all conscience, I can't seriously recommend it!

Business Meetings:

Plan all your meetings with four sacrosanct rules:

- Unambiguous agendas with a time specified for each matter,
- Clearly defined expectations of what you need to achieve,

- Agreement on required post-meeting follow-up actions,
- Mobile Phones/Tablets must be benched during meetings.

In the early 1990s, when mobile phones were still in their infancy and were about the size of a house brick (and cost a great deal more than they do today), I hosted a meeting for a multimillion-dollar commercial loan settlement in St. George Bank's boardroom. One of Sydney's respected solicitors, who I knew well, was there to represent our client, while our senior commercial loans officer talked through the significant conditions-precedent that had to be ticked off before the loan could settle. After the solicitor interrupted us all for a second time to take an incoming call, I pulled him aside (he was in fact seated next to me) and sought his agreement to turn his phone off until we were done. He agreed to do so.

I discovered he'd broken that promise moments later when he took a further call. Without stopping to think about it too much, I snatched the phone from his hand and dropped it in the large water jug sitting on the table between us!

The solicitor inflamed what was already a tense situation when he whispered in my ear that I had just committed a technical act of assault against him! But everyone else at the meeting, including the solicitor's client, seemed quite delighted by my action!

I'll freely admit it was poor behaviour on my part, yet it was a reflex action born out of my extreme frustration. Although the solicitor was not a *happy chappy*, our settlement did proceed quickly after that.

Should I have done what I did? Absolutely not, because two wrongs clearly don't make a right!

Early the next morning, when I was writing up my personal immersion journal, I decided I'd better call the solicitor and clear the air between us, but he beat me to it (at 6 am BTW!). Amazingly, he was apologetic about his behaviour the day before. He admitted his wife had given him a hard time when he told her about it, as I acknowledged Leslie had when I told her about my water-jug caper!

The situation was further complicated for both of us by the fact that Leslie and I were due to go to a dinner party at his home days later! The solicitor and I both had a good laugh about it before hanging up and all was forgiven on both sides. The incident still cost me the price of a new phone, yet the milage I've got out of retelling this tale over the years since (self-deprecatingly, of course!) made it well worth the cost!

Tablet/ mobile phone etiquette in one-on-one meetings:

Just about everyone's had the experience of trying to have a meaningful conversation with someone whose eyes are constantly flicking sideways to glance at their tablet or mobile phone screen. It's disrespectful, and because I value my time, I usually speak up (but I very definitely no longer reach for the water jug!!). The obvious solution is to switch off or place your phone/tablet on silent at those times.

Schedule Set Time for Important Recurring Tasks

These include locking in routine time blocks for your regular must-do tasks, i.e., selling, networking, reading, reviewing daily cash flows, monthly financial results, and dealing with your other front-of-mind projects and priorities.

Schedule Time Blocks for Important Time-Consuming Projects

The University of Southern California (and several others) has broken new ground in their research on the productive management of high-pressure multiple-priority workloads. Their perspectives on the shortcomings of multitasking (i.e., constantly switching focus on more than one task or activity at the same time) and how to alternatively manage competing priorities for maximum outcomes, provides some useful tools for the frenetic, understaffed environment that SMEs typically reside in. The evidence is loud and clear – in periods when we multitask, our IQ can temporarily drop by an extraordinary 15% to 20%!

The 5 Steps of Compartmentalising

Rather than multitasking, the best alternative is to compartmentalise longer blocks of time to each important task to ensure they get done (aka Ian's and my Time Management System).

To explain how this discipline works, I'll reference an excellent Forbes magazine article titled: *The 5 Steps of Compartmentalisation – The Secret Behind Successful Entrepreneurs*, by noted American entrepreneur and author Ryan Blair, Forbes edition: June 26, 2012.

Blair's 5 steps are:

1. Compartmentalise it. Isolate the issue from all other challenges you are dealing with at the time.
2. Apply extreme focus on each compartment for the block of time you have pre-scheduled for it.
3. Move forward in incremental steps. AND once you see good progress….
4. Close the compartment and open the next one.
5. Be willing to say no to things that don't deserve their own compartmental focus.

Take Short Breaks during the day:

I've found a five-minute break every two hours or so is all I need to recharge my batteries. I stand, stretch and go for a brief walk, either through the office or outside in the open air. An alternative is a power nap, ten minutes maximum may help you combat the early afternoon drowsiness and give you an energy boost to get you through the rest of your day. You'll find plenty of valuable advice online about power napping, but my personal preference is always for the five-minute walkabout!

End of Workday Shut Down Routine

These steps will underwrite your capacity to de-stress and disconnect from your workday with a view to ensuring those you care about see the best version of you when you arrive home:

- ✓ Do a late day final email check and record any new commitments for the next day's dairy schedule.
- ✓ Tidy your desk. Close out and back up all your e-files.
- ✓ Build a bridge between work and home by penning a few late-day notes in your personal immersion journal.
- ✓ Every day, commit to *sharing a good slice of affection, enthusiasm and positive energy with those you care about at home, even after the most stressful of work days.*
- ✓ Do *a quick shut-down meditation*: take 15 to 20 very deep circular breaths in through your nose, holding each for three to four seconds, then exhaling out through your mouth while you shut out thoughts of your workday, then
- ✓ Consciously disconnect from work as you turn off the lights and leave.

On Your Way Home

Reinforce your disconnect from work by using this time well to think through matters of importance to those you care about most. During my career, I pretty much always called Leslie as I was driving out of my work carpark to let her know I was on my way home and for us to have a chat about what had happened during our respective days. I called my Mum at least once a week – those calls usually lasted for the entire trip home! I let most incoming calls go to the message bank unless I had been waiting for some critical end-of-day information.

Ban the *Bull Shit* Bag

Despite following my substantially productive time management system, my Bullshit Bag was the enduring Achilles' heel I just couldn't let go of. I took it home most nights for the first two decades of my career. My Bullshit Bag was weighing me down because I religiously tipped in the end-of-day remaining contents of my pre-internet-era in-tray that required my attention. I rarely got through more than a handful of those jobs at home, so all it gave me was a guilty conscience and less precious time with my family. I even carried a Bullshit Bag on my Interstate and Overseas trips, which typically incorporated my accumulated learnings and observations while away.

In the late 1980s, on a US business trip, I had an unplanned but fortuitous catch-up with Stephen R. Covey in an East Coast airport lounge. Steve and I were sitting at adjoining tables, both waiting for flights to be called. When he saw my over-loaded briefcase sitting beside my chair, he nodded towards it and said something like: 'Looks like you're a busy fella'. He smiled politely when I told him it was my Bullshit Bag. Stephen told me he had an academic interest in effectiveness literature, and in our brief time together, he gave me some incredibly valuable advice. His flight was then called and we said our farewells. The internet was just a vague idea to most in the business world back then, and Google was still more than a decade away from becoming a reality, so all I knew about Stephen was that he was a business consultant and academic from Utah. Yet his on-point advice about better managing the personal expectations I placed on myself and better balancing my life choices was priceless.

And soon after that, I substantially ditched my Bullshit Bag!

Postscript: While walking through a Sydney bookstore several years later, I saw *The 7 Habits of Highly Effective People* on a new releases book stand and only then registered that the author was the same Stephen R. Covey I had met at that airport in the US!

Chapter 22: Priorities & Time

"Eisenhower's job was not easy... He commanded the largest multinational force ever assembled, mounted an unprecedented cross-Channel invasion of Europe, mastered logistical problems on a scale never before encountered and came to grips with a battle-hardened German Army fighting on familiar terrain..."

Jean Edwards Smith, Eisenhower in War and Peace, Random House, 2013.

As Supreme Allied Forces Commander, five-star general Dwight D. Eisenhower oversaw the Normandy D-Day invasion, drove Germany's post-war reconstruction, was the first supreme commander of NATO, and from 1953 he served two terms as US President.

The immense challenges he faced in those diverse roles led him to adopt the famous *important/ urgent* rule that had been followed for many years by his good friend, Dr. J. Roscoe Miller, president of North-Western University.

In his address to the Century Association a year after he stepped down from his second presidential term, Eisenhower made the following thoughtful observation:

> *Who can define the difference between the long and the short term! Especially when our affairs seem to be in crisis, we feel most compelled to give our first attention to the urgent present, rather than the important future.*

Eisenhower's *long-term/ short-term* and *important/ urgent* leadership philosophy was to personally focus on his most important tasks while not allowing any of them to reach the stage of becoming urgent, to delegate the less important tasks, and to eliminate the zero value time wasters that were neither important nor urgent.

Eisenhower's *Crusade in Europe: A Personal Account of World War II.* (Double Day Penguin Random House, 1951); and Jean Edwards Smith's: *Eisenhower in War and Peace* (Random House, 2013) relates how Ike applied his urgent/ important decision-making methodology to balance and manage his immense priorities and achieve the best possible outcomes through his life.

I was initially inspired by my mother's habit of keeping a diary and updating her prioritised *to-do lists* every morning of her life. Mum had inherited those habits from her father, who was Managing Director of one of Sydney's large corporates during World War 2, while also having a significant role to play in guiding Australia's small arms munitions contribution to the British Empire.

Although I never met him, my Swedish grandmother, Mormor, loved to tell me stories about Grandpa's life journey, his obsession with following strict routines and habits and grading his priorities according to their *Relevance and Importance*. Mormor assured me those habits and rules were followed at home, as they were by my mother during my sisters and my formative years!

I saw the bare bones of those time management disciplines as a logical starting point for me when I first entered the workforce, and they served me well, particularly when I moved into my mid-career senior leadership roles. I added my complementary *daily personal immersion journal* after attending the Columbia University Program in New York in 1987 and progressively included the other initiatives I've presented in this series of chapters. My time management system also incorporated the embedded disciplines that accompanied the *internet, outlook, email* and *e-diary* capabilities when they started seriously going mainstream in the business world in the mid to late 1990s. Ian has also added many valuable elements to that system.

The SME Priority Planner

The typical SME principal hardly needs reminding that there are never enough hours in any day, nor enough staff on board to do every job. The smartest ones also realise early in their journey that while finding a way to do things faster and more efficiently in isolation may increase output, it won't necessarily solve their broader workload prioritising challenges.

SME Leadership: The 5 Critical Success Factors

The fact is that grading tasks according to their *importance, relevance,* and *urgency* while also mustering the courage to reject those activities that don't add material value to the business is the only sustainable tactic that can possibly allow them to stay on top of their most important jobs.

Our *SME Priority Planner* (Figure 22.1) is a template for grading those Priorities, supported by disciplined work habits and routines, a commitment to programming and prescheduling every facet of the day and of adopting the Time Management System Ian and I have prescribed in this series of CSF 4 chapters.

When you live by this System, I guarantee your days will be more productive, you'll get most of the important things done and you'll consistently take positive steps forward.

Your top priority as an SME principal must be to:

- Retain an experienced bookkeeper or a finance experienced staff or family member to manage all day-to-day *accounting and statutory obligations,*

- Appoint an external tax accountant to guide you on your higher order annual tax and statutory responsibilities,

- Place your personal financial focus on *the financial performance metrics* that will guide you in achieving the best possible outcomes,

- Commit your major time focus to *the Front-Line* income and profit-generating activities because your most important asset is your customer base and your capacity to grow revenues from their patronage.

Urgent tasks and deadlines that are *important and relevant* should preferably be dealt with long before they hit the crisis point.

For back-office priorities, including supply chain management and operational support, the focus is on delegating, automating, and digitising those activities to the maximum degree possible.

Place an A3 copy of the SME Priority Planner (included in your Essentials downloadable Toolkit (Appendix ii) in a prominent position adjacent to your work desk and commit to managing all your priorities in order of their importance.

SME Leadership: The 5 Critical Success Factors

SME PRIORITY PLANNER

MOST IMPORTANT

FRONT LINE PRIORITIES
- The Front Line – Business Planning, Sales, Revenues and Networks
- Growth, Profitability, Cashflow, and Financial Metrics
- Community Engagement
- Supply Chain Performance
- Planning, Strategy and Vision Clarification
- A Mindful "Look Across The Valleys" at future business opportunities
- Team Leadership

PRIORITY LEVEL 1
Knowing that your most important asset is your customer base.

THE FINANCIAL PRIORITIES
- Bookkeeping and Financial Reporting
- Payroll and HR Admin
- Cash Flows, Debtors and Creditors
- Statutory Obligations and Risk Management

PRIORITY LEVEL 1
Ensuring all financial records and reporting are up to date

DEADLINES, PROBLEMS & URGENT TASKS
- Dealing with deadlines and crisis' as they happen
- Timely action on important tasks that are sitting in someone's "too hard basket"

PRIORITY LEVEL 1
Dealing with important tasks **before** they become urgent.

IMPORTANT

BACK OFFICE PRIORITIES
- Supply Chain Management
- Operations and Administration
- Technology and Automation
- Back Office Processes

PRIORITY LEVEL 2
Delegate, Automate, or Digitise all processes and tasks to the maximum degree possible. Keep **Must Do** manual processes **to a minimum.**

NOT IMPORTANT

THE ZERO VALUE TIME WASTERS
THE SYMPTOMS
- Too much time spent on low value tasks and outcomes
- Undisciplined time consuming meetings with no outcomes
- Minimal evidence of good habits and routines
- Poor time management disciplines and too many unscheduled tasks
- Undisciplined, rule free email habits
- No policies on social media and personal phone calls
- Constant shifting of routine tasks
- An entrenched culture of procrastination and bureaucracy

PRIORITY LEVEL ZERO
- Adopt a team based culture of blocking out non value time wasters
- Adopt a team 'code of conduct'

Figure 22.1

Chapter 23: Front-Line Time Management

SMEs come in all shapes and sizes and differ from industry sector to industry sector. Our SME Time Management System adapts well to a broad range of businesses. In larger SMEs, this system may also be followed by multiple team members.

Aim for the time-positive metrics that only emerge when you plan and schedule your most important priorities every day. There's a definite slice of magic in the time you will save by scheduling your day, week and month to the maximum degree possible. In not having to rely on your fragile SME principal's memory, you will undoubtedly eliminate the mountain of stress that goes hand in hand with constantly having to *chase your tail*.

Following this system should be liberating to you and everyone in your team.

The Ground Rules

Use the SME Priority Planner (Figure 22.1) to categorise and schedule all priorities.

Exercise discretion grading every task, especially when there are more jobs than you and your team can handle in any one day.

Beware the risk of unreasonably overloading your team.

Commit to acting on your priorities and rejecting activities that don't add value, AND MOST IMPORTANT, eliminate *the zero-value time wasters*.

Ban bureaucracy and procrastination.

Nurture a dedicated team, all willing to bear their fair share of the workload.

The Principal's Time Management System

1. Know Your Time Availability Boundaries:

For businesses that trade five days a week, there are 19 to 22 weekdays in the average month, excluding public holidays. SMEs in the retail and hospitality sectors tend to be open an additional one to two days a week.

The principal's assumed time on site each day is typically 9 to 11 hours, depending on what time you arrive and leave work.

Take advantage of the four weeks from mid-December to mid-January when many people in the business world take a break and, importantly, when selling opportunities are limited. Use that time wisely to catch up on business planning, budget review and any overdue tasks. But also take a decent slice of those days as leave time with those you care about.

About the Principal's Annual Leave plans: It's important to take scheduled leave breaks away from the business. If staffing constraints or personal circumstances don't justify at least a two-week break each year, consider the following alternative options:

- If you have school-aged children, take several three to four-day long weekends during their school vacations.
- Take several long weekend breaks throughout the year.
- If your business trades 7 days, take at least one of those days away from the business, leaving a senior team member in charge.

2. Schedule Your Must-Do Front-Line Tasks:

All regular business priorities should be automatically diarised as *recurring commitments*. Start by gridding out a typical month with all the things you know you must get done.

Extract a summary from the front-line categories in the *SME Priority Planner* (Figure 22.1). Those priorities include customers and revenues; selling, networking and community engagement; reviewing profitability, cash flows and financial performance; vision, strategy and business planning; quality reading and research time; supply chain performance; and team leadership.

SME Leadership: The 5 Critical Success Factors

Allocate each front-line activity into daily, weekly, monthly, ongoing, and annual tasks. *An example of those tasks may be*:

DAILY:
- *Your* Pre-*Work Daily Review Routine at home*: personal immersion journal reflections, review of the daily journal commitments, and check your accounting software *dashboard* update of cash flows, bank balances, debtors & creditors and other financial data important to you.
- Regular time slots for managing by walking about.

DURING YOUR WORKING WEEK:
- CRM business pipeline review and sales meetings held even when the sales team is just the principal and/ or a business partner – *allow one to two hours.*
- Review back-office priorities and tasks – *allow an hour.*
- Reading, planning & strategies – *allow three hours* a week.
- Selling, networking and community engagement, including business entertaining, your sales plan and accompanying CRM data will dictate the time blocks you need for these activities, but Allow at least two to three blocks of *six hours per week.*

MONTHLY:
- Review with your bookkeeper the monthly financial statements, performance metrics, cash flows, risk management, supply chain performance, and return lodgement payment due dates for statutory compliance obligations – *allow two hours.*
- Business projects review – *allow one to two hours.*
- Chamber of commerce, Rotary, and other similar community meetings.

ONGOING:
- Speaking engagements and/or conferences.

- Periodic meetings with bankers, accountants and others.

ANNUAL:

- Tax time obligations with your tax accountant – allow several days.
- Annual budget reviews/ resets with your bookkeeper – allow 3 to 5 days.
- Staff performance reviews – *allow at least one hour for each review.*

3. Forward Diarise and track your Front-Line Tasks:

- Lock into your diary each of those commitments and others you know you need.
- Allow sensible time gaps between each commitment to allow for time overruns.
- Progressively fine tune those diary commitments over a two to three-month period until you know you can get everything done with time to spare.
- When you are satisfied, formally lock them in as recurring commitments, diarised at least three months in advance.
- Know that being diligent about following the ongoing diary planning routines will underwrite your success.

4. Ongoing Diary Planning Disciplines:

The required resources:

- *For the* Monthly Diary Plan: Open your electronic diary screen with a full month's view.
- For the Weekly Diary Plan: a one-page printout of the next week (Monday through Friday) to include notes and workdays columns in the print menu.
- For the Daily *Diary Plan:* a one-page printout of your diary for the day, to include *notes* in the print menu.

The Monthly Diary Plan

- Make sure all your important recurring commitments are already diarised.

- Add any important additional priorities as needed.

- Ensure scheduled front-line tasks are spread throughout the month. Other important tasks or projects that crop up progressively can be allocated to unfilled time spaces.

The Weekly Diary Plan

- Every Monday morning, review the plan for the next 5 days with your weekly diary printout beside you.

- Double-check that this week's recurring commitments are already scheduled, together with the time you'll need to complete each of them.

- Note down other important tasks and projects that have since cropped up.

- Avoid overloading any one day. It's fine to shift recurring front-line or other tasks to another day, provided there's a good reason to do so.

- Include family/personal commitments in your plan that will occur during workdays.

- Update your diary with any changed priorities.

- Keep your week*ly diary printout* on your desk for the entire week as a reference point to jot down any moving priorities that emerge or new ones that need to be added.

- Let your partner know in advance about any planned *long days* or business trips away during your work week.

The Daily Diary Plan

Your Pre-Work Diary Routine at home:

- Jot down in your personal immersion journal how you went with yesterday's tasks and how could you have done better? Then mentally rehearse your ideal outcomes for each of today's diarised tasks. Then carry out the other routine Journal Reviews summarised in Chapter 18.

- Lock in any late changes to your diary for the day.

- Scan your accounting software *dashboard* and note any required follow-up actions with your bookkeeper.

The Business Projects:

Record and track your major strategic and operational projects by setting up a Microsoft Excel spreadsheet titled *Business Projects* in the following format:

PROJECT TITLE	TASKS	WHO	DUE DATE
1.	• • •		
2.	• • •		
3.	• • •		

Figure 23.1

The spreadsheet accommodates most SME projects, except those with multiple time-dependent tasks (e.g., building & construction sector projects). The current version of Excel includes excellent timeline templates, including Gantt Chart capability.

Be wary of taking on too many live projects at any one time.

SME Leadership: The 5 Critical Success Factors

Weekly Agenda Review Example

📅 Calendar

September								October						
M	T	W	T	F	S	S		M	T	W	T	F	S	S
28	29	30	31	1	2	3		25	26	27	28	29	30	1
4	5	6	7	8	9	10		2	3	4	5	6	7	8
11	12	13	14	15	16	17		9	10	11	12	13	14	15
18	19	20	21	22	23	24		16	17	18	19	20	21	22
25	26	27	28	29	30	1		23	24	25	26	27	28	29
2	3	4	5	6	7	8		30	31	1	2	3	4	5

Monday, September 04
- 05:30 - 06:30 ↻ Read Papers check Markets
- 06:30 - 06:45 ↻ AM Journal
- 07:00 - 07:15 ↻ Weekly work plan
- 09:00 - 09:10 ↻ Daily cash flow review
- 11:00 - 11:30 ↻ Weekly Back Office Review
- 17:30 - 17:45 ↻ PM Journal

Tuesday, September 05
- 05:30 - 06:30 ↻ Read Papers check Markets
- 06:30 - 06:45 ↻ AM Journal
- 07:00 - 07:15 ↻ Day plan
- 09:00 - 09:10 ↻ Daily cash flow review
- 10:00 - 16:00 ↻ Networking & Sales
- 17:30 - 17:45 ↻ PM Journal

Wednesday, September 06
- 05:30 - 06:30 ↻ Read Papers check Markets
- 06:30 - 06:45 ↻ AM Journal
- 07:00 - 07:15 ↻ Day plan
- 09:00 - 09:10 ↻ Daily cash flow review
- 14:00 - 15:00 ↻ Projects & Strategy Review
- 15:00 - 17:00 ↻ Reading, Planning & Strategy
- 17:30 - 17:45 ↻ PM Journal

Thursday, September 07
- 05:30 - 06:30 ↻ Read Papers check Markets
- 06:30 - 06:45 ↻ AM Journal
- 07:00 - 07:15 ↻ Day plan
- 09:00 - 09:10 ↻ Daily cash flow review
- 10:00 - 16:00 ↻ Networking & Sales
- 17:30 - 17:45 ↻ PM Journal

Friday, September 08
- 05:30 - 06:30 ↻ Read Papers check Markets
- 06:30 - 06:45 ↻ AM Journal
- 07:00 - 07:15 ↻ Day plan
- 09:00 - 09:10 ↻ Daily cash flow review
- 17:30 - 17:45 ↻ PM Journal

Saturday, September 09

Sunday, September 10

Figure 23.2

SME Leadership: The 5 Critical Success Factors

Daily Agenda Review Example

📅 Calendar

Wednesday, September 06

■ **Read Papers check Markets**
Wed 06/09   05:30 - 06:30

■ **AM Journal**
Wed 06/09   06:30 - 06:45

■ **Day plan**
Wed 06/09   07:00 - 07:15

■ **Daily cash flow review**
Wed 06/09   09:00 - 09:10

■ **Projects & Strategy Review**
Wed 06/09   14:00 - 15:00

■ **Reading, Planning & Strategy**
Wed 06/09   15:00 - 17:00

■ **PM Journal**
Wed 06/09   17:30 - 17:45

Figure 23.3

Chapter 24: Financial Time Management

Your first must-do decision is to access cloud-based accounting software. Next hire an experienced bookkeeper or allocate that responsibility to a staff member who knows your preferred accounting software solution. It may only be a part-time/casual role or a family member if yours is a micro-business. For large SMEs, a qualified accountant may oversee your books of account.

Your bookkeeper can manage the day-to-day finances using the accounting software to automate most of the financial transactions. This includes the debit credit and double entry bookkeeping entries; building the general ledger and chart of accounts; production of a full set of monthly financial statements; balancing e-commerce software platform transactions; reconciling the bank accounts; extracting financial KPIs; producing compliant tax invoices; GST, sales tax; small business payrolls; debtors and creditors; and meeting statutory compliance obligations with state revenue agencies.

Consider the logical case for also giving your bookkeeper first-line oversight responsibility for the remaining non-financial aspects of the back office (Chapter 25). This supervisory approach often suits smaller SMEs with less than 20 employees on board. I can think of no circumstance that could justify the principal managing these tasks directly, as it would lessen the time they have available to spend generating revenue and managing the other front-line priorities.

The core decisions you make about managing your back office will have a direct impact on your capacity to grow the business. That said, the principal and bookkeeper/ accountant should be metaphorically joined at the hip.

The Bookkeeper's Time Management System

Although the finances diary management commitments are extensive, they are driven substantially by following the automated disciplines that are embedded in the accounting software platform you use.

The Must-Do Tasks

Similar to the front-line time management system, financial priorities should be diarised in advance as recurring commitments. The starting point is to grid out a typical month with the responsibilities you know must be done. Those priorities can be found in the finances chapters and may include:

The recurring daily must-do bookkeeping responsibilities:

- Preparing compliant tax invoices (in larger SMEs, this responsibility may be delegated to someone else on the team).
- Reconciling outstanding items from the daily bank account downloads.
- Allocating debtor repayments to the relevant accounts receivable accounts.
- Following up on overdue debtors.
- Paying creditors by their due date.
- Maintaining a daily updated predictive cash flow for the business.
- Alerting the principal as soon as unexpected cash flow shortfalls emerge.

Pay run responsibilities. Check that:

- Payrolls are completed by the due date (often fortnightly for SMEs).
- Timesheets have been completed by all employees.
- Employees receive a pay slip every pay run.
- Tax file declarations have been completed as required on all new employees.
- Awards: ensure the business is award compliant.
- If the business has a registered workplace agreement, ensure the business complies with that agreement.
- Employee entitlements are automatically updated every pay run.
- Workers Compensation Policy: is paid and up to date.

- Payroll tax is payable once wages exceed the relevant threshold cap for each state. Know what those thresholds are. If they are reached, project the liability, alert the principal and:
  - Complete a payroll tax lodgement return to state treasury (monthly).
  - Pay the state treasury remittance amount by the due date (monthly).
- Remit superannuation/pension deductions to the relevant funds.
- Check that employee income tax deductions have been remitted to the relevant tax authority by the due date.

Other Statutory Obligations: Consult with your tax accountant to confirm the obligation cycles, dates and required actions

Workplace Health & Safety: make sure the business meets WHS obligations.

Schedule brief weekly meetings with the principal to confirm that all the relevant back-office priorities and tasks are up to date.

Download full financial reports, risk management reports and supply chain reviews for the principal's monthly financial performance meeting.

Periodic meetings with bankers and other professional advisors.

Some commitments may also be listed as projects if your commitment requires a full loan or other submission in preparation for the meeting.

Annual tax time information to your tax accountant as required.

Work on annual financial year forward budgets with the principal.

Diarise and Track the Financial Tasks

- Lock into your diary each of those commitments and any others you need.
- Allow sensible time gaps between each commitment to allow for time overruns.
- Progressively fine-tune those diary commitments over a two to three-month period until you know you can get everything done with time to spare.
- When you are satisfied, formally lock them in as recurring commitments, always diarised at least three months in advance.
- Finally, be disciplined about following the ongoing diary planning disciplines.

The Ongoing Diary Planning Disciplines

The required resources:

- For the Monthly Diary Plan: Open your electronic diary screen with a full month's view.
- For the Weekly Diary Plan: a one-page printout of the next week to include notes and workdays columns in the print menu.
- For the Daily Diary Plan: a one-page printout of your diary for the day, to include notes in the print menu.

The Monthly Diary Plan

- Make sure all your recurring commitments are already diarised.
- Add any important additional priorities as needed.
- Ensure all scheduled financial tasks are sensibly spread throughout the month. Other important tasks or projects that crop up progressively can then be allocated to vacant time spaces.

The Weekly Diary Plan

- Every Monday morning, review the plan for the next 5 days with your weekly diary printout beside you.
- Double-check that this week's recurring commitments are already scheduled, together with the time you'll need to complete each of them.
- Note down other important tasks and projects that have since cropped up.
- Avoid overloading any one day. It's fine to shift recurring front-line or other tasks to another day, provided there's a good reason to do so.
- Update your diary with any changed priorities.
- Keep your weekly diary printout on your desk for the entire week as a reference point. Jot down brief notes and follow-up actions as moving priorities come to mind or new ones are added.

The Daily Diary Plan

- Lock in any urgent or late changes to your daily tasks.
- As a bookkeeper, you should maintain your own Personal Immersion Journal. Jot down how you went with each of yesterday's tasks and how could they have done better? Mentally rehearse your ideal outcomes for each of today's diarised tasks. Then carry out the other routine Journal Reviews summarised in Chapter 19.
- Keep the diary clear of any other tasks or commitments on payroll set-up days if you have more than 10 employees on the team.

Chapter 25: Managing the Back Office

From our experience, a significant slice of back-office processing in most SMEs cuts a trail back to how your finances are managed. That's why we recommend allocating day-to-day oversight responsibility of the back-office tasks to the person who does your bookkeeping, as a first point of reference.

Automating the back office is about managing time efficiently and removing unnecessary bottle necks. Consider the compelling argument for automating all non-financial repetitive tasks to the maximum degree possible and delegating those tasks that cannot be automated. When these aspects are handled well, productivity improves out of sight, and individual jobs become less stressful and more meaningful.

Delegation

The number one rule of delegation is DELEGATE, DON'T ABDICATE.

Treat Delegation as an extension of your own responsibility, not something you just give away without retaining accountability. The golden rule for the delegator is to consistently mentor, train, guide, delegate, and then follow up in that continuous five-step rotating loop. Also, make a commitment to manage by walking about (MBWA) to observe, give feedback, offer advice and support your team.

The Benefits of Delegation

Good delegation increases and expands the employees' knowledge, experience and skills. As a result, they feel more engaged, valued, trusted and motivated.

For the principal, good delegation creates a stronger and more resilient business. It empowers your team and is a valuable adjunct to succession planning and is important in identifying and mentoring your pool of potential future leaders.

Do Delegate: when there is too much work to get through, for small recurrent routine jobs, separate tasks related to long-term projects, and any jobs an experienced subordinate is capable of handling.

Don't Delegate: when the staff member doesn't have the requisite skills or capacity to do the job, when they are overloaded, or if they are already dealing with other pressing priorities.

When it's better to 'ask for forgiveness than permission'.

If the boss has to be away for an extended period of time, who takes charge? If it's something significant that needs resolution, call the boss for advice on how to handle it. When it's not, the most competent team member should be given standing authority to deal with it.

The better SME principals I have observed pre-plan for their absences, but the principal must always be contactable to deal with significant matters.

The 'Bless me, Father, for I have sinned' scenario may be a get-out-of-jail card when someone in the team knows the boss has their back if they decide to act outside their delegated authority. It's a great learning medium for emerging leaders in any business. But it only works when the principal believes in their delegatee and is prepared to back them.

The Completed Staff Work Method of Delegation

Former US Secretary of State, Henry Kissinger was a famous early proponent of the *Completed Staff Work Method* and found it to be a key to managing his vast competing priorities. On being offered a solution by one of his minions, Kissinger's standard first line mentoring question was: *Is this the best you can do?* If there was a moment of hesitation or the answer was *No*, he would provide wise counsel, then politely tell the person to take it away and not to return until they were convinced of their own arguments.

When you believe an experienced staff member could benefit from assisting you with the research and groundwork on important higher-level projects, follow the disciplines of *The Completed Staff Work Method*.

The team member should be advised up front that they are required to carry out <u>all</u> the essential subject matter research to a high standard. They should consider and analyse all the alternative solutions, rank each option in order of preference and only then come forward with their final recommendation.

As a talent pool evaluator for future promotion potential, Completed Staff Work is in my view second to none.

Management by Walking About (MBWA)

St. George Bank House in Kogarah, NSW, was officially opened in the early 1990s. One of the largest corporate buildings in Sydney's southern suburbs at that time, it had a vast ground floor atrium with seven head office floors encircling it all the way to the top floor board room and executive offices. During construction, outgoing managing director, Fred Shield, had argued tongue in cheek that there should be no elevators or lifts in the building and that climbing seven flights of stairs would do us all good! My senior team colleagues and I breathed a sigh of relief when our architects confirmed planning rules would not allow that exclusion for a 7 story building. After that, our grand headquarters became affectionately known as *Fred's Shed*!

A couple of months after we moved in, Fred, who had, by then, transitioned to a non-executive directorship of the bank, popped in to see me one morning. He asked if I would agree to clearing a full day in my diary each month with a view to walking through every head office department and listening to what everyone had to say! He confirmed that new Managing Director Jim Sweeney liked the idea of me taking on that role. I already knew this task was Fred's version of Management by Walking About (MBWA) because he had been doing it for many years at our previous corporate headquarters in Hurstville.

The bank's much-loved General Manager of Marketing, Jack Gearin, joined me on those monthly walkabouts prior to his retirement. The bush telegraph was always productive on those days, and we were invariably greeted with morning teas and warm welcomes. It was a good opportunity to reinforce that we cared, but we invariably unearthed issues we were being shielded from as an executive team.

An integral component of an SME principal's regularly scheduled habits is the practice of MBWA. It's an opportunity to address any personal concerns with individual team members and to ask if there are any projects or other responsibilities, they would like to be involved in. Always jot down notes in your personal immersion journal after those meetings and be consistent in following up on anything that requires resolution.

Authors Note: Around the time I commenced my monthly walkabouts through St George Bank's new headquarters, I purchased a small *Phillips Voice Tracer* Dictaphone (which I still have today!) to track my *through the day* thought bites and capture matters requiring specific follow up. I quickly found this strategy complemented my Daily Personal Immersion Journal routine, eliminating the stress of trying to remember everything.

Automate and Digitise

In January 2017, McKinsey Consulting released its global study titled: *Introducing the Next Gen Operating Model*. The focus was on harnessing the capabilities of the digital economy, automating back-office processes and placing the customer experience and innovation at the heart of the business and what it does.

There are now clear opportunities at every business level to automate recurring back-office processes and to adopt enabling technologies that streamline the way repetitive tasks are carried out. Some examples are:

- The significant benefits you'll gain by automating your accounting and financial management cycle with cloud-based accounting software.

- Using CRM software to track and manage the complete sales cycle. *Monday* and *Zoho* are my preferred CRM's.

- Converting filing cabinets to cloud-based storage.

- Maximising automation between the front and back office by better connecting team members with each other, constantly improving customer-facing activities and accelerating service response times. The objective should always be about streamlining customer service, so fulfilment, queries and responses are dealt with seamlessly.

- *Microsoft Office 365 Business Premium* offers valuable productivity tools for the SME including:
  - Personalised web and mobile versions of all Office apps: including Outlook, Word, Excel, Power Point and several other Office apps.
  - Hosted email / calendars: with a dedicated 50 gigabyte mailbox.
  - Your own customer domain name with emails for you and your team: e.g.:
    > your name@yourcompanyname.com, with added functionality to manage your calendar and share/schedule meeting information.
  - File storage and sharing: 1 terabyte of One Drive cloud storage capacity to share files with external contacts with guest links.
  - Full Microsoft Teams functionality: including the capacity to host online meetings and video conferences with up to 300 users and to chat with your team members from your desktop/ laptop.
  - Plus, a raft of compliance and security protection and other useful features.

Google Workspace is also a popular business software solution. Its business options package is similarly priced and offers some similar functionality to Microsoft (including Gmail, Docs, Sheets, Slides and other office apps).

My preference is for Microsoft Office because it's the one most used by the SMEs I have dealt with and because I am personally more accustomed to it. Seek advice from your technology advisor if you are not sure which way to go and look out for other emerging technology solutions.

Be vigilant about tracking emerging technology. Many SME sectors are now able to access multiple automated solutions relevant to their needs.

Managing Supply Chain Efficiency

If your business is a wholesaler or manufacturer that transforms component raw materials or assembles separate product components through several production stages to ready-for-market end-products, then you will need to have disciplined supply chain management protocols and systems in place.

Investopedia defines supply chain management as the management of the flow of goods and services. It includes all processes that transform raw materials into final products. It involves the active streamlining of business process supply-side activities to maximize customer value, minimise production overheads, maximise speed to market, and gain a general competitive advantage in the marketplace.

For a retail business: confirm your wholesale suppliers are providing quality products at the quantities the business requires and that pricing is competitive. To do that, you must be constantly aware of what alternative suppliers can offer.

For wholesalers or manufacturers: map out and flow chart the entire supply chain and confirm at every link point that costs are minimised, production efficiencies and time to production are maximised, and external raw material or component suppliers are delivering quality products at competitive pricing.

Effective supply chain management should always result in:

- Maximum quality,
- Lowest aggregate costs,
- Shortest possible production cycle time,
- A superb end product.

Adopting Franchise Sector Initiatives

"Jeff didn't warm to the menial work, but he did learn some business lessons through direct observation, particularly about how speed could be achieved by automating processes. He watched the way orders, buzzers, friers and other machines were choreographed into ruthlessly efficient processes designed to remove any barriers between customers ordering their food and receiving it in their hands. McDonald's had taught him crucial early life lessons about customer service and customer focus."

Chris McNab, Jeff Bezos, 2022, Arcturus Publishing.

Ray Kroc's first franchised McDonald's store opened in 1955. Today, seven decades on, the numbers are staggering. McDonald's has 42,000 restaurants worldwide and is represented in 120 countries. They sell 100 hamburgers a second and feed over 70 million people each day, i.e., around 1% of the global population pulls into a McDonald's restaurant every day of the year.

There's a clear opportunity to apply some of the core franchising disciplines evident in the better Turnkey franchise systems that improve workflows and efficiencies. In my research, I drew heavily on American sociologist George Ritzer's: The McDonaldization of Society.

Ritzer quite cynically defined McDonaldization as a phenomenon that occurs when: society, its institutions, and its organisations are adapted to have the same characteristics that are found in fast food chains.

My positive take from Ritzer's work is in his validation that McDonald's success story is underpinned by four identifiable dimensions:

Predictability & Standardisation: customers always know exactly what they are going to get, i.e., the same menu, customer service, food quality, taste, mix of ingredients, product look, and appearance.

Calculability: franchisees can rely on McDonald's quantifiable outcomes, including predictable trading and operational overheads, and gross and net profit margins.

Efficiency: with a focus on consistently finding the fastest and lowest cost way to accomplish every task.

Control: employees follow standardised rules on food preparation, dress uniformity, customer service and upselling. The principal who owns the franchise agrees to follow McDonald's disciplined management system.

After reviewing a franchisedirect.com editorial titled: How has McDonald's been so successful for so long I've added a fifth dimension to Reitzer's list:

***Innovation & Continuous Learning*:** McDonald's continues to thrive because of its consistent approach to continuous learning and improvement. They have a well-earned reputation for listening and responding positively to both customers' and local managers/staff feedback. Innovations such as drive-through, McHappy meals, apple pies, McCafé's and McMuffin breakfast options all evolved in response to customer feedback.

Consider how you could adopt some or preferably all those five disciplines in your own business.

Computers Behaving Badly!

I bought my first *Tandy Radio Shack TRS 80* desktop computer in the late 1970s when I was working for the World Bank-funded Papua New Guinea Development Bank in Port Moresby, where I also had a weekly newspaper column and a Saturday morning radio program.

My Tandy computer came with a crude box-shaped black and white screen, a very basic keyboard, a dot matrix printer and a cassette tape recorder for backing up my editorials (MS-DOS and floppy discs were still several years away from release). Back in Australia in the mid-1980s, when I joined St. George Bank's Building Society forbear, I graduated to Apple Macs at home and later to IBM laptops. But with the advent of mainstream online computing in the business world not long before the turn of the century, I found it a lot harder to keep up at home!

At work, I had computer-savvy techies to look after me, but not so at home. So I called in my neighbour, Mark, whose company was quite aptly called *Computers Behaving Badly*! Mark serviced businesses of all sizes but also took on a small number of businesspeople who, like me had no idea how to fix their computer gear at home. With Mark's good counsel, my problems rapidly disappeared!

SME Principals don't need to be tech-savvy experts in dealing with their technology maintenance needs, nor is it necessarily productive use of their time. Your best bet is to access a good technology contractor. They can advise on any system problems and can also carry out necessary maintenance, performance reviews and assist with technology upgrades.

Chapter 26: Making Decisions

Disciplined decision-making is an important trait SME principals should master early in their journey. The basic mechanics are easy enough to grasp, but when the pressure is on, and priorities start mounting, the human brain tends to jettison objectivity all too easily.

Poor decisions invariably crop up because the alternative options have not been considered, important information and criteria have not been weighed, and the costs and benefits have not been adequately measured.

For the average SME, where staff numbers are limited, ultimate decision-making responsibility falls on the principal's shoulders. But there is a definite distinction between finite decision-making and task delegation. Delegated tasks invariably relate to back-office processes. The secret is to automate and/or digitise as much of the back office as possible, but in areas where that is not possible, delegate the responsibility to a competent team member.

Critical Decision-Making Considerations

Other than having primary responsibility for business strategies and tactics, the SME principal needs to personally make critical decisions that emerge from one or more of the following:

- The status quo assumptions the business operates under have changed and no longer hold true,
- There's been a marketplace shift in sentiment for a major product offering(s),
- Other factors, such as improved/ more efficient technology options and/ or to support a change in the way the business operates,
- New employee or capital equipment spends, or other net overhead increases.

Most critical decision-making models encapsulate a series of rational steps leading to a logical conclusion about the preferred

SME Leadership: The 5 Critical Success Factors

outcome. My 6-step model that follows, has served me well for many years:

1. In the simplest language, describe the issue that requires a solution.
2. Summarise what you believe are the logical alternative solutions.
3. Weigh up the pros and cons, the risks, benefits and costs, then rank the assumed best-case outcomes and consider any other factors that may influence each solution.
4. Do a basic cost-benefit and breakeven analyses[4] and decide which is your best solution.
5. Put together an implementation plan and timeline.
6. Track post-implementation outcomes and results and generate further actions/decisions as required.

From an example I gave in Chapter 7, a net additional employee will come on board at an annual salary of $60,000. You already know your gross profit margin is 40% (i.e., every $100,000 of sales produces a gross trading profit of $40,000). You can therefore deduce that you'll need an additional $150,000 (i.e., $150K X 40% = $60,000) of annual sales before that new staff member becomes cost neutral to the business.

Identical 'what if' analyses should also be applied to any non-personnel increases in planned operating expenditure. Make a well-educated guestimate of how long it will take to achieve the additional sales you need to cover those increases and be satisfied you are doing it for the right reasons. Ask yourself: Is the additional expense outlay justified??

---

[4] For all decisions that will result in an increase in overall overheads, get into the good habit of running breakeven analysis to extract what the true economic cost of the intended new outlay is going to be and to analyse what level of additional income you will need before the spend becomes profit/cash flow neutral. To run that analysis, you must first know your gross profit margin.

Too often, I have seen SMEs fall on hard times because they failed to run the true breakeven numbers before committing to such expenditure.

Dealing With Less Consequential Day-To-Day Decision Making

In the 1950s, Nobel Prize-winning scientist Victor Herbert Simon postulated that traditional human judgment and decision-making structures could be subject to limitations because of the time they take to reach a solution. On the back of Simon's hypothesis, Nobel Prize winners Daniel Kahneman and Amos Tversky, who were well known and regarded for their life work on the psychology of decision-making, coined the term Heuristics, from the Greek word Heuriskein, meaning to find, discover, devise, invent, get, gain, or procure.

In Kahneman's book, *Thinking Fast and Slow (2011)*, he addressed the dichotomy between two main time-influenced systems of decision-making:

System 1 decisions tend to be rapid, in the moment, instinctive, habitual, and sometimes impulsive and emotional. System 1 decisions draw heavily on Heuristic reasoning.

System 2 decisions are slower, more deliberate, rational and logical. They consciously weigh all the options with a focus on selecting an optimal outcome.

Well-known examples of System 1 Heuristic thinking are decisions deduced from *trial and error*, *rule of thumb*, or *an educated guess*. Heuristic problem-solving draws heavily on the depth of life experience of the decision maker in dealing with similar recurring problems.

A cold reality of the SME world is that some routine, low consequent decisions must be made on the run and, in need, draw on System 1 Heuristics. That's fine provided the process also incorporates a definite pause for you to consider if there are any other criteria you need to address before proceeding.

I recommend you persevere with the rigours of my 6-step Critical Decision-Making Model when making decisions that may have significant consequences for the business.

Chapter 27: The Organisation Structure

I don't know what the people needs are for each of my readers, but I can lay out for you my time-honoured building blocks that will help you design a people structure that works.

The organisation structure should consider the unique settings of your business and what drives its outcomes. The challenge is to clarify what you need to achieve to be successful and then to build your key people responsibilities around those needs. This requires a willingness to let your evolving and growing business needs define your structural evolution rather than letting the structure dictate those needs in isolation.

You'll know by now my consistent view that the primary driver is about maximising sales, generating revenue and elevating the customer experience to the highest priority because without customers, you have no business. The competing challenge for the typical SME is that there are rarely enough hours in any day, nor enough staff on board, to do every job.

The Stages of Small Business Evolution

In September 1987, I was fortunate to join a dinner at the Harvard Club in New York City at which noted US academics Neil C. Churchill and Virginia L. Lewis spoke about their famous study: *The Five Stages of Small Business Growth.* Their 5 stages are:

GENESIS ➔ *SURVIVAL* ➔ *SUCCESS* ➔ *EXPANSION* ➔ *MATURITY*

Genesis is about attracting your early customers, stepping out to deliver the products or services they want, and having enough cash reserves to ultimately reach the survival stage. It's very definitely a day-by-day proposition at this stage.

Survival is the stage when you've proven your business model is sustainable. The focus is about onboarding adequate sales and revenues to start generating consistent surpluses.

SME Leadership: The 5 Critical Success Factors

Success is the stage where the business is profitable month on month and year on year. The decision facing owners is whether to exploit the achievements to date and expand further or to keep the business as is, freeing up the owner to enjoy a more balanced lifestyle. Many SME principals happily remain at this stage and choose not to diversify.

Expansion is about consciously deciding to grow the business rapidly beyond its already current successful base and working out how to finance that growth.

Maturity arrives when the business has reached significant advantages and economies of scale and size, they have the available financial resources, and they are supported by sound managerial talent. They often become a formidable force in their marketplace, provided they can retain their entrepreneurial spirit. Some may even evolve into successful public corporations.

In the Churchill-Lewis model, each stage is characterized by an index of size, diversity and complexity defined in the context of five core leadership drivers:

- *Leadership style,*
- *Organization structure,*
- *Formal systems and enabling technology,*
- *Major strategic goals, and*
- *The owner's changing role in the business over time.*

For more information, Google, The Five Stages of Small Business Growth, Neil C. Churchill and Virginia L. Lewis (Harvard Business Review editorial May 1983). It's only about eight pages long and is still well worth the read.

Michael Gerber on Building a Structure That Works

Michael Gerber has written a series of bestselling books on what he calls The E-Myth, where he examines why many small businesses don't work and what to do about it. Gerber's analysis of the life cycle of a business from infancy to adolescent growing pains to a mature entrepreneurial perspective is excellent, as is his strongly held view that successful entrepreneurs should follow the philosophical habit of working ON the business rather than just IN the business.

Gerber suggests that if you are in an owner-operated business for the first time, you will soon find yourself having to compete with three diametrically competitive versions of yourself: the technician, the manager, and the entrepreneur. He presents his first E-Myth that just because you're skilled or good at doing something (i.e., *"a good technician"* in Gerber's lingo) doesn't guarantee you'll be able to translate that skill set into a successful journey in your own business.

In The E-Myth Revisited (Harper Collins, 1995), Gerber guides the aspiring business owner towards entrepreneurial mastery through the parable of a struggling bakery/ coffee shop principal called Sarah. He gives her homework each time he visits, and her business starts to evolve and grow as she follows his plan. The entire book is, if you like, a boot camp for Sarah in which Gerber teaches her (and the reader) how to stop being just a great technician (in Sarah's case, a good baker) and how to evolve and transition into becoming a seasoned entrepreneur.

In his final series of chapters, Gerber gives some valuable advice on how to build a small business that works supported by the management and people strategies to go with it.

The E-Myth Revisited is invaluable background reading for any SME principal.

About Individual and Collective Responsibilities

Productive teamwork in SMEs relies on a pragmatic level of shared responsibility, where every staff member has their own role to play and those tasks they share with the rest of the team. There are invariably several shared tasks that cannot justify the luxury of a dedicated specialist driving them. It may be as basic as rotating responsibility for answering incoming phone calls or greeting visitors to the business.

As the business expands and your customer base and bottom line grows, you may need to bring on more people to support that growth. Make sure you evaluate your people's responsibility jigsaw every time. Know what responsibilities will be specific to each new position and what roles can be shared.

Dealing With Bureaucracy

Don't let middle management substructures take hold at any stage of your business evolution. I may be sounding a little like a broken record here, but I always showed a preference for flat reporting lines where each team member has an 'individual' role plus collective 'team-based' responsibilities. When you allow territorial walls to grow around individual or specialist positions, they all too often become barbed wire fences with metaphorical no-trespassing signs all over them. If that happens, I guarantee your operating costs will go up with no relative increases in income. (Chapter 29: Managing Bureaucracy).

Employee Screening

The capacity to objectively identify a prospective employee's personality, skills and competencies, and their ability and willingness to work in a team-based environment, makes psychometric testing useful at the hiring stage to validate or challenge the employer's immediate observations and conclusions following a live interview. The fact is some people are experts at the fine art of outperforming in a job interview, overselling their strengths and underplaying their weaknesses. Referees can also be an unreliable means of validation, given that candidates usually provide testimonial sources from those they know will speak well of them.

In an SME where people resources are limited, and the need for team members to work together as a cohesive, productive working group is a critical success factor, you should consider using these valuable tools.

My two favoured screening sources are The Rogers Group for psychometric and team screening and Herrmann Brain's HBDI® Whole Brain thinking assessments for positively harnessing and capitalising on the different ways people prefer to put their brains to work.

The Rogers Group:

For decades, I have accessed The Rogers Group as the preferred supplier of a broad range of employee screening tests hosted on their high-security web platform. And they're still alive and strong today!

Herrmann Brain's HBDI®

The Herrmann Brain Dominance Instrument (HBDI®) is a powerful assessment tool that describes the degree to which we prefer to think in each of the four quadrants of the Ned Herrmann Whole Brain® Model. Those four preferences are:

The A Quadrant Left Brain Analyser with a preference for logical, analytical, quantitative and fact-based thinking.

The B Quadrant Limbic Brain Safekeeping Organiser with a preference for planning, organising and sequencing information.

The C Quadrant Limbic Brain Feeling Personaliser with a preference for the interpersonal, caring aspects of their thinking.

The D Quadrant, Right Brain Experimental Visualiser with an intuitive and holistic focus on synthesising and integrating.

As discussed in Chapter 15, I have had significant success accessing Herrmann's HBDI® as an aid to maximise sales team outcomes, but HBDI® is also a valuable tool for enhancing team dynamics, strategy development and innovative thinking.

My initial double dominance from the first HBDI® test I took in the US in the early 1990s was in Quadrants A & D, with a lesser mid-level dominance in C and a low score in B, not an uncommon result for the sort of senior executive posts I held over those years. Yet after I took the test and better understood what it measured, I found myself consciously exercising more empathy and understanding for those who were obviously dominant in Quadrant B! In a team-based environment, where I was invariably the senior member, I found an increased opportunity to respond to everyone's relative preference strengths, which invariably improved the quality of our debate. Opposite philosophical disagreements between team members, sometimes peppered with relatively high emotion, soon morphed into healthier *Constructive Contention* as all sides of the argument were given more equitable air space.

The HBDI® survey offers you and your team excellent strategies to enhance your thinking agility and shows you how to construct better mental habits on your journey towards becoming a more productive and complete leader. The collective learnings from the Herrmann team are that when you consciously engage all four HBDI® Quadrants, you'll get the opportunity to work in a larger playing field from which to draw your thinking.

As suggested in Chapter 15, Ned Herrmann and Ann Herrmann Nehdi's Whole Brain Business Book is a must have for any SME principal. Seriously consider the value also of accessing HBDI® screening for you and your SME team.

Roger's Psychometric tests and Herrmann's HBDI® product offerings are each unique in what they offer, and I comfortably endorse both without reservation. Their tests are 21st century digitally accessible and are only a phone call or gigabyte away anywhere within Australia for Rogers and Australia-wide and Internationally for HBDI®. The accompanying debriefs you get after these tests are incredibly valuable.

(https://www.rogersgroup.com.au, https://herrmann.com.au)

I recommend you get in touch with both organisations to discuss your needs. You'll get clear answers and a recommended roadmap to go forward. A good place to start with each of them is to book a test on yourself first!

Employee Induction

Give all new employees a full induction. Ensure they are warmly welcomed and introduced to the team on day one; they understand the job they have been hired to do, what their duties and responsibilities will be and how shared responsibilities operate. Always reinforce the cultural values that unite and drive your team and how you commit to each other. Someone from the team should act as a buddy during their early weeks on the job.

Just Make Things Happen!

My initial job at St. George Building Society before it converted to a Bank was to establish their consumer lending and credit card operating divisions, and they had already chosen Visa as their preferred credit card prior to my arrival. Several years later, when I visited Visa International at their San Mateo Headquarters, not far from San Francisco, I met a rather special senior team driving the business, which, like St. George, had been growing astronomically month on month in their early years.

We sat around their boardroom table as each executive member introduced themselves and told me what part of the business they were responsible for. But interestingly, there was minimal mention of formal job titles from any of the Visa team on that first pass. Even the CEO simply said with a lop-sided grin something like: *I just run the joint*! He then quite eloquently explained that, of course, they all had real titles and fancy business cards but that the decorum of displaying them was discouraged within headquarters because their brief as a senior team was to *strip away the formalities and hierarchies and just make things happen*. I had a memorable couple of hours with them. Our discussions were open and productive. We traded some good war stories and had a bit of fun along the way.

Visa International's egalitarian spirit reminded me of our similarly informal St. George Bank way of getting things done. Our senior team was driven by a collective mindset of getting on with it and just making things happen, and history would reflect that we were pretty good at doing just that. Interestingly, when I joined Rob Hunt's Bendigo Bank senior team a decade or so later, I rapidly discovered they were driven by a similar philosophy and mindset.

My point here is if fast growing corporations can cut through their traditional big business structural hurdles and formalities and can take that collaborative approach to getting important things done, then why shouldn't a successful SME do likewise? And I'm pleased to report I've often seen it happen. When problems need resolution and solutions must be found, many effective SME teams I've known simply scrum together around a table and hash out the details until they have their answer.

The Quest for a Workable Customer-Driven Structure

Before I nail down the nitty-gritty of structural design options, I would recommend the following standard pre-considerations:

- Don't overcomplicate your people's responsibilities with too much formality.
- Don't allow destructive departmental communication barriers to emerge.
- Add new people and skills only when and as you truly need them.
- Make sure everyone has a real job as well as a shared job with the team.
- Avoid overstated grand management titles – keep them simple.
- Narrativise three attitudinal and complementary leadership culture philosophies:
    - We are a *sleeves-rolled-up* team,
    - We are motivated by a *let's just get on with it* mindset,
    - We are at our best when we can *just make things happen*.

Engender in your team a community of like-minded and motivated people who are willing to live by these considerations.

In Chapter 22, I presented my SME Priority Planner (Figure 22.1), a template for grading business priorities according to their relative importance. It's about locking in your most important front office/ front-line priorities, hiring a competent bookkeeper to manage the finances and statutory obligations, systemising and automating the back-office priorities to the greatest degree possible and banning the zero-value time wasters. The SME Priority Planner will also guide your important structural decisions and divisions of responsibility as your team evolves and grows over time.

In the early stages of any SME's business operation, there will be several shared responsibilities, e.g., the principal may do most of the early selling. Sales support and customer service are handled by one person, and the bookkeeper or a financially competent staff member manages both the finances and the back office.

In the introduction to Chapter 15, I began by breaking down the supply chain hierarchy and addressing how businesses in each of those segments operate. The type of business you're in and where it fits in the hierarchy will influence the design of your front and back-office structures, who does what, and where your primary focus is in sourcing customers and generating revenues.

For example, in a fine dining restaurant, your significant sales weapon will be energised by your kitchen team and your front-of-house service team. The only way to consistently attract and grow your patronage is by delivering outstanding, beautifully presented food, quality beverages, and the best customer service. Your reputation will be enhanced by getting those primary building blocks right without fail, and by also harnessing the power of social media as your other key selling medium.

Strip down and gain clarity about what unique business generators drive the success of your business and create an organisation structure with an ethos that capitalises on those identified drivers.

The structural template that follows is a cut-and-paste master plan that starts with all the business roles you may need to cater for. It can then be trimmed to suit the needs of a micro-SME with less than five on the team right through to a large SME with over one hundred on board.

The template (Figure 27.1) has two components: The business structure and the monitoring and control framework.

SME Leadership: The 5 Critical Success Factors

The Generic Structural Template
THE CUSTOMER FOCUSED BUSINESS STRUCTURE

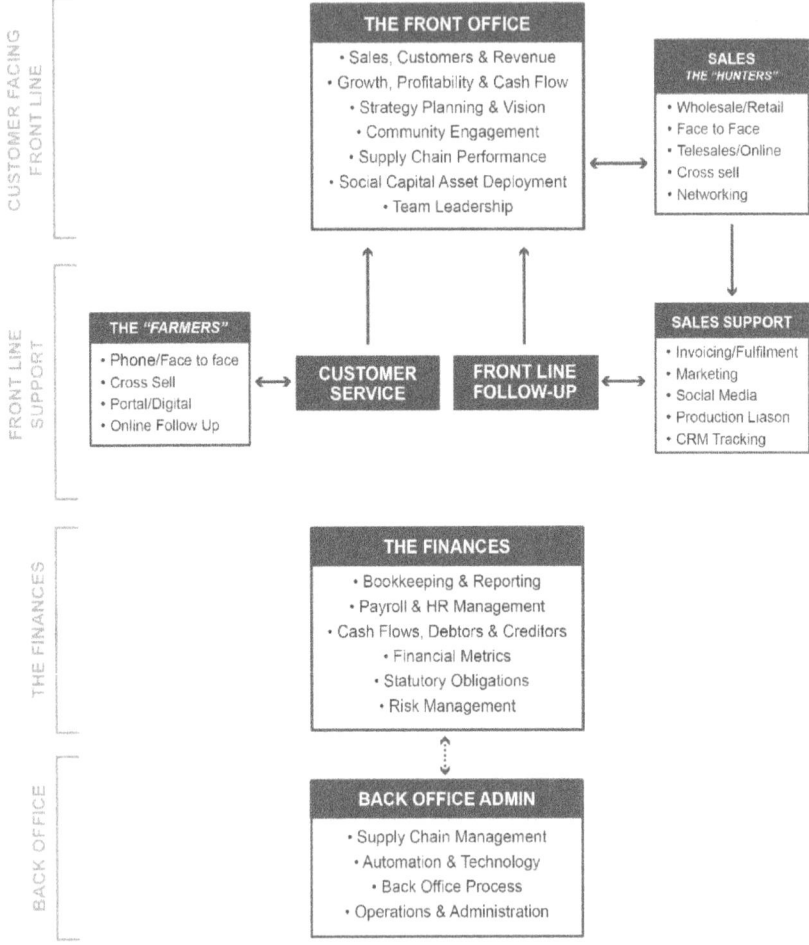

MONITOR & CONTROL FRAMEWORK

- Weekly Sales Meetings
- Monthly Financial Reviews
- Monthly Supply Chain Review
- Monthly Risk Management Review
- All Staff Meetings (As Required)
- Annual Staff Performance Reviews
- Day to Day "Management By Walking About" (MBWA)

Figure 27.1

The Business Structure

The Front-Line Includes:

The Front Office: sales, customers & revenues, growth, profitability & cash flows, strategy planning & vision, supply chain performance, networking & community engagement and your social capital asset deployment.

The Hunters: the sales team who source new customers.

The Front-Line Support team includes:

Sales Support: invoicing, fulfilment and product delivery, operations and production liaison, marketing and social media, and CRM tracking.

The Farmers: deal with aftersales customer service.

The Finance Tasks:

These tasks include bookkeeping, financial reporting, HR/payroll, statutory obligations, cash flows/debtors/creditors, financial performance metrics and risk management.

The Inwardly focussed Back Office Team includes:

The Non-Financial Tasks: production & supply chain management, automation/technology, back-office processes, operations & administration.

The customer-focussed organisation's structure assumes at its core that the workflow and back-office tasks are substantially managed on auto drive, maximising the time the principal can spend at the front line growing the business and its bottom line.

The Monitoring and Control Framework:

This step involves locking in standard meeting controls and follow-up protocols to ensure timely management and review of all aspects of the business.

Regular meetings locked into your diary are weekly sales meetings, monthly financial review meetings, monthly reviews of supply chain management, statutory compliance, risk management, staff performance reviews, all staff team meetings and day-to-day Management by Walking About (MBWA).

The Meeting Rules

The non-negotiable protocols are:

- An unambiguous agenda with time set aside for each item.
- Clearly defined expectations of what you want to achieve.
- Agreement on follow-up actions.
- The first item is an update on carry-forward items from previous meetings.
- Ban mobile phones and tablets.

Chapter 28: The Power of One

The Sole Trader

I'm consistently underwhelmed by the tendency to categorise sole traders as the poor cousins of the SME world. To me, these practitioners represent the proud community of courageous, hardworking entrepreneurs who account for a good percentage of the SME sector globally and who make a significant contribution to GDP. I hold them in the highest esteem and believe they are deserving of every bit of support we can throw their way.

The ranks of successful sole traders are traditionally dominated by subject matter specialists and artisans who have consciously chosen to be self-employed in their chosen profession. Examples include specialist business consultants, finance brokers, builders/property developers, beauty therapists, allied health therapists, building industry *tradies* (electricians, plumbers, carpenters/plasterers, painters, etc), small family run agricultural SMEs, landscape gardeners, mechanical repairers and so on.

In the previous chapter, I presented the Churchill-Lewis Five Stages of Small Business Growth model. Their evolutionary stages were identified as:

Genesis, Survival, Success, Expansion, and *Maturity.*

The Success stage emerges when the business is consistently generating adequate income and surplus cash flows to satisfy the needs of the owner and those they financially support at home. The decision they then face is whether to further expand or to keep the business as is, freeing them up to enjoy a more balanced lifestyle. Sole traders more often than not operate their business from a home office, and many receive at least some degree of support from family members and life partners.

A lot of sole trader principals quite happily choose to remain at that *Success Stage* and not to diversify further.

Managing their time and staying focussed are the perennial existential challenges for the sole trader. The common thread is their challenge to be relentlessly obsessive about how they pursue outcomes and get things done. As sole traders, they accept that the buck stops with them. As proof positive that necessity is the mother of invention, most of these people have a definite penchant for doing whatever it takes to survive and thrive.

Being relentless and doubling down on following and living by every aspect of the time management system we've laid out in the Critical Success Factor 4 chapters is vital if you are going to be successful as a sole trader. Most particularly, you should place your major focus on:

- Being obsessive about pre-planning and pre-scheduling every workday, week and month,
- Locking down disciplined work habits and routines.
- Constantly looking for the most productive way to get things done.
- Going out of your way to automate all repetitive tasks.
- Steering clear of unnecessary distractions during working hours.
- Not wasting your time doing things that don't contribute or add value to your business.
- Not multitasking. Instead, single tasking to get every important job done without distraction.
- Maintaining a daily personal immersion journal to track and guide you to better connect with the things that truly matter, to add clarity and substance to your values, visions, goals and actions, and to constantly challenge yourself to do better.

When you do these things well, you'll learn how to consistently:

- Turn hard work into smart work.
- Remain in control of every aspect of your workday.
- Gain back many valuable hours each week by automating productive work habits rather than having to rely on your memory.
- Gain the clear head space that will enable you, as principal, to focus on the income generating, big picture, growth and future-proofing business priorities that count.

CRITICAL SUCCESS FACTOR 5:

LEADERSHIP

'If your actions inspire others to dream more, do more and become more, then you are a Leader.'

John Quincy Adams, 6th United States President.

'True leaders who work most effectively never say "I". They say "we' and they think "team". They know their job is to make the team function. They accept responsibility and don't sidestep it, but "we" always gets the credit. This is what creates trust, and what enables you to get the task done.

Peter Drucker, famous 20th Century American business consultant.

SME Leadership: The 5 Critical Success Factors

Rapid changes in 21st century business leadership are being driven by an increasing emphasis on genuine collaboration and shared-value work cultures.

Jim Clifton and Jim Harter's 'It's the Manager' (The Gallop Press, 2019) has distilled three decades of Gallop Research Group workplace tracking that included millions of in-depth interviews of employees and managers across 160 countries. Their findings are summarised in 52 easy-to-digest leadership insights, spread across five subject matter headings: *Strategy, Culture, Employment Brand, Boss to Coach*, and *The Future of Work*. The last of these is represented below.

Gallop's most recent research found that millennials (born between 1980 and 1996) and Generation Z (born in 1997 or later) have disrupted how people communicate, read, write and relate.

The significant changes Gallop noted were:

1. *Millennials and Generation Z don't just want to work for a salary. They want a purpose:*
   Compensation is important to them, and it must be fair, but it's not their primary motivation. They want to work for an organisation with a clear mission and a defined purpose.

2. *They are no longer pursuing job satisfaction in isolation.*
   They are pursuing personal development: They care less about the bells and whistles and the fluff. They want the substance.

2. *They don't want a boss. They want a coach:*
   The old-style boss is driven by an outdated command and control mindset. They seek a modern leader who will help them grow and build on their strengths.

3. *They don't want annual reviews. They want ongoing dialogue:*
   This generation is hooked on instant communication via social media. Although still important, they know intuitively that once-a-year reviews can't work in

isolation. They also seek rolling communication and feedback so they can grow and learn incrementally.

4. *Globally, millennials and Gen Z have transformed the definition of what it means to have a great job.*
They're more tech-savvy and socially aware. They seek roles with a greater sense of purpose that offer meaningful learning opportunities and the potential to participate in a positive workplace culture.

By 2030, millennials and Gen Z will represent over 70% of people in full-time employment throughout the Developed World, but their positive influence on sustainable and collaborative styles of leadership is already being felt.

Chapter 29: The Leadership Basics

"If your actions inspire others to dream more, do more and become more, then you are a Leader."

John Quincy Adams, 6th United States President.

Some of you may be going through your maiden experience of being a fully accountable boss when you open your doors for the first time. Reinforcing positive goals and institutionalising consistent behaviour and actions from day one is a critical starting point.

From my leadership experience, when you treat your people fairly, show respect, give them encouragement and let them know when they do something well and tell them in positive terms how they could have done better, you will more often than not be rewarded with a stronger commitment to good performance. In creating a productive workplace, it's just so important to look for balance, sensible compromise and a good dose of seat-of-the-pants humanity. The bonus is your team will invariably become stronger.

However, I will always support the principal's right to remove any team member who is not truly committed to the business.

The Pre-hire Stage.

If you are new to your venture and still at the micro business stage, it may well be just you and perhaps a business or life partner and a part-time contract bookkeeper on your team. It's all sleeves rolled up, and it may seem like you are dealing with a million priorities at once.

It's in this micro business stage that your initial hirings are going to be so important to your early runs on the board. Take care to select people who are willing to seriously put in, who will complement rather than compete with your own skills and experience. Your new recruits must be energetic, driven, flexible and willing to bear their share of the workload.

Hiring Friends and Family

Take the greatest care if you are considering or indeed confronted with the pressure to hire friends or family members. You will need to ask yourself: *What if it doesn't work out or if times get tough? Am I willing to give them their marching orders?* If the answer is no, then my advice is do not hire them.

Your best approach is to be up front in laying out the possibility that the job may not be right for them, or the business may not be able to afford to keep them on board. Make it clear what the ramifications of such an outcome could be. Do not create false expectations and be clear that the job is not guaranteed because of the personal connection they have with you.

Ban the Annual Review!

And, of course, I don't mean that literally! But annual review time should be about the big picture, a review of the past year and constructive discussion about the forward objectives and challenges for the employee's position for the next 12 months. There should never be any shocks, surprises or *get even messages* saved up for those reviews.

Respectful, honest communication and feedback should occur every day, as and when it happens.

Annual reviews are best done on the anniversary date of each staff member's employment to spread the load through the year. Develop a standard review template all your team members can follow. You'll find plenty of good ones online.

The employee should initially complete their own self-assessment of their performance, their competencies, their contribution to the team and their overall achievements during the year in review. The principal discusses these comments with the employee, adding any additional observations, before having an open discussion and review of the position objectives for the year ahead.

Dealing With Negativity

St. George Bank acquired several large building societies in New South Wales and Victoria in the wake of the devastating Farrow

Pyramid Building Society collapse in Victoria in the early 1990s. It was a huge job integrating those businesses plus several others we had recently acquired.

We had bucket loads of experience in managing mergers & acquisitions and were pretty good at dealing with the usual jockeying for territory that tends to occur when you merge large companies and combine huge Headquarter departments and divisions that carry out virtually identical tasks.

But around that time, we were also seeing more negative blowback than usual. So we decided to tackle it at our second quarter 1992 managers' conference held in the main auditorium of the St. George Rugby Leagues Club, not far from our Southern Sydney Corporate Headquarters. Managing Director Jim Sweeney was at his usual best in clarifying our forward vision and painting a clear picture of what we had to achieve over the coming year. I followed Jim with some strategies about collaborative leadership and harnessing the power of positive thinking. I then finished off with a light-hearted take on the movie: *Network* where, like Peter Finch, I got all our managers in the auditorium to stand up and shout several times: *I'm as mad as hell, and I'm not going to put up with it anymore!*

The vibes were good to that stage and we followed with an on-stage round table forum joined by each of our guest speakers on the day.

Jim Sweeney's opening question to the panel was: *How can we turn around the negativity that is holding us up at this time?*

A well regarded National Rugby League Coach was the first to weigh in on his approach to managing negativity.

As summarised from our recordings of the day's speeches, this is what he said:

> *'Please know that negativity in any business is like rust in a car. While it only ever starts as a tiny spec, if you don't address the symptoms rapidly, it's pretty much guaranteed to radiate out until it consumes and destroys the entire car.*
>
> *I've seen infectious negativity take hold in several elite sporting teams over the years and know from*

experience that when it's not muzzled rapidly, it's potentially 'season over' for the team.

So these are my four no-exception golden rules of engagement when I have that problem in one of the teams I have charge of:
1. *urgently unearth what is driving that negative mindset,*
2. *take hold of the root cause of the problem head-on and excise it rapidly,*
3. *co-opt the captain and his/her respected senior leadership group to take ownership and instruct them to make sure it doesn't recur.*
4. *AND if that strategy doesn't work then it may be time to start replacing some of those senior leaders with people who can and will get the job done!*

In my view, it should be pretty much the same process for Big Corporations like St. George.

SO MY ADVICE IS THIS: JUST BAN NEGATIVITY ACROSS ST GEORGE BANK, PERIOD, AND SACK ANYBODY WHO REFUSES TO ABIDE BY THAT EDICT!'

The Coach then stood, pointed to those seated in the auditorium on the day, and said:

Given the leadership of the Bank is significantly represented here today, please know that YOU people are the important drivers of St George's culture and ultimate success. So please know that the buck must always stop with you!

There was plenty of humour in his 'sacking' punch line and tone of voice to keep it all on a positive track, so much so, that he got a standing ovation from every one of our managers.

After that conference, we saw an immediate and positive turnaround in attitude across the Bank. And whenever we picked up on the grapevine that any two of our managers were talking negatively about each other or even about the Bank at large, Jim Sweeney would invite the antagonists to his office for one of his famous fireside chats, with me also there to observe. With a practiced and demonstrably dour look on his face, he would tell them explicitly what they had been saying behind each other's backs – warts and all! He'd then stand, eyeball each of them and simply say, '*FIX IT, and don't you dare think about leaving my office until you've kissed and made up!*' Jim and I would then walk out and leave them to it!

So, there it is! Just ban negativity, period! And know that it is indeed like rust in a car if left unchecked. Importantly, adopt the good habit of Management by Walking About (MBWA), so you always know precisely what's going on in your business.

Show That You Care

'Do you know The President?' a journalist asked a small-town labourer attending a rally of 20,000 or so citizens at which Franklin Roosevelt had just been speaking. 'No,' replied the labourer, 'but I can guarantee he knows me!'

That exchange speaks volumes about one of the great US Presidents. During his 15 years in office, Franklin D. Roosevelt was loved by Republican and Democratic voters alike because they knew without a doubt that he cared. He journeyed with the American people through the very tough years following the Depression, dealing with the seemingly impossible challenge of finding gainful employment for tens of millions of unemployed citizens. He had the courage to roll out the magnanimous employment-generating *New Deal* initiatives when both sides of Congress and the Senate were ruminating about the massive cost to the economy. He then guided his nation through the equally challenging years of World War 2. But no one had any doubt that the well-being of the American people was always Roosevelt's number one priority.

Genuine Gestures Do Count

Although I never had the privilege of knowing him, my maternal grandfather cared for those who worked for him. He was very much loved by all the staff at Wormald Brothers, the Sydney based corporation he headed up. He was also a proud Freemason and a generous philanthropist.

It was only after his passing that my grandmother became aware of a number of his substantial personal acts of benevolence. People came out of the woodwork, a good many of them from Wormald Brothers, sending their condolences but also passing on their heartfelt thanks for the generous assistance he had given them in a time of need. To a person, they confirmed his support had come with only one condition, that it should remain between them. But of course, his generosity was well known across the Sydney business community because people invariably do talk about good deeds as they do about people who care.

The real fact in the business world, is that genuine gestures do count. Good bosses get into the habit of showing interest in their employees' personal lives. Without being intrusive in any way, they make a point of knowing something special about each employees' family, their partners, their kids and their personal likes and hobbies. They also share something back about themselves. This exchange builds trust but also garners a stronger commitment to the job. This reciprocal interchange makes your people feel important, valued, safe and trusted. Indeed, they know that you care.

Sounds like a very real and genuine win-win to me!

Chapter 30: Sustainable Collaborative Leadership

"There are those who look at things the way they are, and ask, 'Why?' I dream of things that never were, and ask 'Why not"

George Bernard Shaw.

Figure 30.1

As human beings, the society we live in is energised and animated by the product of social human interaction, ordered and organised by collective behaviour between those who share common interests, values and goals. Socially, those close connections are the nexus that allows groups of people to follow largely unwritten yet well-understood rituals and traditions, defining how they behave and create order and predictability when they come together.

Those collective behaviour norms are found in every tier of society that includes life partnerships, immediate family, extended family hubs, groups of close friends, student cohorts, sporting teams, social clubs, and religious or cultural affiliations. As social beings, we feel a sense of security and belonging when we are able to connect with those we care about.

So how do those socialisation norms translate into good business leadership? Well, for a start, getting a job and joining a business team doesn't guarantee the people you'll be working with will have similar interests or values to yourself.

The fact is that the core leadership style of the principal will undoubtedly influence how easy or how difficult it is to feel and experience that true sense of belonging.

Outdated command and control business leadership models, driven exclusively top-down by the boss, limit the opportunity for individual team members to actively work together to achieve better outcomes. Fortunately, there's now a plethora of contemporary evidence affirming that collaborative leadership consistently produces better outcomes and more productive team environments.

In my experience, sustainable collaborative leadership is driven consistently by six important building blocks (Figure 30.1):

- The Cultural Value Drivers
- The Capital Leadership Drivers
- The Team Leadership Drivers
- Team and Stakeholder Trust
- A Proactive Mindset, and
- Daily Reflection and Personal Accountability

The Cultural Value Drivers

Our values are the beliefs, principles and ethical standards we live by and care about deeply. In the business world, your core values should drive your conscious choices, decisions and actions, and how you treat and wish to be treated by your team, your customers and in the broader marketplace. Consistently honoured and followed values have a quite huge role in driving your leadership culture. Indeed they reflect how your actions, behaviours and outcomes match your aspirations.

Dynamic business strategies and goals will evolve over time, but your values should represent the solid foundations of your business culture. Those core values may include traits such as:

- Consistently showing strength of character.
- Being empathetic in all your dealings with others.
- Behaving ethically and acting with integrity and honesty.
- Balancing mental and emotional toughness.
- A core commitment to being a team player.
- Consistently treating others as you would like them to treat you.
- Knowing that the *sum of us* invariably garners greater scope to achieve positive outcomes than *just me doing it without help* from the rest of the team.
- Consciously finding ways to work in concert with others in achieving mutually satisfactory outcomes.
- Knowing that to survive and thrive you must have a productive revenue generating sales and service mindset.

The best business leaders I have known have a resolute commitment to their core values. They promote and support those values and behaviours throughout their teams and in the way they deal with their broader business community.

Engage with your team to define and clarify the important values that drive your business and how it operates. Reinforce those values in a Code of Conduct Statement and seek the whole team's positive commitment to support them.

The Capital Leadership Drivers

Social Capital Assets

The notion of social capital first seriously emerged in the 18th Century, with a theme of harnessing social networks to solve collective community challenges.

Since the dawn of the 21st century, the constructs of *social capital*, *corporate social responsibility*, *good corporate citizenship* and *sustainability* have increasingly been recognised as valuable business drivers. In fact, there's now a strong body of evidence to suggest that having a social conscience in business can be incrementally beneficial to the bottom line for the simple reason that people prefer to trade with a business that can demonstrate that it truly cares.

There are several definitions of social capital assets. My version for the SME sector identifies five distinct components:

- *The Team* addresses the collective strengths of the team, including their combined skills, education, experience, drive, judgement and, most importantly, their willingness to work cooperatively together to achieve the best possible outcomes for the business.

- *The Customer* embraces your resolve to grow the business but also, importantly, to make sure that every touch point with your customers is underwritten by an unwavering commitment to excellence.

- *The Networks* focus on the important collaborative relationships that enable you to maximise your customer acquisition, growth and retention outcomes.

- *The Community* defines your commitment to embrace the principle of engaged citizenship and support of community enriching initiatives in the region you do business in. Done well, this commitment generates customer loyalty and increased patronage because people prefer to trade with a business that can show it cares about their local needs and the causes that are closest to their hearts.

- *The Time and Priority Management Disciplines* are those actions and decisions that will complement and enable your team to optimise their capacity to function at their best, and that will ultimately contribute to a more fulfilling workplace environment. Those disciplines include ongoing refinement of *work habits*, streamlining *back office processes*, eliminating *bureaucracy* and *non-value tasks*, and productively *accessing technology* to create a more resilient front line, *customer driven organisation*.

Embedded in all five of our Critical Success Factors is the recognition that SME organisation structures continually evolve as the business grows and expands its reach. Please know there is nothing esoteric about reinforcing the role social capital plays during that evolution and in the ultimate successes that follow.

Financial Capital Assets

The focus here is on Critical Success Factor 2, the Finances. The important priority is to access cloud-based accounting software, to hire an experienced bookkeeper to manage your transactional accounting, cash flows, debtors, creditors and statutory compliance obligations, and to appoint an external account to advise on the higher order annual taxation and statutory obligations.

Other than ensuring all those tasks are being managed well, the principal's financial focus is then on tracking profitability and overall financial performance and maximising their available time at the front line to grow the business.

Strategic Capital Assets

Strategic capital is significantly about Critical Success Factor 3, the Front Line. It encompasses your vision, business planning, brand and business building strategies and tactics that will aid you in maximising your projected customer and revenue outcomes.

SME Leadership: The 5 Critical Success Factors

The Team Leadership Drivers

"For the strength of the Pack is the Wolf, and the strength of the Wolf is the Pack."

Rudyard Kipling, The Jungle Book. Circa 1894.

For many decades, my favourite team leadership mantra has been:
We only have an A Team. There are no second-class citizens in our team.

This mindset promotes an environment and a culture in which each individual gains as much from the team as the team gains from each individual.

In the SME world, the A-Team philosophy is not about creating a team of rock stars but rather about entrenching a whole-of-team collective mindset focussed on achieving the best possible outcomes together. In that environment, the team genuinely believes *we are the best team in the business world* because they know it's about *consistently putting team before individual.*

Am I setting the bar a little too high for the SME principal and their team?? Absolutely not! Doing these things well lays down the ultimate foundations for achievable success.

Team and Stakeholder Trust

A lack trust in any business team is pretty much always visible for all to see. At its very worst, poor trust may be driven by a combination of unprofessional behaviour, overblown egos, biased rivalries, bullying, lack of clarity about individual roles and responsibilities, backstabbing and/or a general atmosphere of fear and suspicion. When those symptoms are not addressed head on, decision making tends to grind to a halt because people become fearful of what will happen if they get it wrong. A poor trust environment may also be the result of a business that has lost its way financially and is struggling to recover and generate the income it needs to carry on and survive.

When left unchecked, a persistently low trust culture ultimately bleaches into every crevasse of the business. Regardless of the

SME Leadership: The 5 Critical Success Factors

cause, when the whole team is unhappy and feels insecure, be aware their body language alone has the potential to paint a thousand words of discontent in the marketplace without them uttering a single word. Customers spot the symptoms when service standards slip as they invariably do. This leads to increasing levels of customer dissatisfaction. When the situation doesn't improve, customers eventually vote with their feet and go elsewhere.

In my experience, those trust shortcomings frequently come from the top down where the principal is either the instigator of the underlying problems or is failing to act on those who are directly driving aberrant behaviour down the line.

These leadership chapters focus on a commitment to shared values, collaborative work cultures, the power of a productive team and the importance of a strong sense of responsibility and *belonging* among each of the team members.

And of course, trust sits at the core of each of those drivers.

The Team Trust Generators

Dealing with the subtleties of Power vs Influence: Having a leader's title doesn't confer on the team leader the presumptive right to be respected by the team. You earn that right by the way you consciously choose to lead. Your preference should always be to lead by positive influence and to use raw positional power only when it's truly justified.

It's also important to know when you don't need to lead. When a team member takes the positive initiative to act, give them the breathing space they need. Offer guidance, support, and positive encouragement when they ask for it. And don't forget to congratulate them when the job is ultimately done well.

Run your team meetings in the spirit of *Constructive Contention* where the dialogue is genuine, and everyone is given a voice (even on occasions when they may have a respectfully different view to the boss!).

Inclusion and Respect

"Just because I'm a woman, I must make unusual efforts to succeed. If I fail, no one will say: 'She doesn't have what it takes.' They will say: 'Women don't have what it takes.'"

Clare Booth Luce, US Stateswoman & Author.

Treat your employees on their merits, without bias to sex, race, age, religion, relationship status, or any other factors that should have no bearing or influence on the work they do. Value your employees by how well they perform their duties, how they contribute to good camaraderie in the team and on their ability to maintain consistently high standards of service.

Drive strong and fair values from the top down and mean it. Your employees want to feel safe and secure in the knowledge they are working in an environment free of discrimination, victimisation, sexual harassment, or vilification of any kind. Provide a safe and healthy workplace. Be genuine about driving a culture of inclusion and respect throughout the business. These values should be clearly stated in an employee Code of Conduct, signed by you, and countersigned by every staff member.

Empowerment, Responsibility, and Accountability

In SMEs, *Empowerment* is about the Principal's willingness to delegate important tasks to capable team members and providing them with the necessary back up support, guidance and tools to ensure those tasks are carried out well. Taking on that *Responsibility* represents the team member's willingness to carry out the assigned task. *Accountability* is the 'X Factor' that ensures they put their nose to the grindstone and complete the task well.

Acting responsibly, the team member gains the support not only of the boss, but also of their fellow team members as they have a well-earned reputation of doing what they have promised to do. When executed with integrity, linking *Empowerment*, *Responsibility* and *Accountability* is the ultimate trust builder.

When business teams reach the maturity stage of being accountable to and supportive of each other collectively, as tends to happen in elite sporting teams during live game time, the consequent watching each other's back bond of trust is powerful and they hone a natural tendency to automatically exercise more autonomy in their thinking.

Aligning Leadership Drivers with Business Priorities

A successful business team operating at its best is made up of a group of passionate people with individual talents and skills and a willingness to grow, collaborate and share responsibility with their fellow team members.

Early in your journey, when staff numbers are constrained by the limits of the income the business can generate, you will undoubtedly start with several hard-working generalists whose special talent is that they can carry out multiple tasks well and are willing to work together to get things done. Over time, as income and profits grow, you will likely create several skillset specific roles to drive critical parts of the business.

The cultural challenge is not to allow negative middle management substructures to take hold at any stage of your business evolution. When territorial walls are allowed to grow around specialist positions, they all too often become brick walls with no trespassing signs all over them. Do not let that happen!

Bottom line, there is a certain social magic that can drive and motivate a group of like-minded, passionate people. A productive team sitting in a substantially flat structure but with entry/exit doors left ajar on all sides, has the potential to become one of your most valuable trust building assets, provided you nurture, support, and treat them well and promote a business wide culture that concurrently balances, values and celebrates:

- Individual achievement with
- Collaborative mutual achievement.

'Shared Responsibility' Delegation

Treat Delegation as an extension of your own responsibility, not something you just give away without retaining accountability: Continuously Mentor, Train, Guide, Delegate, then Follow Up, in that continuous order.

Management by Walking About (MBWA):

This is about taking periodic walks through your workplace, observing, offering feedback and advice, supporting your team, and building that two-way bond of trust with each of them.

The Stakeholder Trust Generators

Taking a balanced stakeholder's view

The vision for your business should encompass all your key stakeholders with a genuine intent to address their combined needs. In Chapter 12, I referenced an example from a stakeholder statement I saw many decades ago that I particularly liked: *We aim to be a great company to work for, to be a shareholder in, to be a customer of, and to be a supplier to.*

The Importance of Social Capital

Investing in your Social Capital is about moulding your team to maximise their individual and collective contributions to the business. The important Social Capital dimensions are the Team, the Customers, the Networks, the Community you do business in, and the Time and Priority Management Disciplines that empower your team to optimise their capacity to function at their best.

The Customer's Perspective

> "In some important business meetings with Partners and Investors, Bezos would somewhat theatrically leave an unoccupied chair around the table – he called it 'The Customer's Chair!' "
>
> **Chris McNab, Jeff Bezos, Arcturus Publishing, 2022.**

SME Leadership: The 5 Critical Success Factors

The Bezos 'Vacant Chair' strategy serves as a metaphor and reminder that the big decisions in any business should ultimately have a complimentary respect for customer value!

Understanding the Buyer's Viewpoint

The metrics of attracting customers, closing sales, and generating revenues is about connecting and building a bond of trust with the other person, identifying common ground, and responding to what motivates and drives them and their needs.

Being Aware of What Drives Your Brand

Brand is about the promises you make and your customer's reactions and responses to those promises. It's about how you attract customer loyalty and build trust, and how you engender a desire for them to continue doing business with you. Most importantly, it's about not promising more than you can deliver, and always delivering more than you promise.

Collaborative Networking

Your networking focus should be on building a bond of trust with the important collaborative relationships that will enable you to maximise your customer acquisition, growth, and retention outcomes.

Engaged Citizenship

This is about your commitment to actively engage with the community you do business in. Genuine engagement generates customer loyalty and increased patronage because people prefer to trade with a business that can show it cares about the causes that are close to their hearts.

Crafting a Proactive Mindset

We who lived in the concentration camps can remember the men who walked through the huts comforting others, giving away their last piece of bread. They may have been few in number, but they offered sufficient proof that everything can be taken from a man but one thing, the last of the human freedoms – to choose one's attitude in any given set of circumstances, to choose one's own way.

Extract Victor E. Frankl, *Man's Search for Meaning*.

Prominent neurologist, psychiatrist, author, and Holocaust survivor Victor Frankl endured devastating traumas during his three years of concentration camp internment during World War 2. He witnessed firsthand the death of his father, mother, and sister and learned of the passing of his wife in a nearby Camp. Frankl never knew if he would survive to the next day, yet, in his darkest moments of despair, he came to the realisation that there was one thing his jailers could never take from him – his freedom and his right to decide how he would react to his dire privations.

After the war, Frankl returned to his medical practice in Austria and released his international bestseller about his wartime experiences, *Man's Search for Meaning*. He drew on those learnings to develop the new science of Logotherapy and Existential Analysis, with a focus on finding the true meaning in life and exploring man's capacity to exercise free will during critical life moments. Frankl's acknowledgement of life meaning as a motivational factor in mental health was later recognised as his enduring contribution to the field of psychology.

So how do I underwrite my capacity to be proactive and objective in the moment rather than reactive.

When I'm about to exchange views with an individual or group of people, or am considering taking an important action, I consciously pause for a second or so to check off what the voice of my conscience is telling me. In those moments, a quick breath in is all it takes for me and a personal commitment to truly think about the implications of what I'm about to say or do.

And, of course, I sometimes fluff my lines and allow subjectivity and emotionality to affect my capacity to be proactive. But in those moments, the voice of my conscience generally gives me a nudge, holds me to account, and gives me a cue to make amends before it's too late.

But sometimes, particularly after a long and busy day, that moment of self-reflection doesn't register with me until the next morning when I am jotting down in my *Personal Immersion Journal* how I did with each of yesterday's tasks and communications. But it's never too late to make amends, and it's frankly an act of extraordinary arrogance not to do so when you know you've pressed the wrong buttons, reacted poorly, or have simply said or done the wrong thing. From my Catholic origins, I call those admissions my *Bless me, Father, for I have sinned* moments!

So, what's my core message? In the constantly evolving and frequently emotive atmosphere of the SME world, your capacity to think and act proactively in the moment is a critical trait to hone.

Don't Cheat *the Guy in the Glass*

In introducing my *Personal Immersion Journal* routine in Chapter 20, I referred to those reflections as my daily deep dive into the voice of my conscience, in how they guide me to:

- Better connect with the things that truly matter.

- Constantly add clarity and substance to my values, visions, goals and accompanying actions.

- Consider how I could have done better with the previous day's tasks and incorporate those learnings in planning out today's commitments.

- Consistently eliminate unnecessary emotionality and subjectivity by choosing to be Proactive rather than Reactive in my dealings with others.

A critical component of recording your daily reflections is to constantly work at sharpening your capacity to be straight and honest with yourself. And frankly, if you're not prepared to do so, then sadly, my best advice is don't bother keeping a journal!

One of my favourite poems puts the case for honing and sharpening your capacity for honest self-reflection:

The Guy in the Glass

When you get what you want in your struggle for self and the world makes you king for a day, just go to the mirror and look at yourself and see what that man has to say.

For it isn't your father, or mother or wife whose judgement upon you must pass. The fellow whose verdict counts most in your life is the one staring back from the glass.

He's the fellow to please – never mind all the rest. For he's with you clear to the end, and you've passed your most difficult, dangerous test, if the man in the glass is your friend.

You may fool the whole world down the pathway of years, and get pats on the back as you pass, but your final reward will be heartache and tears if you've cheated the man in the glass.

Peter Dale Wimbrow 1934.

Some Unique Leadership Lessons from Elite Sport

Aside from the various examples I've given throughout the book, I have three other stories that go to the heart of good leadership in team sport, which can also translate to good business leadership.

Go to my Chapter 32 nine *Inspiring Tales From the Trenches*. My first tale relates how former champion international rugby union player Daniel Herbert transitioned through several careers before becoming a consummate and successful CEO in the business world. Dan's thirteen life lessons are inspiring and demonstrate the

SME Leadership: The 5 Critical Success Factors

common ground nexus between Elite Team Sport and Business Leadership.

My test cricket story is what former champion Australian wicketkeeper, Adam Gilchrist, said on day one of the 2021 Ashes first Test between Australia and England. In presenting Alex Carey with his Baggy Green Cap on his maiden outing for Australia, Gilchrist's advice was this:

There's a lot of value placed in this cap, but not for a moment is there any entitlement that comes with it. It doesn't make you any more special than anyone else in society. But if you play with humility, if you play with integrity, honesty and complete commitment to this group of people, society will ride with you in the highs. More importantly when the lows come along, they will pick you up and carry you.

Humility, Integrity, Honesty and complete *Commitment to the Team*! Gilchrist's words represent the grand spirit of team leadership in both sports and in those businesses brave enough to adopt those sorts of values.

Author's note: The Baggy Green Cap may only be worn by Australian test cricketers, past and present, and was first made available to players over a century ago.

In 2010, author James Kerr was invited to join the New Zealand All Blacks' inner sanctum for five weeks as they were preparing for the 2011 Rugby World Cup, which they subsequently won. Bottom line, the All Blacks have been consistently rated by prominent commentators as one of the most successful professional global sporting franchises in history.

In James Kerr's book LEGACY: *What the All Blacks Can Teach Us About the Business of Life* (Constable Publishers, UK, 2013), Kerr explores the All-Blacks' successful journey over the past century and presents their 15 Lessons of Leadership. As it happens, a Rugby team also comprises 15 players who work together with a common purpose – to win! Kerr's 15 lessons work in the same way. Those lessons are:

SME Leadership: The 5 Critical Success Factors

1. *SWEEP THE SHEDS: Never be too big to do the small things that need to be done*

2. *GO FOR THE GAP: When you are on top of your game, change your game*

3. *PLAY WITH PURPOSE: Always ask why?*

4. *PASS THE BALL: Leaders create leaders*

5. *CREATE A LEARNING ENVIRONMENT: Leaders are teachers*

6. *NO DICKHEADS: Follow the spearhead*

7. *EMBRACE EXPECTATIONS: Aim for the highest cloud*

8. *PREPARATION – TRAIN TO WIN: Practice under pressure*

9. *PRESSURE – KEEP A BLUE HEAD: Control your attention at critical times*

10. *AUTHENTICITY – KNOW THYSELF: Keep it real*

11. *SACRIFICE: Find something real you would die for and give your life to it*

12. *INVENT YOUR OWN LANGUAGE: Sing your world into existence*

13. *RITUALISE TO ACTUALISE: Create a culture*

14. *BE A GOOD ANCESTOR: Plant trees you'll never see*

15. *WRITE YOUR LEGACY: This is your time*

The 5 Qs for Thriving as a Leader

In 2019, Ali Qassim Jawad and Andrew Kakabadse released Leadership Intelligence: The 5 Q's for Thriving as a Leader (Bloomsbury Publishing, 2019). The authors speak of two leadership mindsets in creating value. One is pursuing a value proposition. The other is about delivered value. They prefer the latter mindset (as do I) because it's characterised by closeness to customers and stakeholders.

The authors' 5 Qs are:

IQ Cognitive Intelligence: thinking your way to competitive advantage.

EQ Emotional Intelligence: harnessing emotions, enhancing relationships.

PQ Political Intelligence: navigating diverse stakeholder agendas.

RQ Resilience Intelligence: sustaining high performance under pressure and diversity.

MQ Moral Intelligence: competitive decision making through moral decision making and doing what's right.

The wisdoms presented in this concise 180 page, easy-to-read guide are logically presented and includes an excellent 5 Q's checklist with an opportunity to test yourself, your business and your team on each of the five questions.

Chapter 31: Managing Emotions

In this chapter, I lay out the demographics of Stress and Trauma in the Australian workplace and the Mental Health and Crisis Support Services that are publicly available. You'll find similar Crisis Support challenges and services available in all other Developed and Developing World economies.

My first job after completing my higher school certificate was as a trainee with a major bank in Sydney. As I returned from lunch one day, I failed to spot two men slipping into the branch just behind me. One grabbed me in a headlock and held a gun to my head, while the other one chained the door, drew the blinds and told the branch staff what would happen if their demands were not met!

Back in those days bank Head Tellers generally had a pistol hidden in the back of their cash drawers! ... But thankfully our tellers willingly responded to those demands and rapidly emptied their cash drawer contents into calico bags. I collapsed to the floor as both gunmen took off with their booty soon after. The whole incident had taken only minutes.

The branch manager, who was many decades my senior, took me to his upstairs office and gave me a cup of tea. Draining his cup in record time, he stood up and told me it was time to get back to work!! No real words of comfort or advice were offered other than his tacit assumption that being in his sacred presence would make me feel better. I left that bank weeks later and joined a mid-city accounting firm to get an early start on my Chartered Accounting studies. At that time, I figured it was a much safer profession to pursue!

I had nightmares of that experience for several months, and sometimes the gun actually went off during my dreams! But when I woke each time to discover I was still a member of the human race, I was able to reduce their impact by compartmentalising those dreams.

I later learnt from a clinical psychologist that my unique version of compartmentalising can in fact be a legitimate defence mechanism for dealing with conflicting thoughts and feelings during times of high stress. This version of compartmentalisation then became a valuable empowering strategy for me throughout my career.

For the record, the banking industry no longer arms it's Head Tellers, and it today takes its responsibility of protecting and supporting branch staff with professional support and counselling services that would abhor and never countenance the lack of support I experienced way back when!

Authors Note: While the observations that follow relate principally to the Australian workplace environment, there is undoubtedly a universality of those reflections in managing work related stress just about anywhere internationally.

More About Stress and Trauma

The Australian Institute of Health and Welfare released its Stress and Trauma Snapshot in July 2020. That report defines trauma as an experience of extreme stress or shock. Traumatic events are sometimes life-threatening and may include natural disasters, serious motor vehicle accidents, the illness or loss of a family member or close friend, sexual assault or, indeed, experiencing an armed holdup. Most people will go through at least one serious traumatic event during their lifetime.

Stress is defined as a reaction to less dramatic life events such as job loss, pressing deadlines, financial difficulties or a partner breakup. Stress may initiate a *fight or flight response*, while continuous ongoing stress without relief may transition to distress.

Mental health in Australia

- 20% of Australians between 16 and 85 years of age experience some form of mental illness every year.
- 54% of people with mental illness do NOT seek professional advice or treatment. Yet access to treatment has been proven to be important, given that 75% of people are admitted to

the public health system for psychological support improvement.

- Suicide accounts for 1.6% of all deaths in Australia. Males account for 75% of those deaths, yet they are least inclined to seek help.

Mental Health in the Typical Workplace

Untreated mental health conditions cost the collective Australian workplace $10.9 billion in absenteeism and lost productivity each year. Promoting a mentally healthy workplace is a shared responsibility, ideally based on the team's commitment to watch each other's backs. But it must primarily be driven from the top down with the principal's commitment to establish appropriate policies in their workplace.

A recent study of Australian employers conducted by TNS Social Research found that:

- 91% of respondents believe their mental health is more important than their physical health and safety at work.
- 52% of respondents feel their workplace does not value mental health.
- 56% believe their principal/ CEO does not value mental health.
- Employees who believe their workplace is mentally unhealthy are unlikely to disclose to their employer that they suffer from a mental health condition, fearing this disclosure may have the potential to negatively impact their future.
- 81% of employers say they have Workplace Mental health Policies, yet 35% of employees say they don't know what those policies are.
- THE BIG NUMBER: when mental health is valued by the employer, the level of absenteeism halves!

Common Workplace Stress Symptoms

As a responsible principal, you need to be on the lookout for observable indicative symptoms that may include fatigue, muscular tension, headaches, sleeping difficulties, anxiety, irritability, pessimism, feelings of being overwhelmed, inability to cope, increased sick days, or a drop in work performance.

Common causes of stress at work are an inconsistent uncaring organisation culture, a lack of core values, unreasonable job demands, heavy workloads, overlong working hours, tight deadlines, job insecurity, over-supervision, team relationship tensions, bullying, harassment and/ or discrimination.

Every one of these causes is within a responsible principal's domain to manage.

Useful Mental Health Resources in Australia

Beyond Blue is a highly regarded mental health organisation that focuses on supporting people who are affected by anxiety, depression and suicide. Beyond Blue is committed to ensuring everyone has greater knowledge about their mental health and to feel comfortable about seeking help.

Beyond Blue actively promotes its Big Blue Door as a safe place for those with mental health conditions to go for help. Go to: www.beyondblue.org.au. You will find some valuable tools and resources, including:

- Their Anxiety and Depression 10 Question Checklist – a multiple choice questionnaire completed and submitted online. The response arrives back immediately with advice on what steps and actions to take next.
- Their New Access I'm OK/ Not OK program is a free and confidential mental health support program designed to help you manage life challenges and get you back on track. It's available via phone, video call, or face-to-face. Go to: www.wellways.org/newaccess or call 1300 921 535.
- Beyond Blue's 24-hour Crisis Support Line (1300 224 636) is available for anyone in need of crisis support or advice.

Lifeline's education, advocacy and crisis support options provide compassionate support for people in crisis. No judgement, no conditions, just a human connection to help people get through their darkest moments. Lifeline Digital offers crisis support across three unique platforms that give everyone a chance to speak and to be heard:

- Lifeline 24-hour Crisis Support Line (13 11 14) connects the caller directly with a trained crisis support worker. This is their most popular service.
- Lifeline Text (0477 13 11 14). Available nightly, it connects the caller with a crisis support worker.
- Online chat. Available nightly, the chat service is available for people who prefer to type than talk.

Other Lifeline support programs include:

- Holding on to Hope Podcast: encourages help-seeking resources by sharing masked stories of people who have struggled with suicide.
- Face to Face Counselling: offered through many of Lifeline's 40 Australian centres.
- Bereavement Support Groups: bring people together to safely share their experience of coping with the loss of a loved one.
- Eclipse Support Groups: an 8-week evidence-based program for survivors of suicide.
- Financial Counselling: a financial counselling support service to assist people with responsible budgeting and ways to relieve financial burden.

The Mentally Healthy Workplace Alliance is a collaboration of national organisations from the business, union, community and government sectors with a brief to foster mentally healthy workplaces. This alliance is an invaluable source. Go to: www.mentallyhealthyworkplacealliance.org.au.

How to Promote a Mentally Healthy Workplace

If you don't already have a mental health policy document for your business, download The Mentally Healthy Workplace Alliance 'Heads up Mental Health and Well-being Policy Template' It will give you all you need to create a robust policy. Make a personal commitment to positively support that policy. Ensure everyone in your team sees the document and periodically reinforces those policies at team meetings. All team members should be encouraged to positively support each other.

Be on the alert for any signs of mental stress in your team. You'll find excellent guidance at www.beyondblue.org.au on how to spot the more obvious signs and symptoms of stress and depression, the recognisable behaviours, the feelings, the thoughts and the physical symptoms.

As a principal, do not present yourself as an expert on mental health but rather as a supportive boss who simply wants to help. Practice several opening questions to allow you to gently broach the subject in an understanding and non-threatening way. For example: 'I've noticed you haven't been yourself lately. Is there anything I can do to help?' Your role from there is to be a good listener.

Your employee should not feel any sense that sharing their problems with you is going to be a threat to their career or career progression. If the source of their stress is mainly work-related, such as bullying, unreasonable work demands, discontent in the team, and so on, assure them the matters will be dealt with confidentially.

If you form the view the source is not work-related, encourage them to see their GP, or if you believe their level of stress requires urgent help, suggest they call the Lifeline or Beyond Blue 24-hour Support Lines.

Your loyal trained team members are integral assets in your business and you need to let a stressed employee know how important they are and just how much you value them.

Research Sources for This Chapter:

www.abs.gov.au: (Go to: Mental Health; then First insights from the National Study of Mental Health and Wellbeing 2021)

www.beyondblue.org.au

www.lifeline.org.au
www.mentallyhealthyworkplacealliance.org.au/
www.tnsglobal: TNS report: State of Mental Health in Australia

NB: You'll be able to download dedicated Mental Health and Crisis Support Services available in most international locations.

Chapter 32: Nine Inspiring Leadership Tales from the Trenches

Daniel Herbert, *CEO SSKB Property Group and Chairman of the Australian Rugby Union.*

Daniel Herbert has been the CEO of SSKB since 2017. One of Australia's leading property firms specialising in strata management, SSKB employs 130 people across Australia's Eastern Seaboard.

Before that, Daniel spent eight years with the Queensland Rugby Union in various management and executive roles. Prior to his career in sports administration, he was a professional rugby player for the Queensland Reds and the Australian Wallabies during a golden era for the code when the Wallabies won five consecutive Bledisloe Cups, a Tri-Nations Cup, a Rugby World Cup and secured the first ever series victory over the British & Irish Lions.

During his playing days, Daniel played 67 tests for the Wallabies, 124 caps for the Qld Reds and was awarded the coveted Équipe International Player of the Year in 1999.

They used to say the average person has three careers during their working lifetime. If that's the case, I'm on my third now. Sports taught me many lessons which prepared me for life after sports. The pressurised environment can super-charge your learning or leave you exposed. Below are a few of the lessons I learnt by playing a team sport at an elite level over a decade.

Lesson 1: Turn up – I was selected in my first senior representative squad when I was observing the training of the Qld Reds squad one pre-season. I was 18 years old, and it was in between Uni classes at Ballymore Stadium, a 3-Wood drive from my Uni campus, that I would turn up to watch the Reds training. If the teams were uneven, I would play in the traditional warm-up game of touch, fetch the balls for the kicker, practising shots at goal... wherever I could join in. One day someone didn't turn up, and the coach approached me and asked what position I played. When I told him, he threw a singlet at me and said: "You're in the squad; go warm-up."

So, turning up and being there can be one of the most important things you do.

Lesson 2: Get noticed – by the right people and for the right things. The coach and senior players in a sporting environment are the most influential. In a business environment, it's usually the executive and management team. Most good leaders I've known place attitude and hard work above all else. Talent is overrated, and most skills can be taught if the person is willing. Pre-season became about demonstrating I could handle whatever was thrown at me and putting in the discretionary effort, staying around and working after everyone else left to go home.

Lesson 3: Show respect – if there's something senior players/ workers really dislike, is their environment being sullied by a young upstart who thinks they know better but has none of the life experience to justify thinking that. Take your time and sit up the front of the bus 'til you're invited down the back. Chip away, get results, show respect, and in time you'll earn their respect.

Lesson 4: Be humble – you're going to need support at some stage of your career; best you have people who want to support you through thick and thin. We like confidence, but we detest arrogance; know the difference.

Lesson 5: Be a sponge – we all benefit from coaching and mentoring, and coaches and mentors love nothing more than to share their collective experiences and insights so they can feel they are giving back to their passion or profession. Soak it up!

Lesson 6: All shapes and sizes – a rugby team is made up of specialists filling roles and comes in all shapes and sizes, all performing a unique role for the team's benefit. Some secure the ball, some advance it, and some protect it so it can be advanced again. Everyone plays their part, and if one part breaks down, the whole breaks down. For me, it's a metaphor for the workplace where there is a mix of specialists, generalists, and coaches.

Lesson 7: Have an X factor – work out what you can be the best at and where the team/ coach places real value. It's a bit like Jim

Collins' 'Hedgehog Concept' based on the ancient Greek parable that states, "A fox knows many things, but a hedgehog knows one big thing." As an aspiring rugby player, I knew the coach wanted to play a certain game style which relied on large bodies advancing the ball and bending the defensive line. I knew I could do that better than most, but it required a lot of gym work and additional training to get there and stand out from the others.

Lesson 8: Be the glue – dressing rooms can be more pressurised than most workplaces and can be emotion-charged at times. People are strange animals and are motivated by different things, react in different ways and can perform tasks quite uniquely to one another. These differences can lead to disagreements, and if there's no peacekeeper or leader, things can become toxic quite quickly. Different is not only ok, it is preferred – diversity gives strength and flexibility to adapt, but it needs the glue that binds it all together in stressful times.

Lesson 9: Have a plan – it's quite amazing how many workplaces operate without a plan, or if there is one, it isn't communicated to all. This should never happen in any elite sport or business. Failing to plan is planning to fail.

Lesson 10: Over-communicate – the best teams are in sync, knowing their own and each other's roles. They know how to adapt when things don't go to plan because they have spent time with each other and learnt how to connect and communicate. I grew up deaf in my left ear (mumps as a 3yo), and due to this disability, I had to constantly talk to people around me on the field to know what was going on. When you're deaf, you learn to be a good listener as well.

Lesson 11: Today's news is tomorrow's fish & chip wrapper – don't go looking for the criticism; it will find you soon enough. Critics have a job to do too, but you can't take it personally, and tomorrow there will be a new story to write. Only a few people's opinions matter. Stay close to them.

Lesson 12: Keep going – it will be tough, you'll fail, you'll get criticised, and then the cycle will repeat. Eventually, things will fall into place for those who have bothered to keep going. Talent is overrated; grit will win the day.

SME Leadership: The 5 Critical Success Factors

Lesson 13: Hold people accountable – if you do your part (Lessons 1 thru 12), then you need others to do theirs to ensure you get to where you're going. If they are critical to your success and aren't meeting you halfway, change them or change teams. Don't hang around sooking about it.

Footnote from Tim Sheehan, Shareholder and Director of SSKB:

Daniel Herbert is the CEO of our group of businesses. It isn't an easy job, and the day-to-day experience of leading a body corporate management business with over 100 staff servicing 50,000 apartment owners is far from the cheering adulation of a packed stadium watching a Rugby Union International. Nobody gives us a cheer as we leave in the lift at the end of our workday. Dan has been able to excel at both business and sports. In business, the quality I think that helps him excel is thoughtfulness: the ability to listen to all the stakeholders and consider situations from all points of view, then make decisions which balance all the competing interests. Running our business is a long game. The stakeholders are many: clients, staff, third-party contractors, and other shareholders. Emotion and passion from time-to-time help, but passion is not always sustainable. Moreover, an overdose of passion can be a blunt instrument. It can lead to impulsive reactions. However, thoughtfulness is a laser that can be sustained, and Daniel is a consummate and thoughtful leader.

SME Leadership: The 5 Critical Success Factors

John Mangos, *Managing Director, Megisti Media.*

John Mangos has been a highly respected print and broadcast journalist and a household name in Australian mainstream commercial television for over forty years. With a strong SME ethos in his DNA, John founded Megisti Media, and as its Managing Director, has successfully developed a presentation and media training company that operates with associates in all the Australian capital cities.

John's Journey Begins

I'm a proud Greek descendant who grew up in the Melbourne suburbs in the 1960s. My maiden employment experience was working in our family café, and those early learnings gifted me with entrepreneurial instincts that have never left me.

After studying journalism at RMIT, I completed a cadetship at the Herald and Weekly Times but later transitioned to television, joining the Nine Network. The newspaper game had been struggling to find its raison d'etre at that time, and I was excited about the opportunity to engage in the optimistic dynamism television was offering me.

I dealt with the pressure of being the first non-Anglo-Saxon face on mainstream television news in the late 1970s by working harder than anyone else to justify my presence. Happily, my efforts paid off when I was offered Nine's prestigious Canberra correspondents' job, reporting on federal politics.

Hooray for Hollywood

I was promoted again three years later when I took on responsibility for the Nine Network's US bureau. Based in Los Angeles, I had the pleasure of broadcasting America's top stories of the day to Australia each evening. My LA sojourn was a definite life changer for me, and I was starting to imagine I could broaden my horizons beyond just broadcast journalism.

SME Leadership: The 5 Critical Success Factors

The King and I

My big break came when Australia's King of television, Graham Kennedy, invited me to return home to become his co-host for a ground-breaking new program called "Coast to Coast". This was my transformation from an 'on the road reporter' to a respected 'anchor'. My personal brand was thrust rapidly into the living rooms of millions of Australians, and I would continue to enjoy that anchor's prestige for Nine, Seven, and Sky News over the next 25 years.

The Flying Swan

At the height of my career, I enjoyed an excellent national profile and was frequently invited to MC events for corporations and charities alike. One of those was an Italian Opera Foundation fundraiser, where I first met John Goddard, who was then CEO of the Italian Bank, Cassa Commerciale Ltd and a Director of Opera Foundation Australia. Driven by my belief that the more you give, the more you get, I did a lot of those jobs on a pro bono basis.

One of those roles was with my favourite footy club, the Sydney Swans AFL team. The Swans were languishing at the time (1990) and were struggling to find a friend in the media for love nor money. When they reached out to me, I was delighted and honoured to take on the role of MC of the club's corporate functions before every home game.

Little did I know that for the next 32 years, I would not only proudly serve my club, but as a bonus, I would also be exposed to 200 to 300 senior corporate leaders every second weekend of the season. It was pure networking gold for me.

By the turn of the century, technology was spreading its reach in every direction. Computers, the internet, mobile phones, niche pay TV television channels, and web-based streaming services were all coming into prominence. I was seeing an insatiable yet unsatisfied thirst for content and soon realised that few had the professional expertise to capitalise on those opportunities. It was an ideal gap for me to pursue when I realised those corporate leaders had a clear need to be professionally trained if they were to get the most out of their media interviews and presentations.

SME Leadership: The 5 Critical Success Factors

"Luck Is What Happens When Opportunity Meets Preparation." This quote from the Roman philosopher Seneca resonated perfectly for me during a chance meeting in 2001 with Air Chief Marshall Angus Houston, who was then Chief of the Australian Air Force. He was the special guest at one of the Swans football functions I was hosting, and we were seated together. I told him I was in the process of setting up a media training company, and he was all ears. He listened to my plans, and when I finished, he eyeballed me and said: "You should definitely go ahead with this venture. You'll be perfect at it." That was all the endorsement I needed to go ahead full steam!

I had already established Megisti Media (romantically named after the Greek island of my origins) and had the coveted prime-time role at Sky News as their evening anchor. It left me with all the daylight hours I needed to pursue my passion.

Time to Hang Out The Shingle

Armed with the contacts I had developed at the upper end of the corporate world, I started working the phones, but there was indeed a pot of gold already sitting in my own backyard. During the news bulletins I was presenting, I was crossing live to economists and senior executives from the major banks and stockbroking firms, and it was clear for all to see they were simply not up to scratch as 'on-air talent'! I offered to train them, they enthusiastically accepted, and fortunately for me, they all rapidly lifted their game. So I realised I was onto something special.

Word of Mouth

Yes, I ramped up my social media profile, and yes, I began offering my services to my corporate contacts, yet by far and away, my best endorsements were word of mouth. Fairly soon, within the banking and financial services industry, I had developed a good reputation for delivering positive outcomes, and the work flowed in rapidly from there. At that time, there was little competition, and I was able to forge an excellent reputation among the big players.

My significant learning was that CEOs, COOs, and CFOs with billion-dollar budgets and thousands of staff under their care were very competent at the business of generating revenues and maximising their share price but were seriously lacking in media communication skills.

I found myself rapidly accumulating clients, including two of the big four banks, major financial institutions, property groups, a major supermarket chain and other ASX-listed companies. At the heart of my training model was advice from my early mentor, the legendary political reporter Peter Harvey, who gave this most prescient pearl of wisdom: "It's all very well to have great information, but if you can't communicate it effectively, it's like pissing in a wet suit. You'll get a nice warm feeling, but nobody will ever know about it!"

Leverage Your Loop

Over dinner at a Greek taverna with my friend George Dalaras, Greece's most famous vocalist of the modern era and a star of international fame, I was reminded that he had performed at The Royal Albert Hall in London and Carnegie Hall in New York, but not at Sydney's Opera House!

My entrepreneurial spirit kicked in, and I immediately accepted the challenge. As a first-time impresario, not only did I pull off a successful tour, but I went on to bring him and his entourage to Australia on three further tours. Unquestionably my public profile helped me pull it off, and so too did my respected status within the Greek community. But no one knew about the risks I took, borrowing against my home. I 'channelled' Walt Disney and was driven by my successful business-centred ethos: "If you want something done well, then you'd better do it yourself because no one else can possibly have the same passion and drive as you!"

The Organ Grinder, Not The Monkey

I learnt early on in business that everyone wants to meet and do business with the boss. As my company grew, I formed valuable connections with the best producers, directors, camera operators and sound recordists in every capital city. I can call on them at the drop of a hat when a crisis hits. But when it comes to the essence of my core offering, my clients want to deal directly with the 'organ grinder'! My mantra is, if you are going to be the face of your business, you must be at the front line and be present when they need you.

Zero Sugar

If you've read this far, please don't presume my inspiring tale is just the success story of someone famous. It took me 14 years of hard work for Megisti Media to become an 'overnight success'. Having a public name and profile offered no guarantee of success, and there were occasions when I had to ask creditors for extra time when unscrupulous clients refused to pay and even times when their cheques bounced!

No two SMEs will ever be the same. The reason yours can succeed always comes down to one essential ingredient ...YOU!

Ross McQuinn, *Principal, Pilot Restaurant Group.*

I graduated from Australian National University with a combined Bachelor of Commerce/ Bachelor of Laws degree and an expectation to enter the traditional workforce. I hated the graduate application process and didn't understand why for some time. Eventually, I came to the realisation it was because I wanted to work for myself in whatever form that would take. I had been working in restaurants and bars while studying and fell in love with the food and drink industry. Once I put two and two together, I set a clear goal with a definite time frame. I would open my own venue within five years. This allowed me to focus and meant I dedicated every decision towards achieving that goal.

My partner Dash and I opened Pilot Restaurant in September 2018 in Ainslie, an inner northern suburb of Canberra. We set out to offer a premium style of food and hospitality that we felt was missing from Canberra's dining scene. This culminated in a successful awards season in 2019, claiming a Good Food Guide Chef's Hat and being listed 8th in the country by Delicious Magazine. As with any new business, there were significant challenges; however, we have been able to navigate these effectively while staying true to our core concept.

Surround Yourself With People Smarter Than You

I will not claim to be the first person to cite this philosophy; however, I truly believe in it and have attempted to apply it to all aspects of my life. I used to want to work in talent management. I grew up thinking my dream career would start at William Morris Agency in Los Angeles. To an extent, this is essentially what I still do. I'm not the best restaurant manager, and I am not a restaurant chef by any stretch of the imagination. However, we have managed to assemble a very talented team of individuals. Some of them have had issues with former employers, being designated as 'difficult to manage,' but in my opinion, this was simply because they were not given an opportunity to shine and grow. Recognising talent within someone and creating a workplace environment that gives that person the best chance to succeed sets the foundation for a business to thrive before it even opens.

I am constantly learning from our employees, which means I'm constantly being challenged by most of them, and I think that's great! I'm surprised when contemporaries in other venues exclusively employ yes men and yes women. Frankly, an entrepreneur who only wants to be told that they're right and how smart they are will more often than not fail to evolve and grow – the key is surely having the willingness to learn from others!

There Are Only Two Questions That Really Matter

During the first three years of our business, at times, I struggled with anxiety and feeling overwhelmed. Pilot only began to find its feet (financially speaking) just over a year into operation, which coincided with COVID-19 spreading around the world and adding a new level of stress and insecurity. This meant that for close to two years, we weren't seeing the financial results that we had hoped for, and I would question the concept and its implementation. Were we doing the right thing? What could I do better? In the end, I realised there were two questions I kept asking myself:

Are We Proud Of What We're Doing?

And Can We Keep Doing It?

I've found these are the only things that count, and the rest are simply garnishing. The first question allows you to set your own parameters for success. Your pride can come from financial goals, contribution to society, or financial KPIs. However, you need to be unambiguous as to what drives you. For us, it was creating a premium venue on par with the best in Australia.

The second question is on the business side of the equation. Is your model sustainable? It doesn't matter if you create the greatest restaurant in the world if no one comes! Obviously, there can be a conflict between the two, and balancing them is the key to operating a successful business. In difficult times, I always find myself coming back to those two questions, and so long as my answer is yes to both, the results will speak for themselves.

I write this from a second lockdown in the ACT, as millions of Australians are similarly under restrictions. That said, I am prouder of my team than I ever have been. Prior to the lockdown, we doubled down on our mission to be the best restaurant that we could be and felt a huge amount of support from the community within Canberra and around Australia. In fact, we have just begun negotiations on a second site, with the aim to open our next venue early in 2023.

How Do We Manage Our Team Responsibilities?

Dash is the restaurant manager and the face of our business. I drive longer-term strategic planning and the financial aspects of the business. We also have a talented head chef, who we are in the process of making a business partner.

Our employees include six full-time chefs; two kitchen hands; and three full-time, four part-time and three casual front-of-house employees.

Our Team Leadership Philosophy

We do several things to support and nurture our positive team culture. For example, the whole team goes out for dinner at least every other month, for birthdays, to celebrate significant occasions such as winning an award, or simply because we feel a team outing is overdue.

SME Leadership: The 5 Critical Success Factors

Michael Morgan, *CEO Asia, Herrmann Brain International.*

In 1975, I was working as a young livestock officer (Dairy Cattle) with the NSW Department of Agriculture, based in Lismore. My job was to offer help, support and advice to the dairy farmers in the Northern Rivers. I would spend my days driving from farm to farm in some of the most beautiful country in New South Wales. Why would I ever want to leave?

Early on a frosty June day Ben Hall, the regional director of agriculture, knocked on my office door and invited me to join him at the Civic Hotel. My heart stopped. He was the boss, it was only 10 am, yet he wanted to share a drink with me. I had to be in trouble! As we sat on our bar stools soon after, my beer remained untouched and was starting to go flat.

"Michael, may I give you some advice?" Ben finally said. "Of course," I replied quite hypnotically, and then he dropped the clanger. "I have watched you over the past 3 years, and I think it's time for you to move on. Stay any longer in your current job, and I guarantee it'll kill you, your spirit, and your innovative flair. I want you to find a job where you can grow, flourish, and succeed. The department is far too procedural and conservative for you." That's when I finally downed my beer in a couple of gulps!

Over the next year or so, Ben was true to his word and helped me in many ways. I transferred to the head office in Sydney, I moved divisions and continued to apply for various jobs, armed with the CV Ben had written for me. A job did finally come along from a company with 2 employees which had just acquired a franchise for a management training program from America.

My colleagues at the department told me I was mad. Throwing away a career, throwing away 9 years of service and for what? A company with only 2 people and a questionable future? 'Think of the risk, Michael,' they all said!

Thanks to Ben Hall, I was thinking quite rationally about the risk – the risk of staying! I couldn't think of even one risk in deciding to go for it.

Two months later, I found myself in Pittsburgh, Pennsylvania, at a conference organised by the US parent company. I was one of 300 delegates. I didn't know a soul, but I sat there full of excitement and

SME Leadership: The 5 Critical Success Factors

anticipation. It was, in fact, the beginning of what would ultimately become my life career and proud raison d'etre.

On the podium, the speaker was talking about how people channel their thinking in varying ways and how given identical scenarios, they will often use different thought pathways to find their solution. He explained why some people like a structured environment and a predictable career path while others like the freedom and excitement of small business and the general thrill of living by their wits and ideas. In that lightbulb moment, I knew I was in the right place and doing the right thing. Those who said I was throwing a career away were right. In truth, I didn't want one. I wanted to be in business for myself, to build something special, and to succeed by my own efforts.

The speaker that day was Ned Herrmann, author and creator of the Whole Brain® Thinking Model and the HBDI®.

As soon as Ned finished speaking, I tracked him down and introduced myself. I told him I was from Sydney and that I wanted to work with him to bring his thinking to our part of the world. We had that discussion in 1979.

In the 42 years since that meeting, I have introduced Whole Brain Thinking® to a vast number of businesses, both large and small. I have introduced it to IT companies, finance companies, mining companies, government departments, beauty salons, printing companies and many family businesses. I have also introduced it to most countries in the Asia Pacific region. In every case, I am reminded of Ned's parting words to me all those years ago. "Be careful, Michael," he said, "because this stuff actually works."

He was right, and HBDI® has become a dominant phenomenon used globally by small and large corporations alike.

SME Leadership: The 5 Critical Success Factors

Tim Sheehan, *Principal/Shareholder SSKB Property Group.*

Tips I learnt about being an SME Principal Shareholder – ITS ALL ABOUT LUCK. I was a very unhappy lawyer. But that's not unusual. Sometimes it takes being very unhappy to snap you into action. Being moderately unhappy and even moderately happy can be the curse of mediocrity.

Tip 1: Be lucky enough to be so unhappy you are prepared to do something about it:

I remember my business starting point clearly. It was a Sunday at the end of the Christmas holidays, and I was driving back from the Gold Coast to Brisbane after two fabulous weeks of vacation, and out of the blue, I said to my wife, "I am going to work tomorrow, and I am going to resign." During our vacation, I hadn't even mentioned work to my wife. It must have been playing on my subconscious. Without hesitation, my wife jumped in: "Definitely. You do it." Brave words considering we had a mortgage, and she was an articled clerk on a small salary who would be our sole income.

Tip 2: Be lucky enough to be surrounded by people who will love you and support you when you make your decisions:

I left my secure job and launched into a world of uncertainty. I knew that I had "a particular set of skills" (thanks, Liam Neeson). But I also knew they weren't the complete set of skills I needed to have a successful business. Too many years of looking at books and not enough time dealing with people made me realise I needed to improve my people skills. I concluded I would get a real-world course in dealing with people if I took a job in selling. Selling is communication, compromise, and cooperation wrapped up into a neat bundle.

Tip 3: Be unlucky enough to have shortcomings which you recognise, and be prepared to work on them:

I spent 12 months in a commission-only sales job. Commission-only sales positions aren't really jobs; they are micro-businesses. No sales = no business = no money. I earnt very little during the first 9 months, but I was fortunate enough to make some good sales towards the end. One of the people I came across while working as a salesman liked me. He offered me an opportunity to join his business. The money on offer was about 30% of what I was earning as a lawyer. However, I took the opportunity.

Tip 4: Be lucky enough to meet good people and when you do, get involved with them even if it means going backwards before you go forwards again:

Take on opportunities where there are no guarantees, but there are upsides which reward hard work. The opportunity was in the field of body corporate management. I told my new partner, Howard, that there was no way I wanted to spend the rest of my life listening to Mr Smith complain about Mrs Jones' dog barking - which is how I viewed body corporate management. Howard explained to me that I had a big misconception. As a body corporate manager, you weren't a bureaucrat pushing paper. You were actually helping people. Most importantly, you were helping people with something important to them, where they lived. In their community!

Tip 5: Be lucky enough to pick a field where you are helping people with something that is vital and important:

It was 1999. Howard explained to me that he believed Australia was at the start of a big change. Australians were going to accept that living on a quarter-acre land subdivision in the suburbs was not the only way to live. There was great utility and amenity in embracing apartment living, and as more people embraced apartments, there would be a dramatic increase in the need for good body corporate management.

Tip 6: Be lucky enough to do something in an industry where the tide is coming in – it floats all boats.

Don't be in a business delivering ice to homes when everyone is buying refrigerators.

Only 3 months into my new business, a person named Paul joined the business. He was different to me. An accountant. A tough negotiator. Very steady with strong opinions. Changes his mind reluctantly. After a heated exchange of opinions, he is quick to move on and forgive. Paul and I have been business partners for 20 years, and we are still going.

SME Leadership: The 5 Critical Success Factors

Tip 7: Be lucky enough to create lasting relationships with people who are different to you:

Early on in running our business, Paul and I realised that we had some ordinary clients. People who were difficult to deal with and didn't appreciate the efforts we put in and the quality of our work. Conversely, we had some awesome clients. People who made us excited to go to work. We enjoyed serving them. They provided us with challenges. It wasn't always easy, but there was mutual respect and appreciation. We took the punt on putting our energy into the good ones and moving on from the others.

Tip 8: Be unlucky enough to have some bad clients and lucky enough to have some good ones:

Realise you cannot be all things to all people. Pick the good ones, find out what makes them good for you and for your business, and then double down on those clients.

These lessons I identified at the start still apply every day in our ongoing operation of the business. There is no "one path" to have a good SME, but on whatever path you are on, you will be both very lucky and very unlucky. All you need to do is to think a lot about the luck, then take some action.

SME Leadership: The 5 Critical Success Factors

Mick Devine, *CEO, Calxa Accounting Software.*

My wandering start!

When I left school, many of my friends embarked on lifelong careers. A couple of them are still working for the same organisations, but others had change imposed upon them more than once over the past 40 years.

For me, there was a big world to see and explore, and I was out the door and on the road at the first opportunity. Those early years took me to the west coast of Scotland, the North East of Scotland, Amsterdam, and Adelaide. I made a living doing manual labour, cleaning schools, selling this and that, delivering telegrams and more. Gradually I learnt that working outside in 40-degree heat was no more fun than doing it in snow, ice and harsh winds!

While picking up a degree in politics and philosophy, I gravitated to bar and hotel work and that brought me from Europe to Australia again.

The Accidental Accountant

While I enjoyed the people aspect of hospitality, a couple of years of night shifts while I had 2 young children took the gloss off it. I found a graduate diploma in accounting course in Hobart that I could complete in 16 months with a few 4 am starts. Within a few weeks of starting, I had a desk job, working 9 to 5 for the first time at the age of 30. I'd achieved the first goal!

However, while I liked the business management aspect of accounting, tax and audit left me cold entirely. I figured that with a graduate diploma in computer science, I wouldn't have to be an accountant forever. During this time, I didn't stop travelling and exploring, ending up in Adelaide in the late 90s.

Start-Ups Before They Were Fashionable

It was during my second stint in Adelaide, while consulting many small businesses and not-for-profits that I became heavily involved in cash flow forecasting and management reporting. I considered myself pretty clever with a spreadsheet, but it was still always hard work. And even clever people made far too many mistakes!

In early 2000, MYOB announced the release of an ODBC driver. This enabled programmatic access to the data in the accounting system. I knew instantly what I wanted to use it for. I wanted to build an app to make budgeting and cash flow forecasting easier. I knew I didn't have the skills or experience, or the time, to do all the coding myself, so I hired a software developer. We discussed my outline plans and estimated we could complete it in 6-8 weeks. 10 months later, we released version 1 of Money Manager.

Money Manager was the first add-on for MYOB before we even knew the word "add-on". There were no start-up incubators in those days and no government assistance. In fact, the advice I did get from the South Australian government was that it would be better to stick to consulting and not waste my time and money.

Being the stubborn kind of person I am, I persisted, and we eventually built a moderately successful business with a few hundred happy customers.

Building a team

Being my first serious app, Money Manager had its flaws, and by 2008 we realised it was limited in how we could grow and expand it. Now based in sunny Townsville, my partner and I sat down and decided to start from scratch and build something new and better.

We struggled to find the development talent we needed locally, so we had a distributed team right from the beginning and had to find ways to communicate and keep in touch. Building a team in Townsville to help and support our customers was easier, and that team has grown over the years. Still, when we moved Calxa online in 2016-17, we found our UX (User Experience) designer in Wellington.

Building a software business hasn't been easy. As they say, it takes a long time to become an overnight success. We learnt a lot managing our own cash flow over the years. From time to time, we looked into getting external investors, but we couldn't find any with values that matched ours. Our goal wasn't to become billionaires. Yes, we needed to grow and make a living and not be stressed about cash, but that wasn't the only goal.

Working with not-for-profit organisations, we've had the opportunity to help many of them improve their efficiency and save days on their monthly reporting. Early on, we realised that the small ones often had the same complex reporting requirements of the big ones but with fewer resources. To help them out, we launched a donation program in 2011 and gave away Calxa to small and medium ones. Making a difference to hundreds of charities and community groups over the years is one of our major achievements.

So, now we run a global business from a North Queensland base. In the 21st century, that's not hard to do. Yes, we travel a little bit more than if we were in a capital city but with a good internet connection, we can help our customers from Singapore to Norway, from Chicago to Nairobi.

Looking Back, Looking Forward

I've been lucky to surround myself with good people throughout my life. They make the difference and help you through the hard times. None of us can do this on our own, and every venture is a team effort. There's often one person who gets to be the public face of an organisation, but we all know they didn't get there unaided. It takes a lot of hard work from the whole team working together to build success.

SME Leadership: The 5 Critical Success Factors

Antonio Avolio, *Principal, ACB Project Solutions Pty. Ltd.*

My Beginnings

After completing my higher school certificate in 2003, I commenced a finance/ accounting degree with the intention of ultimately linking up with my father and starting our own family accounting practice. But after a couple of years of study and undertaking some work experience, I quickly realised that the accounting world wasn't for me.

After much thought, I transitioned to a degree in construction management, specialising in quantity surveying. As a graduate quantity surveyor, I moved through several jobs trying to work my way up the corporate ladder. With each new position came a new set of experiences, more responsibility and ultimately, a more substantial income.

But the idea of starting my own business and becoming the master of my own destiny had always excited me. Initially, I had two not-so-successful startups, but each experience positively influenced my progressive learning, and I finally found success the third time around!

What follows is a summary of my accumulated learnings as a self-employed commercial builder:

Align Yourself With People You Trust

My current business was created around a bar room table in an inner-city pub with two like-minded pals. What made this business different for me was linking up with friends I had known, trusted and respected during our long association together.

With three equal shareholders, we have managed to build a successful boutique building company, specialising in the design and construction of commercial, industrial and retail projects throughout South-East Queensland.

Have a Clear View of What's Going to Drive Your Successful Outcomes

Going into business together, my partners and I focussed early on deciding what we seriously wanted to achieve, to frame up our Grand Vision for the future and to lay out the critical building blocks that would enable us to succeed.

Be Collaborative in Your Decision Making

We reached an early accord about how we would make important decisions for the business. We knew it was a given that we wouldn't always be able to agree unanimously on every decision. What guided us, though, was a commitment to ensure that our debate was respectful. The important thing to us is that there's always a clear understanding of how our decisions are reached and how the outcomes can be assured.

Yes, you may be disappointed for a while when decisions don't go your way; however, this brings me back to the initial point of aligning yourself with business partners who have similar values, goals and motivations. This firm understanding has allowed us to see things from each other's viewpoint with understanding and compassion.

Just Get Started

Once the three of us had agreed in principle to go ahead, the significant issue for me was in deciding if moving away from my comfortable and safe salary was the right thing to do. Both my partners had started small businesses before, and the best advice I received from them was to have some faith and 'just get started'.

Overcoming those pressures can be difficult. Whether it's personal, financial, or professional, you'll always find compelling reasons NOT to go ahead.

Personally, the inner voice in my head battled with the following thoughts:

- Is the timing right, given what is happening in the economy?
- Should I be starting a business in an industry that will almost certainly be affected by the COVID shutdowns.
- I have a young family to support, so do I need this pressure and the inevitable stress that comes with it?
- Do I want to place my family under the financial burdens and risks that go hand in hand with running a business?
- I have already built a successful career in the corporate world. Do I want to sacrifice all that hard work to go out on my own?

Ultimately, while these things weighed on me, I consciously chose not to let fear and worries about security stop me. The key ingredient in this step quickly became to 'just get started'!

So, what happened after that? The truth is the business has gone better than we could have hoped for during its early years, we three partners have each been able to draw a good income from it, and our contracted forward business continues to grow!

Yes, there's been lots of lost sleep, and yes, I've worked long hours. But I've got to say it feels pretty damn good after each project is completed to be able to proudly stand back and visually see the finished product of our good work.

Build a Track Record

In reality, we are still relatively early in our business life cycle, and in the very early days, there was, at times, a fine line between success and failure. One of the obvious downsides was the lack of a track record – each of the directors had very successful CVs in the construction industry, but the company's lack of a track record was ultimately what clients looked to when making their forward business decisions.

Never forget that your early clients are taking a risk in backing you. Our initial service offering wasn't so much in the delivery of construction projects. We spent many months undertaking valuable cost-planning analyses for potential clients at no cost to them as a means of building trust. And all too often, we were overlooked for the project, but we never took those hits personally and knew it was just 'a cold hard reality of our learning curve'.

We also had to lower our expectations initially and build our track record by undertaking minor refurbishment works and small shop fit outs. The good news was that those projects allowed our company to enhance its credentials until, eventually, we found a client willing to take a chance on a larger project – and then the business grew rapidly from that base!

Have Strong Personal Support Networks

Building a business can be difficult and, for the most part, lonely. For me, this has been the most challenging process I have encountered – dealing with the sleepless nights, the rejections and the risk of failure can really wear you down.

Never overlook the value and importance of having a strong support base to lean on in difficult times. I've been fortunate to have a great group of friends and family supporting me. But undoubtedly, my biggest and most important supporter has been my wife.

Don't Overlook the Importance of Work-Life Balance

My wife is a strong, independent and loyal woman who always tells me how it is, but without fail, she has my back when things get difficult. She is also my greatest supporter. Without her by my side, there would be no way I would have been able to achieve half of what I have. Most importantly, there is no one else on the planet I would rather share this experience with.

While it's difficult at times, I am constantly trying to get the balance right between work and family. Too often, I fail miserably, but this is definitely a work in progress and of critical importance because, ultimately, my family is my motivation to keep going and to chase success.

SME Leadership: The 5 Critical Success Factors

Jo Pollard, *Principal, Samford Design & Print. (Written by John Goddard)*

Jo Pollard is the owner and principal of Samford Design and Print, located in Brisbane's Samford Valley.

Jo and her team deliver well on the traditional range of print shop products and services, but their true point of difference lies in their rapidly growing document design business. Jo had over a decade of corporate marketing experience before taking on her SME venture, so she knows and understands the language and nuances of business creativity. From business cards to new logos, eye-catching marketing material, posters and signs, or simply her wise creative input and counsel, Jo delivers well.

In a 21st-century digital working relationship, distance is simply not a hurdle! My writing base has been 1,200 kilometres south of Brisbane, yet I would not have considered going anywhere else for my needs. Jo has produced many of the graphics for this book. We communicated by phone and swapped documents via email and text. After emailing my rough concept drawings, Jo understood the nub of what I wanted to communicate and translated my rough sketches into professional graphics.

I compliment Jo and her team at Samford Design and Print in helping me realise my dream of writing this book.

Andrew Cooper, *Managing Director, The Cooper Property Group.*

Extract from John Goddard's Biography: *'The House That Jeff Built'* (2011).

The story of The Cooper Property Group is a definitive rags-to-riches tale. After an abusive childhood, my friend Jeff Cooper left his family home west of Ipswich at age 15 to join the telecommunications division of the Postmaster Generals Department (PMG) in Brisbane. There wasn't any support system to get him started in life, just a recycled Qantas cabin bag which held all his worldly belongings. Drawing on his natural charm, Jeff found modest lodgings and a caring landlady in one of Brisbane's inner northern suburbs.

By 16, while still working for the PMG, Jeff started airfreighting freshwater baby crocodiles into Brisbane from the Gulf of Carpentaria and successfully offloading them to local pet shops. Years later, while I was penning Jeff's biography, Jeff's wife Ros showed me some amusing old news clips about Jeff's little critters being spotted, wriggling around suburban backyards! Jeff tried his damnest to convince me that, unlike their country-cousin Salties, Fresh Water Crocks were quite tame as pets, but I had my serious doubts! Importantly to Jeff, though, he was turning over a very tidy $2,000 a month from those sales when the average wage at the time was barely 10% of that.

Driven by his will to succeed, Jeff bought his first investment property at the tender age of 18, and by 21, he owned a further four houses, five laundromats and 200 space-invader slot machines. Around the same time, he met and married the formidable Roslyn Hughes, and they subsequently reared three strapping sons (Talbot, Andrew, and Cameron).

By 25, Jeff was an Alderman on the Morton Shire Council, and the Coopers opened their first Caravan Park soon after that. Then over the following three decades, Jeff and Ros literally went out and built an empire together that would eventually span over 30 companies, including shopping centres, caravan parks, motels, industrial estates, commercial office rentals, and their other significant undeveloped land holdings in the Ipswich region. The Cooper Family also purchased and renovated the historic 19th

Century Woodlands of Marburg Mansion. Jeff went on to become a local vigneron of note when he established vineyards on the acreage surrounding Woodlands.

Notwithstanding his extraordinary drive and will to succeed, Jeff's longstanding battle with Parkinson's Disease took its toll, and he finally stepped down from an active role in the business in 2009, passing the baton to his son, Andrew.

With the GFC raging at its worst and the global financial services industry in a fragile state, the Australian commercial property market took its own hit, our local Banks tightened their lending guidelines significantly, and times were indeed tough. Taking responsibility for the family business over those years was undoubtedly Andrew's baptism of fire! Yet he rose to those challenges and rapidly demonstrated he had inherited every bit of his old man's DNA and nose for the property development game. Indeed, under his leadership, the business survived those challenging times well and emerged stronger than ever.

Over the years since I penned Jeff's biography, the parallel story of Andrew's success has been in the powerful collaborations he has built with Cooper CEO Graham Harding and Senior Property Planner Mark Mahaffey over the 29 years the three of them have been working together. I believe there are few business partnerships around today that could lay claim to that sort of longevity and continuity of leadership.

I was non-executive chairman of the Cooper Property Group for a decade from 2007, and so I had a bird's eye view of how Andrew, Graeme and Mark learnt progressively from each other's skills and knowledge and how as a team, they became highly competent generalists. There were no hidden secrets or agendas. Their weekly property meetings and monthly board meetings had all the hallmarks of good stewardship. There was never any doubt in my mind that their passionate level of debate contributed positively to the quality of the robust decisions they were making for the business week in and week out.

Andrew continues to be an outstanding leader of one of South-East Queensland's successful large family trading SME enterprises and I rate his leadership competency as superior. I'm sure Andrew would also agree that many of his ultimate *successes have been* underwritten along the way by his valuable collaborations with Graeme and Mark.

I catch up with Andrew several times a year and continue to marvel at his achievements. He undoubtedly exemplifies the power of having mastered all my 5 Critical Success Factors and sits very comfortably in the top tier of Highly Competent Generalists I have known.

Andrew's Dad Jeff would be so very proud of what he has achieved.

Appendix (i)
The 5 Critical Success Factors Rapid Learning Guide

The 5 Critical Success Factors are interdependent, so to achieve peak performance it's most important to master all five of them over time.

This Quick Start Learning Guide will help you get there faster. Once you've successfully mastered and implemented the first four Critical Success Factors, Critical Success Factor 5, the Leadership fundamentals will serve you well and guide you over time in becoming a *Consummate Business Leader*.

Our Quick Start Learning Guide aims to rapidly maximise your learnings with some solid early strategies and runs on the board:

Tier 1: Critical Success Factor 1

The Foundations subject matter is much more about what you should do than what you should learn.

Your first priority is to retain an external tax accountant (Chapter 1) who will provide you with valuable advice on the ideal Trading Structure (Chapter 2), your Capital Formation Decisions (Chapter 3), your major Corporate Law Business Responsibilities and Liabilities (Chapter 4) and your Basic Tax and Compliance Obligations (Chapter 9).

Tier 2: Place Critical Success Factors 2 & 4 on Auto Drive ASAP

Unless you have productive systems and controls in place for efficiently dealing with *The Finances* and *Time Management* aspects of your business, those responsibilities will weigh you down and limit your valuable time at the Front Line gaining new business and generating the revenues so important to the ultimate success of your business.

The Finances and Time Management Responsibilities are best managed by establishing a series of *Prescriptive Systems* with regimented, logical and easy to follow habits and routines that will ensure all essential tasks can be carried out efficiently.

The composite bonus with well managed prescriptive systems is their emphasis on placing a high percentage of the essential individual steps on *auto-drive*. This *Prescriptive* approach is traditionally followed in fields such as medicine, law, accounting, banking, education and so on. In effectively managed successful larger SMEs, the Finance and Back Office procedures invariably already have established standards, systems and routines in place to maximise the highest efficient potential for a business to predictably underwrite ideal outcomes.

The challenge then for smaller SME's is to find a way to replicate those systems with similar philosophies, without incurring significant additional expenditure.

CRITICAL SUCCESS FACTOR 2: THE FINANCES:

The overwhelming *MUST DO* Prescriptive priority is to subscribe to *a cloud-based bookkeeping software solution* and to *contract an experienced bookkeeper or delegate that responsibility to a finance-literate staff member*. This may only need to be a part-time or casual role, depending on the volume of transactions and the size of the business. In smaller SME's, this role is sometimes carried out by a family member of the Principal (Chapters 5 & 6). In large SMEs, a qualified on board accountant may manage those functions.

Following that prescriptive protocol, your bookkeeper/accountant will be able to manage the lion's share of your routine daily financial transactions and the ongoing statutory compliance obligations of the business.

Your external tax advisor will deal with your annual tax returns and any other higher order tax compliance obligations (Chapter 9), and the general operational efficiencies of the typical accounting practice will be able to schedule those activities so the fee you pay is not prohibitive yet fairly reflects the value of the work done.

With the routine daily financial responsibilities so delegated and on auto drive, the Principal's residual Critical Success Factor 2 priorities are to focus mainly on

- strategies that maximise the financial performance of the business (Chapter 7), and,
- deal personally with your preferred banker (Chapter 10).

See Book Buyer's Essential Toolkit Rapid Learning Guide:

The Financial Statements & The Key Performance Metrics

CRITICAL SUCCESS FACTOR 4: MANAGING TIME:

Unless you're managing your time productively, there's little chance you'll be able to spend enough time at the Front Line, generating the revenues vital to the success of your business.

For that reason, you and your Senior Team Members should make an early commitment to follow our prescriptive *Nine Frontline Management Priorities* with particular focus on:

- Adopting a culture of Continuous Learning (Chapter 19),
- Keeping a *Personal Immersion Journal* (Chapter 20), and
- Adopting *Daily, Weekly and Monthly Time Management System and Routines* laid out in Chapters 21 to 28).

See Book Buyer's Essential Toolkit Rapid Learning Guide:

Time Focus Time Management.

Tier 3: Critical Success Factor 3 The Front Line:

Critical Success Factor 3 (Customers and Revenues) has its focus on building a productive revenue generating *Front Line Selling Machine*. This is where the Principal needs to allocate a substantial proportion of their time.

SME Leadership: The 5 Critical Success Factors

To be successful, you should be obsessive about following our *9 Tenets of Front Line Leadership* and ensure you are well versed in the subject matter in all of the Front Line chapters.

See Book Buyer's Essential Toolkit Rapid Learning Guide:

> *The 9 Tenets of Front Line Leadership.*

Tier 4: Progressively Hone Your Leadership Capabilities

Twenty First Century business leadership is driven by a commitment to shared values and collaborative work cultures that focus on the power of a productive team and underwritten by an unwavering sense of personal responsibility, accountability and belonging by every team member.

Chapters 29 and 30 focus on the benefits of creating a culture of *Sustainable Collaborative Leadership.*

Chapter 31 provides guidance on how to *Manage Emotions* within the team.

Chapter 32 rounds out the Leadership Chapters, presenting our nine *Inspiring Leadership Tales from the Trenches.* All these entrepreneurs have built their businesses from the ground up and are successful leaders today because they consciously chose to invest in both their business and leadership capabilities.

Appendix (ii)
Access to the Book Buyer's Essentials Toolkit

The Book Buyers *Essentials Toolkit* includes our special *workbook that will allow you to pace yourself and maximise your learning ASAP.*

The Book Buyer *Essential Toolkit* subjects are:

- ✓ *The Financial Statements & Key Performance Metrics* (Critical Success Factor 2),
- ✓ *The Time Focus Time Management System* (Critical Success Factor 4),
- ✓ The *9 Tenets of Front Line Selling* (Critical Success Factor 3), and
- ✓ How to Effectively *Double your Reading Speed in 5 days.*

Our Essentials Toolkit includes access to a downloadable set of *Graphics* from the book (formatted to print in A3 or A4 format).

The *Essentials Toolkit* is a complementary offering to all book buyers to help get you started and may be accessed at:

smekeystone.com/essentialstoolkit

Appendix (iii)
SME Keystone Web Platform Initiatives

Ian Hubert's SME Keystone Web Platform emerged from a collaboration between Ian and John and the Platform will progressively present the following range of products and services:

1. *SME Leadership: The 5 Critical Success Factors:* softback & eBook versions, with an audio book version to follow.

2. Book Buyers *Downloadable Essentials Toolkit*

3. *Multi-Media Digital Learning:* Accelerated learning modules, presented by subject matter experts.

4. *Community Connect:* a valuable portal for two-way conversation and learning.

5. *Resources Hub:* an extensive database of templates, worksheets, standard documents and regular research.

6. *SME Keystone Recommended Reading:* regular book summaries and recommended reading for our members.

7. *SME Keystone Media:* Frequent Blogs/Vlogs, Podcasts and entrepreneurial interviews.

8. Ian's book, *Time Focus Time Management System*, will be released via the SMEK Platform in 2026, together with release of a fully digitised on-line version of the system.

9. John's book, *The 9 Tenets of Front Line Selling,* will be released via the SMEK platform in 2026, together with release of a fully digitised on-line version of the system.

The first stage of the SME Keystone Platform will be open to new members by end of 2025. For further information go to: smekeystone.com

Dedication to Sam Goddard

My son, Sam, who passed away early 2018, was the definitive high achiever. Etched deep in his DNA was the core belief he could achieve anything in life, provided he never stopped trying. From an early age, he was fearless with the self-imposed imprimatur there would be no regrets, no missed opportunities and no stones left unturned in pursuit of his goals.

By 23, Sam had trekked in three continents other than Australia. He was a scratch golfer, had secured a Finance Degree from QUT, and had a good job as a graduate accountant with Pitcher Partners in Brisbane. Sam and fiancé Sal had also purchased their first home.

Then on Valentine's Day 2010, Sam suffered a number of devastating strokes after heading goals in a charity soccer match. He was in a deep coma and his prognosis and survival odds were as bad as they could be. Sam's medical team said it was as though a grenade had gone off in his head. Yet driven by his innate fighting spirit and our subsequent discovery of two spectacularly successful offshore off-label drug treatments, he recovered enough to keep up the good fight for a further eight years. In 2011 and 2017 Sam and Sal spoke lucidly about their inspiring journey in a series of documentaries on ABC's Australian Story, 60 Minutes and NBC New York. (Google: *Sam Goddard: Love and Other Drugs*).

In 2009 at the launch of my book, *The House that Jeff Built*, Sam urged me to get an early start on *The 5 Critical Success Factors*. He knew I had a mountain of research yet to complete and that the book was realistically still years away from completion. Yet armed with his finance degree and an abundance of self-confidence, 23-year-old Sam was convinced he should be my co-writer! Of course I couldn't say no, but unfortunately his strokes followed only weeks later and my writing plans had to be set aside indefinitely. And Ian Hulbert has since most capably filled that important co writers role.

Let there be no doubt Sam would have given our book his most fulsome tick of approval and would have been our grandest advocate .... so I proudly dedicate this one to you, my boy!

Bibliography

Acemoglu, Daren & Johnson Simon. *Power & Progress, a Thousand Year Struggle Over Technology & Prosperity*. John Murray Books, 2024

Anderson, Michael & Jefferson, Miranda. *Transforming Organizations: Engaging the 4 C's*. Bloomsbury Business, 2019.

Apps, Judy. *The Art of Conversation*. Wiley, 2014.

Aurelias, Marcus. *Meditations*. Penguin, 2011.

Banerjee, Abhijit & Duflo, Esther. *Good Economics for Hard Times*. Penguin Random House, 2019.

Churchill, Neil C, Lewis Virginia L. *The Five Stages of Small Business Growth*, Harvard Business Review, May 1983.

Clear James. *Atomic Habits*. Penguin Random House UK. 2018.

Clifton, Jim & Harter, Jim K. *It's the Manager*. Gallup Press, 2019.

Collins, Jim. *Good to Great*: *Why Some Companies Make the Leap and Others Don't*. Random House Business, 2009.

Comey, James. *A Higher Loyalty: Truth, Lies and Leadership*. Pan Macmillan, 2018.

Coverdale, David. *The Bank of Dave, How I took on the Banks*. EMI Music Publishing, 2023

Covey, Stephen M. R. *The Speed of Trust: The One Thing That Changes Everything*. Simon & Schuster, 2018.

Covey, Stephen, R. *The 7 Habits of Highly Effective People: Powerful Lessons in Personal Change*. Simon & Schuster, 1989.

Covey, Stephen R & Merrill, Roger A. & Merrill, Rebecca R. *First Things First*. Simon & Schuster, 1996.

Dyer, Jeff, Gregersen, Hal & Christensen, Clayton, M. *The Innovator's DNA: Mastering the Five Skills of Disruptive Innovators.* Harvard Business Review Press, 2011.

Drucker, Peter F. *Managing One's Self.* Harvard Business Review, 2008.

Duhigg, Charles. *The Power of Habit.* Random House, 2012.

Eisenhower Dwight D. *Crusade in Europe: A Personal Account of World War II.* Double Day – Penguin Random House, 1951.

Frankl, Viktor, E. *Man's Search for Meaning.* Beacon, 2008.

Galloway, Scott. *The Four: The Hidden DNA of Amazon, Apple, Facebook and Google.* Penguin Random House, 2017.

Gerber, Michael E. *The E Myth Revisited: Why Most Small Businesses Don't Work and What to do about it.* Harper Collins Business, 1995.

Gittins, Ross. *A Life Among Budgets, Bulldust and Bastardry.* Allen and Unwin, 2015.

Gittins, Ross. *Gittins Guide to Economics.* Allen and Unwin, 2006

Jocelyn K. Glei, Jocelyn K. *Manage your Day-to-Day: Build Your Routine, Find Your Focus & Sharpen Your Creative Mind.* Amazon, 2013.

Goleman, Daniel. *Emotional Intelligence: Why it can matter more than IQ.* Bantam Books, 1995.

Graham, Douglas & Bachmann, Thomas T. *Ideation: The Birth and Death of Ideas.* John Wiley & Sons, 2004.

Herrmann, Ned. *The Whole Brain® Thinking Model, 1st edition.* McGraw Hill, 1996.

Herrmann, Ned A. & Herrmann-Nehdi, Ann. *The Whole Brain Business Book: Unlocking the Power of Whole Brain Thinking in Organizations, Teams, and Individuals.* McGraw Hill, 2nd ed., 2015.

Housel, Morgan. *The Psychology of Money.* Harriman House, 2020

Kalanatar, Jahan. *Talk Your Way Out of Trouble.* McMillan Books, 2025

Kennedy, Shannah, *The Life Plan*, Penguin Random House, 2015.

Kerr, James. Legacy: *What The All Blacks Can Teach Us About the Business of Life.* Constable, 2nd ed., 2013.

Kubler-Ross, Elizabeth & Kessler, David. *On Grief & Grieving.* Scribner, a Division of Simmon & Schuster, 2014.

Kwik, Jim. Limitless: *Upgrade Your Brain, Learn Anything Faster And Unlock Your Exceptional Life.* Hay House, 2020.

Lencioni, Patrick. *The Five Dysfunctions of a Team.* Jossey, Wiley Books, 2002.

McDonald, Hector. *Truth: How the Many Sides to Every Story Shape our Reality.* Little Brown and Company, 2018.

McNab, Chris. *Jeff Bezos: The World-Changing Entrepreneur.* Arcturus Publishing, 2022.

McRae, Hamish. *The World in 2050: How to Think About the Future.* Bloomsbury Publishing, 2022.

McRaven, Admiral William H. *The Hero Code.* Penguin Random House, 2021.

Murphy, Shawn. *Work Tribes.* Harper Collins Leadership, 2019.

Obama, Barack. *The Audacity of Hope.* Penguin Random House, 2006.

Ozenc, Kursat & Hagan, Margaret. *Rituals for Work.* Wiley, 2019.

Peterson, Jordan B. *12 Rules of Life: An Antidote to Chaos.* Penguin, 2018.

Peterson, Jordan B. *Beyond Order: 12 More Rules for Life.* Penguin, 2021.

Jawad, Ali Qassim & Kakabadse, Andrew. *Leadership Intelligence: The 5 Q's for Thriving as a Leader.* Bloomsbury Business, 2019.

Ritzer, George. *The McDonaldization of Society.* Sage Publishing, 2000.

Robbins, Anthony. *Personal Power 2: The Driving Force*! Robbins International, 1996.

Schramm, Carl J. *Burn the Business Plan: What Great Entrepreneurs Really Do*. Simon & Schuster, 2018.

Smith, Jean E. *Eisenhower. In War and Peace*. Random House, 2013.

Son, Joonmo. *Social Capital*. Wiley, 2020.

Spinks, David. *The Business of Belonging, How to Make Community Your Competitive Advantage*. Wiley Publishers, 2021.

Stiglitz, Joseph E. *People, Power and Profits*. W.W. Norton & Company, 2019.

Taleb, Nassim Nicholas. *Skin in the Game, Hidden Asymmetries in Daily Life*. Penguin Random House, 2018.

Tipler, Christopher J. *Corpus Rios. The How and What of Business Strategy*. Rios Press, 2010.

Walsh, Toby. *The Shortest History of AI*. Swartz Books, 2025

Willink, Jocko & Babin, Leif. *The Dichotomy of Leadership*. Macmillan, 2018.

www.ingramcontent.com/pod-product-compliance
Lightning Source LLC
Chambersburg PA
CBHW071950070526
44583CB00015B/1131